THE CHURCH AND SOCIAL ORDER

Frontispiece

THE CHURCH AND SOCIAL ORDER

Social Thought in the Church of England, 1918-1939

JOHN OLIVER

283.061 OLI

LONDON
A. R. MOWBRAY & CO LTD

24335

© A. R. Mowbray & Co. Ltd. 1968

Printed in Great Britain by
Alden & Mowbray Ltd.
at the Alden Press, Oxford

SBN 264 65560 5

First published in 1968

EDUCATION & HUMANITIES
LIBRARY
THE POLYTECHNIC
WOLVERHAMPTON

261

DY 1264 8590

701076

283.061
OLI

Foreword

BY THE REV. DR. A. R. VIDLER
Formerly Dean of King's College, Cambridge

THIS BOOK throws much light on the history of the Church of England between the two world wars. It originated in an academic thesis at Cambridge but has been so recast and expanded that it is now not only a piece of scholarship but a work of wide interest and very readable. The subject has not hitherto been investigated with the thoroughness and impartiality that Mr. Oliver has devoted to it. I myself lived through the period which he covers and was not indifferent to Christian social thought and action: his book has reminded me of things which I had forgotten and made me aware of things of which I was ignorant at the time. Not only, so far as I can judge, is his record of facts accurate, but his presentation and interpretation of them are fair and free from bias. In comment and criticism he is shrewd, but he does not tediously obtrude his own opinions.

While he does not moralize, I am sure he is right in suggesting that Christians today have much to learn from the experiences of this quite recent period. There was far too much that was ineptly said or done. Seldom was a satisfactory balance struck between idealism and realism. There was an awful amount of amateurishness and lack of expertise in those who sought to bring their faith to bear upon the needs of society. They meant well, but to mean well is never enough. Above all, there was a lamentable state of indifference in the rank and file of churchpeople and of preoccupation with narrowly ecclesiastical interests. At the same time, there were areas of solid and creditable achievement which constitute an example to us all.

The so-called Christian Socialism of 1848–54 is now fairly well known and its sequels in the latter part of the nineteenth century have been considerably canvassed. I apprehend that much more instruction for the present is to be derived from this study of a comparatively unexplored period. The principal lesson that I have learned since those days is that Christian social action is primarily a matter of laypeople *doing* things in the various walks of life in which they hold responsibility and of which they have first-hand knowledge, and not of clerics and ecclesiastical assemblies *saying* things or passing well-intentioned resolutions about what other people might do. Mr. Oliver's book, which has to be predominantly a tale of the latter kind of inaction, goes to show how little this point of vital importance was appreciated between the wars.

October 1967 ALEC VIDLER

Contents

List of illustrations

Preface

MANY PEOPLE have provided invaluable help in the preparation of this book, but my special thanks are due to Canon V. A. Demant, of Christ Church, Oxford; Bishop L. S. Hunter; Dr. W. J. Macpherson, of Caius College, Cambridge; Mr. D. L. Munby, of Nuffield College, Oxford; Canon Ronald Preston, of Manchester; the late Canon C. E. Raven; Mr. M. B. Reckitt; and the late Sir Dennis Robertson, all of whom were kind enough to grant personal interviews, although of course they bear no responsibility for any of the opinions or judgments which I have expressed.

I am also indebted to the staff of the Industrial Christian Fellowship, and especially Mr. Norman Barnes, for allowing me to see much useful material in their possession.

Above all I am grateful to Dr. A. R. Vidler for his inspiration, encouragement and constant help.

J. O.

I

Introduction: Christian Social Thought 1877–1918

'IF THE present social situation is to be controlled by Christian principles, thoughts will be necessary which have not yet been thought.'[1] So wrote Ernst Troeltsch at the end of his magisterial survey of nineteen centuries of Christian social thought, and his conclusion still holds good. But social problems have an unwelcome habit of persistence. Slums, homelessness, poverty, hospital waiting-lists, bad schools, strikes and unemployment are still melancholy features of the social scene, despite the fact that the Welfare State has more than come of age. International tension, the arms race, and the difficulty of establishing a workable system of world-wide collective security have been banished neither by two world wars nor by the most strenuous efforts of the United Nations Organization. And Christian witness on these matters is still divided and uncertain.

Behind this survey of social thought in the Church of England between the wars lies the conviction that any attempt to apply Christian principles to the present social situation must be based on the most thorough and intimate knowledge of the recent past; much effort can be spared, and many mistakes avoided, if the experience of recent years is taken into account. The origins of many of our contemporary social problems, particularly in the spheres of international affairs, labour relations, and the relative importance of the public and private sectors in industry and the provision of welfare services, can be traced to the inter-war period, so that this study is of more than academic interest for those who are concerned with the new thoughts which will be necessary if current issues are to be dealt with in the light of Christian principles.

[1] E. Troeltsch, *The Social Teaching of the Christian Churches*, Vol. II, p. 1012.

WOLVERHAMPTON TEACHERS
COLLEGE LIBRARY

For this same reason, in order to understand the Christian social thought of the inter-war years it is important first to look briefly at the most important movements and personalities in the period which led up to the First World War. It is also perhaps necessary to explain that the limitation of the scope of this survey to the Church of England is for two reasons: to make the field a manageable one, and because the contribution of other Christians in this country to this field of thought can in most cases be dealt with in references to work which was undertaken on an ecumenical basis. The influence of Continental and American Christian social thought was slight, at least until well on into the thirties, but occasional references to this influence will also be found in the text.

It is not easy to distinguish the moment to which the rebirth of Christian social thought in England may be traced, for rebirth it undoubtedly was. As has often been pointed out, this was an area of Christian concern which suffered a period of prolonged and disastrous neglect from the time of the Renaissance to the middle of the nineteenth century.[2] The short-lived experiments of the Christian Socialists of 1848–54 have been fully described,[3] and it is perhaps to the year 1877 that the student of twentieth-century Christian social thought should first turn. That year saw the first explicit fusion of the two dominant streams of theological thinking in the Church of England during the second half of the nineteenth century, the Maurician and the Tractarian—a combination which was to prove particularly valuable in the field of Christian social thought. It was in 1877 that Stewart Headlam was dismissed from his curacy at Bethnal Green, for praising with an enthusiasm offensive to the Christian conscience of the day the charms of the dancers at the Gaiety Theatre.[4] The end of his parochial career might well have meant also the end of the Guild of St. Matthew, which he had founded a few months earlier for young communicants in the parish; but, driven out into the ecclesiastical wilderness, Headlam decided to transform the Guild from a local organization into an active propaganda society, open to all church-

[2] See especially R. H. Tawney, *Religion and the Rise of Capitalism.*
[3] T. Christensen, *The Origins and History of Christian Socialism, 1848-54.*
[4] F. G. Bettany, *Stewart Headlam*, pp. 43f.

men, and dedicated to the recovery of the Church's right to criticize and if possible modify the social order in the light of Christian principles and to awaken in churchmen an understanding of the social implications of their faith.

Headlam owed much to F. D. Maurice's theology of the Incarnation and the Kingdom, and to the example of the first Christian Socialist movement of 1848–54, but he added to this a Tractarian emphasis on the devotional life, a love of beauty and colour in worship, and a high doctrine of the sacraments. The Socialist spirit of the Guild was exemplified by a resolution passed at a public meeting in Trafalgar Square in 1884, asserting that 'the present contrast between the great body of the workers who produce much and consume little, and of those classes which produce little and consume much is contrary to the Christian doctrines of brotherhood and justice.'[5]

This was a radical pronouncement, and in 1886 Headlam committed himself to the extent of joining the Fabian Society, but his attitude towards secular Socialism nevertheless remained ambivalent. He once said: 'Yes, I am a Socialist, but I thank God I am a Liberal as well',[6] and he was always more anxious to expound the social implications of Christianity than to preach a political remedy for the ills of society, or to stir up sentimental pity for the poor: 'What we want to do is to call your attention to the fact not that these evils can be alleviated by Christian charity, but that they can be prevented by Christian justice.'[7] Although this refusal to identify himself with a particular political party was a position later adopted by many of the most radical Christian thinkers on social questions,[8] there were many members of the Guild who wanted it to pursue an explicitly Socialist policy, while the more conventional spirits found Headlam's idiosyncratic and combative temperament both tiresome and embarrassing. A widening division of opinion within the Guild, and the fact that

[5] *Ibid.*, p. 83 [6] *Ibid.*, p. 214.

[7] S. D. Headlam, *The Guild of St. Matthew: An Appeal to Churchmen* (a sermon preached on the 13th annual festival of the Guild), p. 9.

[8] It did not escape the notice of Munro Miller, one of Headlam's closest associates in the G.S.M., that the Church Socialist League, founded in 1906 with an explicit political allegiance, later reverted to a position more like that of Headlam and the G.S.M. (Bettany, *op. cit.*, pp. 92f.)

Headlam so dominated its affairs as to prevent the emergence of a successor to him as Warden, led Headlam to disband it in 1909.

The failure of the Christian Socialist movement in 1854 had seemed complete, but the seed sown by Maurice, Kingsley, Ludlow, Vansittart Neale and Thomas Hughes continued to grow, and an increasing number of churchmen, quite apart from the group which gathered round Headlam, became persuaded of the need to study the structure and problems of society in the light of their faith, and to criticize both the assumptions on which it was based and its practical results, particularly when these took the form of poverty, sickness, squalor, sweated labour or unemployment. The appendix to *Lux Mundi*, published in 1889, on *Some Aspects of Christian Duty* pointed to the significance of the transition from political to ethical economics; a man's rights must be limited, in a social context, by the claims of others, but among the rights which the worker may fairly claim are good working conditions, security of maintenance, and opportunities for recreation and culture.[9] There was a ready audience among the clergy for a course of lectures given by Wilfrid Richmond at Sion College in Lent, 1889, on Economic Morals, and as a result of these lectures a meeting was held on June 14th, 1889, under the chairmanship of Henry Scott Holland, to discuss the formation of a society to work out a Christian political economy.[10] It was suggested that the G.S.M. was already in existence to deal with such matters, but, as Charles Gore tactfully pointed out: 'While we felt very grateful to it, it did not in some ways suit our purposes.'[11] Headlam made a magnanimous reference to the projected new society when he addressed the annual general meeting of the Guild on September

[9] *Lux Mundi*, edited by C. Gore, pp. 523f. of the 10th edition of 1890.

[10] This account of the foundation of the Christian Social Union is taken from Percy Dearmer, *The Beginnings of the C.S.U.*, pp. 5–10. Henry Scott Holland, 1847–1918; Canon of St. Paul's 1884–1911, Regius Professor of Divinity at Oxford 1911–18, Editor of *Commonwealth* 1896–1918, was perhaps the outstanding representative of the spirit of the C.S.U. in its most active and constructive form.

[11] C. Gore, in the chapter *Holland and the C.S.U.*, which he contributed to *Henry Scott Holland: Memoir and Letters*, edited by S. Paget, p. 242. Charles Gore, 1853–1932; Librarian of the Pusey House 1884–93, Vicar of Radley 1893–4, Canon of Westminster 1894–1902, Bishop of Worcester 1902–5, of Birmingham 1905–11, and of Oxford 1911–19; Founder, and from 1892 to 1901 the first Superior, of the Community of the Resurrection; President of the C.S.U. 1902–11.

23rd, 1889; he wished the venture Godspeed: 'Let us, I charge you, have no petty jealousy in this matter. We have laboured and they are welcome to enter into the fruits of our labour.'[12]

The Christian Social Union came into being in November 1889. B. F. Westcott was elected President[13] and Scott Holland Chairman. Its objects were:

1. To claim for the Christian Law the ultimate authority to rule social practice.
2. To study in common how to apply the moral truths and principles of Christianity to the social and economic difficulties of the present time.
3. To present Christ in practical life as living Master and King, the enemy of wrong and selfishness, the power of righteousness and love.

These objects clearly allowed a good deal of latitude in interpretation, and in practice the C.S.U. never tackled the task which it had originally envisaged, the formulation of a Christian political economy. It was prevented from pursuing any such ambitious course by the anxiety of its leaders to accommodate as many different points of view as possible. It was non-political, and avoided identification with any particular ecclesiastical party, but membership was restricted to Anglicans, since it saw its work primarily as the awakening of the national Church to an awareness of the social implications of its creed and sacraments. It was led from the beginning by academic theologians, and never lost a certain donnish air; patronized by many bishops, it exercised a considerable influence on the representative utterances of the Church of England in successive Lambeth Reports, but it failed both in its object of creating a lively social conscience in the majority of the clergy and laity, and in extending its influence to the trade unions far enough to make any effective impression on the labour movement.

The C.S.U. was socialist only in so far as it was opposed to unbridled individualism. In his famous address to the Church

[12] Quoted by P. Dearmer, *op. cit.*, p. 8.

[13] Brooke Fosse Westcott, 1825–1901; Canon of Peterborough 1869–83, Regius Professor of Divinity at Cambridge 1870–90, Canon of Westminster 1883–90, Bishop of Durham 1890–1901. Westcott created a notable precedent in the Church of England by his successful intervention in the Durham coal strike of 1892, as a result of which a settlement was reached.

Congress of 1890, Westcott attempted to rescue the word socialism from its connection with extravagant and revolutionary schemes, to use it for nobler purposes, to describe a theory of life rather than of economics. Socialism in this sense regards humanity as 'an organic whole, a vital unity formed by the combination of contributory members, mutually interdependent.'[14] Contrasting it with individualism, Westcott saw its method as co-operation, its aim as the fulfilment of service, and its object as an organization of life which would secure for everyone the most complete development of his powers. It is not altogether clear what form Westcott would have wished to see society take; certainly he repudiated the still popular belief in *laissez-faire* and the benevolent workings of self-interest, but despite his startling judgment on the wage system[15] he committed himself no further than to say: 'We can see the direction of social movement. We wait for the next stage in the growth of the State, when in free and generous co-operation each citizen shall offer the fulness of his own life that he may rejoice in the fulness of the life of the body.'[16] Gore perhaps understood most clearly the great upheaval of society which would be necessary if the objects of the C.S.U. were to be realized, and he often felt it necessary to emphasize the need for corporate penitence, or to urge impulsive Christian social prophets to count the cost of their enthusiasm,[17] but he was as reluctant as any to commit the Church to an open alliance with the Labour Party.[18]

The work of the C.S.U. was in practice divided between the intellectual and the practical. Its influence on Lambeth Conferences was considerable, and became quite unmistakable in 1908, although it was not the only factor in persuading the bishops of the need to consider social questions. The 1888 Encyclical maintained that 'No more important problems can well occupy the attention, whether of Clergy or Laity, than such as are connected with what

[14] *Report of the Church Congress, Hull, 1890*, p. 320.

[15] Westcott looked forward to the time when wage-labour would be seen to be 'as little fitted to represent finally or adequately the connection of man with man in the production of wealth, as at earlier times slavery or serfdom' (*Ibid.*, p. 321).

[16] *Ibid.*, pp. 321f.

[17] Notably at the Pan-Anglican Congress of 1908 (*Pan-Anglican Papers*, S.A.6.a., on Socialism) and at Copec in 1924 (see below, Chapter 3).

[18] See G. L. Prestige, *The Life of Charles Gore*, p. 94.

is popularly called Socialism',[19] but the report of the committee which considered the Church's practical work in relation to Socialism, after tentatively suggesting ways in which state action to protect the working-class from the evil effects of competition might be extended, concluded that 'the best help is self-help'.[20]

The report to the 1897 Conference of the committee on *The Office of the Church with respect to Industrial Problems* went further, emphasizing four principles on which a Christian social order should be based: brotherhood, as a counterpoise to the instinct of competition; labour, the task and privilege of all; justice, including the opportunity for all to lead a happy and useful life; and public responsibility for the character of the economic and social order.[21] The same committee also explicitly repudiated the *laissez-faire* doctrine that 'economic conditions are to be left to the action of material causes and mechanical laws, uncontrolled by any moral responsibility'.[22]

In 1907 the Convocation of Canterbury accepted the report of its committee on *The Moral Witness of the Church on Economic Subjects*, the Upper House with scarcely a murmur of dissent, but the Lower House only in the face of vigorous protests from its more reactionary members,[23] thus setting a pattern of behaviour in the two houses which persisted with unfailing regularity when social and industrial issues came to be discussed more fully after the 1914–18 War. This report of 1907 was notable for its introduction of the principle that the first charge upon industry should be the adequate maintenance of its employees, commonly known as the doctrine of the living wage. This was to be one of the chief corner-stones of Christian social propaganda for the next thirty years, despite the opposition of industrialists and despite the Church's failure to prove its feasibility by economic reasoning. *The Moral Witness of the Church*, a similar report to the 1908 Lambeth

[19] *The Five Lambeth Conferences, 1867–1908*, p. 109.

[20] *Ibid.*, p. 140. A more ambitious note was struck by the suggestion that the Church might require some knowledge of economic science from her candidates for orders.

[21] *Ibid.*, pp. 266f. [22] *Ibid.*, p. 267.

[23] See the *Chronicle of Convocation*, 1907, especially pp. 111–15. It is significant that all five episcopal members of the committee which produced the report (C. Gore, E. S. Talbot, J. Percival, E. Hoskyns and J. R. Harmer) were members of the C.S.U.

Conference, included as an appendix an important extract from the 1907 Convocation report,[24] and spoke of the Church's attitude to social affairs in language borrowed directly from the official objects of the C.S.U.[25]

It is sometimes unjustly observed that the C.S.U., having claimed that the Christian Law should rule social practice, omitted to say what the Christian Law actually was.[26] Westcott did in fact set himself the task of defining it, as in his presidential address to the C.S.U. at Manchester on November 25th, 1895, in which he described the Christian Law as 'the embodiment of the Truth for action in forms answering to the conditions of society from age to age. The embodiment takes place slowly, and it can never be complete. It is impossible for us to rest indolently in the conclusions of the past. In each generation the obligation is laid on Christians to bring new problems of conduct and duty into the Divine light, and to find their solution under the teaching of the Spirit.'[27] Two conclusions seem to emerge from this: political measures are necessary if the Christian law is to be applied to society, but political action must not be revolutionary. Westcott accepts the Fabian doctrine, later endorsed by the Labour Party, of the inevitability of gradualness. This definition of the Christian Law was still imprecise, but the failure of the majority of C.S.U. members to do anything to hasten 'the embodiment of the Truth' by political means must be attributed not so much to genuine mystification as to a ready acquiescence in the status quo.

The task of bringing 'new problems of conduct and duty into the Divine Light' was one which particularly appealed to Gore, who looked forward to the enunciation, by groups of churchmen collaborating with secular economists, of a new Christian casuistry, filling a gap in the teaching of the Church which had been a source of weakness to it ever since the decay of the medieval principles of social justice in the face of a capitalism and industrialism to which they could not be applied. Only one such study was in fact carried

[24] *The Five Lambeth Conferences, 1867–1908*, pp. 413–15.

[25] *Ibid.*, p. 410.

[26] This dictum appeared originally in G. C. Binyon, *The Christian Socialist Movement in England*, p. 197. It is used by many writers of the C.S.U., but almost always without consideration of the qualification which Binyon himself adds.

[27] B. F. Westcott, *Christian Social Union Addresses*, p. 18.

out, a symposium on the subject of property, edited by Gore himself, but this has remained a definitive expression of the Christian attitude on the subject.[28] In his introduction Gore acknowledges that property is necessary for the expression of personality, but he sets clear limits to the right of property, claiming that the state should be free to intervene and regulate it in such a way as will best promote the welfare of all its citizens; in his own judgment the time was ripe for such intervention.[29] The advantages of private property-holding are acknowledged, but some modification of the system is needed which will avoid the inequalities, hardships and uncertainties which prevail at present.[30] Perhaps the most important essay is L. T. Hobhouse's *The Historical Evolution of Property, in Fact and in Idea*, which makes the important distinction (much used in later attempts to formulate a Christian philosophy of society) between property for use and property for power. In the former case property is 'the material basis of a permanent, ordered, purposeful, and self-directed activity', which the Christian must judge to be perfectly legitimate; in the latter it is 'a form of social organization, whereby the labour of those who have it not is directed by and for the enjoyment of those that have'—a dangerous and unjust arrangement.[31]

The problem of reconciling the advantages of individual ownership with the necessities of the method and organization of large-scale industry was one which was to bring unhealed divisions into the Christian social camp. Scott Holland, in his essay *Property and Personality*, looks forward to an extension of the benefits of ownership by collective means, but he does not deny the difficulty of making this generally acceptable, and he doubts whether collective ownership will work on the individual conscience and imagination as effectively as private ownership.[32]

In 1896 Scott Holland founded the magazine *Commonwealth*, and edited it himself, or shared in the task, until his death in 1918. It provided a useful platform for the dissemination and discussion of C.S.U. views, and an instrument of propaganda to help its more

[28] *Property: its Duties and Rights*, edited by C. Gore (1913).
[29] *Ibid.*, pp. xi–xviii.
[30] *Ibid.*, p. 64 in the essay by Hastings Rashdall, *The Philosophical Theory of Property*.
[31] *Ibid.*, p. 10. [32] *Ibid.*, p. 190.

practical activities. These were largely concerned with the most obvious industrial evils of the day, particularly sweated labour, and the C.S.U. drew up 'white lists' of firms which Christians could patronize in the knowledge that their employees worked under satisfactory conditions and received a fair wage. Sweating was particularly prevalent in the tailoring trade, and it was here that white lists were most effective, although the number of customers whose choice was governed by them was naturally so small that no significant impression was made on the problem. More constructive and influential was the C.S.U. contribution to the campaign for industrial legislation, notably to prevent lead-poisoning in the pottery industry. It helped to secure the passage of the Factory and Workshops Act of 1901 and the first Trade Boards Act of 1909, which established minimum wage-rates in certain industries whose workers lacked the protection of strong trade union organization,[33] and the C.S.U. research committee also investigated bad housing and drunkenness.

Despite the range of its activities, the episcopal support which it enjoyed, its lack of partisan colouring and its relatively large membership (rising to 6000; the G.S.M. never boasted more than 400),[34] there were many areas of Christian activity into which the C.S.U. failed to penetrate. For nearly twenty years one such was, rather surprisingly, the Student Christian Movement. Its evangelical origin, missionary orientation and solidly middle-class membership (which meant that its members were effectively insulated from contact with the harsher sides of life) contrived to prevent it from giving serious attention to social problems until 1909, when a conference was held in April to discuss the subject of Discipleship and the Social Problem.[35] William Temple[36] was

[33] The Trade Boards Act of 1909 covered the tailoring, chain-making, box-making and lace-finishing industries. By 1921 there were 63 boards, covering 39 trades and three million workers.

[34] The figures are quoted by M. B. Reckitt in *Maurice to Temple*, p. 160.

[35] Tissington Tatlow, *The Story of the S.C.M. of Great Britain and Ireland*, pp. 346–54.

[36] William Temple, 1881–1944; Fellow of the Queen's College, Oxford 1904–10, Headmaster of Repton School 1910–14, Vicar of St. James's Piccadilly 1914–17, Leader of the Life and Liberty movement 1917–19, Canon of Westminster 1919–20, Bishop of Manchester 1920–9, Archbishop of York 1929–42 and of Canterbury 1942–4; President of the Workers' Educational Association 1908–24, Editor of *The Pilgrim* 1920–7, Chairman of Copec 1924, of the Edinburgh Faith and Order Conference 1937, and of the Malvern Conference 1941.

present at this conference, and later came to have a warm appreciation of the influence of the S.C.M. in encouraging an attitude in students which led on naturally to the study of social problems.[37] After the 1909 conference a group of senior S.C.M. members formed the Collegium, a group under Temple's leadership which devoted itself to study and corporate prayer about the will of God for modern society.[38] There seemed to be no real understanding of the Christian doctrine of society, and the group's object was to rectify this state of affairs by publishing essays on general aspects of society similar to the work envisaged by Gore for the C.S.U. Like the C.S.U., the Collegium in fact tackled only one subject, competition,[39] but this study was another outstanding contribution to Christian social thought.

The first half of the book deals with the nature of competition itself. Modern industry is built upon a competitive basis, which, although originally a moral one, has been abused in such a way as to exaggerate its inherent defects to the exclusion of its virtues, and to lead finally to the establishment of a system of vested interests and economic privilege which is incompatible with a Christian ideal of society.[40] The authors admit that substantial

[37] Tatlow (*op. cit.*, p. 670) records that at the time of the Copec conference of 1924 Temple expressed the opinion that, had it not been for the S.C.M., Copec would have been impossible. F. A. Cockin, writing in the *Torch* (the monthly magazine of the Industrial Christian Fellowship), in May 1928, (p. 70) estimated that more than half the delegates at Copec were former members of the S.C.M., citing this as evidence of the S.C.M.'s concern with social matters. For the later history of the S.C.M.'s work in this sphere, see Hugh Martin, 'A Widening Horizon', in *Stockholm*, Vol. 4, 1931, pp. 133–8.

[38] The Collegium was a very small body, with only eleven members in 1913. For details of its beginnings see Temple's introduction to *The Industrial Unrest and the Living Wage* (a collection of lectures given at the 1912 Summer School of the Interdenominational Conference of Social Service Unions). As a result of the discussions at this Summer School an organization was formed in 1913 known as the Council for Christian Witness on Social Questions. After the 1920 Lambeth Conference this body was known as the Christian Social Crusade; Gore was its Chairman, and it worked through local interdenominational Social Service Unions.

[39] *Competition, a Study in Human Motive*, by John Harvey, J. St. G. C. Heath, Malcolm Spencer, William Temple and H. G. Wood (1917).

[40] This critique includes (p. 45) a favourable estimate of the break with the medieval Christian view of society which is unusual in Christian social writing (but *cf.* Eli Heckscher, 'Ethics and Economics,' in *Stockholm*, Vol. 1, 1928, pp. 38–48). Despair at the condition of industrial society increasingly led many Christian social thinkers to look, however unrealistically, for some sort of return to the past rather than to further development of the existing system. This tendency is discussed in more detail in Chapter 6.

advantages can be claimed for a competitive system; it leads to a high level of production and efficiency, provides a constant incentive to ingenuity and research, and theoretically ensures the maintenance of the greatest measure of personal liberty by allowing production to be controlled by public demand. It is efficiently selective, matching men and occupations in the best possible way, and the authors recall the impetus given to *laissez-faire* economics by Darwin's discovery of the principle of natural selection, which seemed to provide a cosmic imprimatur for the principle of competition. Finally, competition has a beneficial effect on character, encouraging endurance, self-reliance, energy and initiative.

Against these advantages, it is argued, there are many drawbacks. There is a tendency for the best to be eliminated, for if the taste of the majority is the arbiter of everything, there is little hope that the highest standards will be reached or maintained. Many valuable services remain unprovided and resources unutilized, because private profit does not stand to benefit. The excellences of a competitive system are bought at great cost; the success of some means the failure of others, and this involves appalling social misery. The analogy with the principle of natural selection is not even valid, since society is not callous enough to permit the ruthless extermination of the failures. They simply become parasitic, lowering the general level of society and absorbing not only much of the profits of competitive industry, in the form of expenditure on Poor Law relief and the treatment of disease, degeneracy and crime, but also the energies of many of the most capable citizens in the administration of these services. And the effect of competition on character is by no means one-sided, since it may also foster despair, suspicion, greed, cunning, enmity, pride and hardness of heart.

The competitive system could, it is claimed, be either modified by social reform legislation or replaced by the introduction of a collectivist or syndicalist social order. The authors point out that the first method was being pursued with some vigour by the Liberal government between 1906 and the outbreak of war in 1914, with its programme of legislation which, although leading to many important social reforms, was not socialist in the collectivist sense. This could, they feel, be extended, particularly by the improvement of maternity and infant welfare services, and of education, measures which would have the effect of increasing the equality of opportunity on the basis of which the advantages of competition most readily develop. In short, 'through a more stringent system of graduated taxation and through an increase in the death duties all undue profits would be transferred to the community as a whole, and out of the fund thus raised far-reaching communal experiments in education, sanitation, housing, and the like would be carried out.'[41] In dealing with the objection that such piecemeal reform would not go far enough, the authors weigh the merits of thorough-going collectivism, and tentatively suggest that the most hopeful course may lie in the adoption of guild socialism, a compromise between collectivism and the anarchic form of syndicalism which originated as a political theory in France. Guild socialism was widely canvassed in various forms from 1912 onwards, and won strong support from a number of Christians who were attracted neither by private capitalism nor by collectivism.[42]

The difficulties in the way of any radical recasting of society lead the authors of *Competition* to the almost inevitable conclusion that no lasting improvement is possible without a transformation of human nature, but they point out that this is not necessarily a vain utopian hope. Although a Christian ideal must take account of the facts as they are, it need not avoid the note of genuine demand, and it must not acquiesce in the common illusion that society is static and unchanging; social institutions mould character hardly less than they are moulded by it, and small improvements may make possible more important advances.[43]

Competition is a forgotten and neglected book, but it ranges over many difficult social problems and takes account of the most important suggestions for dealing with them which were to be

[41] *Competition*, p. 127. The Liberal legislation to which reference is made included the Trade Disputes Act (1906); provision for a school meals service (1906) and the medical inspection of schoolchildren (1907); regulation of the employment of children outside school hours (1908); an eight-hour day for miners (1908); the Housing and Town Planning Act, and the first Trade Boards Act (1909); and, most important of all in that it was the first large-scale application of the principle of redistributive taxation, the introduction of non-contributory old age pensions in 1908.

[42] Guild socialism is not fully discussed in *Competition*. Its exposition from a Christian point of view is considered in Chapter 3, as part of the Christian response to the problems and opportunities which emerged in a new form at the end of the 1914–18 War.

[43] *Competition*, pp. 159–66.

hotly disputed, not least by Christian writers, in the post-war period. It also shows a spirit of impartiality and fair judgment in discussing them which was not often maintained in the treatment of such subjects by Christian social thinkers.

To complement this brief outline of the theoretical discussion of social problems within the Church of England, some account must be given of the practical attempts which were being made, with the help of churchmen, to mitigate the most obvious evils of the existing social system, and for this purpose it is necessary to go back to the sixties of the last century. The charitable relief of suffering, accepted as a Christian duty since the earliest days of the Church, had become an enormous undertaking in industrial Britain, and one which was in a state of chaotic disorganization. Numerous small societies, using different methods, inspired by different ideals and accepting different standards, attempted to deal with the worst poverty, but they hardly touched the problem as a whole. There was much overlapping and waste, and plenty of scope for unscrupulous applicants to exploit the often gullible visitors, while for many of the most deserving cases there was no alternative to the justifiably dreaded workhouse.[44] Above all, there was little attempt to deal with each case sympathetically, constructively and with understanding. In 1869, in an attempt to rectify this state of affairs, a group of philanthropists founded the Charity Organization Society. Among the founders were Octavia Hill, whose pioneering work in housing and system of housing management strongly influenced later specifically Christian attempts to deal with the problem, C. S. Loch, the secretary, and two Anglican priests, W. H. Fremantle and S. A. Barnett.[45] The

[44] The deterrent principle on which the Poor Law was administered after 1834 was that of 'less eligibility'; in order to avoid the worst effects of pauperism caused by indiscriminate out-relief, and to reduce the burden on the rates, it was laid down that the lot of anyone maintained at public expense must be 'less eligible' than that of the lowest-paid independent workman. In principle no out-relief was to be given, which meant that a family, even though destitute by no fault of its own, was ruthlessly broken up and condemned to the rigours—and frequently horrors—of the 'House'. The guardians did not always act in accordance with this principle, but the administration of relief was harsh enough to earn the universal hatred of the poor.

[45] Samuel Augustus Barnett, 1844–1913; Vicar of St. Jude's, Whitechapel 1873–94, Warden of Toynbee Hall 1884–96, Canon of Bristol 1894–1906, and of Westminster 1906–13; Poor Law Guardian 1875–1904, Founder of the Children's Country Holiday Fund 1877.

work of the C.O.S. was based on three principles: patient and persistent personal service; personal responsibility for the consequences, both individual and social, of charity; and scientific investigation of each case to forecast the effect of charity on the character and circumstances of the recipient.[46] This was a praiseworthy attempt to provide a useful outlet for the philanthropic energy of the well-to-do, without the pauperizing effect of indiscriminate charity of which Barnett himself wrote in 1874: 'The relief of the poor is a matter which I hold to be of the greatest importance. Indiscriminate charity is among the curses of London. To put the result of our observation in the strongest form, I would say that "the poor starve because of the alms they receive".'[47]

If the worthy principles of the C.O.S. were to be put into practice, it was apparent that a distinction must be made between the deserving and the undeserving, but this proved to be in most cases impossible, and before long the criterion came to be whether an applicant could be adequately helped by what the C.O.S. could offer. Anyone, however deserving and virtuous, who could not be restored by the C.O.S. to the ranks of the self-supporting was denied help, and the effect of this policy development was not unnaturally to alienate many Christian supporters of the Society, notably Barnett and his wife, who broke finally with the central organization of the C.O.S. in 1895.[48] His work in Whitechapel, and the inability of the C.O.S. to make any significant impression on the problem of poverty in London, convinced Barnett that there must be an extension of state-provided services, particularly medical treatment, housing, education and old age pensions, on a scale hitherto thought quite unnecessary by the predominantly *laissez-faire* opinion of the day. The C.O.S. persevered in a rigid policy of opposition to any extension of state or municipal action to relieve poverty, maintaining even in the face of such convincing evidence as that provided by Charles Booth that self-help was the only

[46] Beatrice Webb, *My Apprenticeship*, pp. 196–201.

[47] *Canon Barnett, his Life, Work and Friends*, by his wife, Vol. I, p. 83. In support of this judgment was the fact that eight million pounds was spent annually in London alone by charitable institutions without reducing the numbers of the poor. (Quoted in S. A. Barnett, *The Perils of Wealth and Poverty*, p. 58. The figure of eight million pounds applied in 1913.)

[48] *Canon Barnett, his Life, Work and Friends*, Vol. II, pp. 263–9.

remedy for poverty and distress.[49] Barnett never abandoned his opposition to indiscriminate charity, but he came to see that voluntary action, no matter how enlightened, and self-help, no matter how valiant, were incapable of raising everybody's standard of living to an acceptable level so long as the organization of society and industry remained unchanged.

There were two lessons to be drawn from Barnett's work. First, doles and charity do tend to pauperize, and in some cases to draw capable and able-bodied men into the vicious circle of dependence on charity, disinclination for work, inability to work, and even more complete dependence on charity. But, secondly, it is possible to act rigorously in the spirit of this conclusion and withdraw charitable help only if society is organized in such a way as to offer to the able-bodied a good education, a job, a living wage, a reasonable house and the prospect of security in old age, and to the sick the certain knowledge that they will receive the medical treatment they need. There are, of course, many dangers in collective security and welfare services of the kind to which Barnett's experience logically points, but it was a common fault, even among Christian thinkers, when the opportunity presented itself from 1918 onwards to provide some of these desirable social services, to remember the first of Barnett's lessons but forget the second. Many made the same mistake as C. S. Loch, who taunted Barnett with inconsistency in declaring his opposition to out-relief, and then his support of it in another guise—a reference to Barnett's campaign for old age pensions.[50] The distinction between charity and welfare services was not always clearly grasped.

Expressed in terms of the choice defined by the authors of *Competition*, Barnett undoubtedly favoured social reform legislation rather than full-scale Socialism. In *The Perils of Wealth and Poverty* there is only one disparaging reference to Socialism as a

[49] Charles Booth, *The Life and Labour of the People in London*, nine volumes, 1892–7; the first results of his research were published in 1889. It is interesting to note that Booth's refutation of the Malthusian doctrine of the necessity of poverty and insecurity to keep down the population level was also widely ignored, and opposition to the principle of family allowances continued to be based partly on Malthusian grounds until the 1920s.

[50] *Canon Barnett, his Life, Work and Friends*, Vol. II, p. 267.

political method of bringing about the desired increase in the means of the poor,[51] but there is nothing half-hearted about Barnett's enthusiasm for redistributive taxation. The main burden of his message to the middle-class Christian is that the role of the taxpayer is one which should be cheerfully accepted: 'In the days when our brothers' needs were met only by charity it was said that "God loveth a cheerful giver". Now that they are more efficiently met by the State it can be equally well said that "God loveth a cheerful taxpayer".'[52]

Barnett's cautious attitude towards political remedies, and his uneasy relations with the C.O.S., earned him a good deal of criticism. Beatrice Webb was impatient with what she regarded as his confused outlook: 'Intellectually he has no system of thought, no consistent bias.'[53] From a different point of view George Lansbury could write: 'How heartless and brutal in its effect on the lives of the poor was the Charity Organization policy of men like Canon Barnett. . . .'[54] That Barnett was unable to win sympathy for his position, or distinguish it from that officially adopted by the C.O.S., even in the eyes of Lansbury, a man moved by the same religious and emotional impulse and equally well aware of the facts, is a measure of the difficulties with which he had to contend.

An increasing number of Christians wanted to go further than Barnett, avoiding his paternalist spirit and showing a deeper consideration for the status and personal dignity of the worker. They wanted to narrow down Westcott's broad definition of socialism, and link the Church's social effort with that being made by the Labour Party. Such a course appeared to many Christians as the natural expression of their social enthusiasm, for the labour movement in Britain, thanks partly to the efforts of J. M. Ludlow, had never been hostile to Christianity. It was certainly severely critical of the Church, but the I.L.P. under Keir Hardie maintained

[51] S. A. Barnett, *The Perils of Wealth and Poverty*, p. 67.
[52] *Ibid.*, p. 92. [53] Beatrice Webb, *My Apprenticeship*, p. 212.
[54] George Lansbury, *My Life*, p. 132. George Lansbury, 1859–1940; Labour M.P. for Bow and Bromley 1910–12 and 1922–40, First Commissioner of Works 1929–31, Leader of the Labour Party 1931–5, Signatory of the Minority Report of the Royal Commission on the Poor Law 1909, Editor of the *Daily Herald* 1913–14 and 1919–22 and of the weekly *Herald* 1914–19; imprisoned as a Poplar councillor for contempt of court 1921.

a fully Christian moral outlook. Theologically, idealistic Socialism was strongly immanentist, even pantheist, but its Christian inspiration was undeniable. This is well seen in Philip Snowden's pamphlet, *The Christ that is to be*, which, while pointing out the extent of the Church's failure, claims that the survival of Christianity is a proof of the appeal which it makes to the 'eternal needs of humanity' and of the satisfaction which it can offer to the 'cravings of the human heart'.[55] But 'if Christianity is to be of any use it must be applied to our everyday life, and the only way in which principles, either Christian or otherwise, can be applied to social and industrial conditions is through the agency of political means'.[56]

Snowden's position shows the influence of an extreme form of liberal protestantism, but most of those Christians whose theology was of this kind were reluctant to read into it any social implications at all. It was left to a group of predominantly high church clergy from parishes in the North and Midlands to meet at Morecambe in 1906 to form the Church Socialist League. One of their leaders was P. E. T. Widdrington,[57] who traced the origin of the enthusiasm for Socialism among the northern clergy to a charge delivered to them by Westcott in 1892.[58] The electoral success of the Labour Party in 1906, when it gained twenty-nine seats in parliament, further increased the number of clergy who saw in Socialism the political embodiment of Christian ideals, and it was a leading member of the C.S.L., Lewis Donaldson,[59] who first expressed this conviction in the form of the slogan 'Christianity is the religion of which Socialism is the practice.' Widdrington, however, pointed out in retrospect that the Labour Party of 1906 was still a party of idealists who had not settled down to the serious business of politics; Socialism 'was not, certainly for the average Labour voter, so much a formulated system of economics as a burning protest against social injustice. It owed little to Karl Marx, but much to the Bible.'[60]

[55] Philip Snowden, *The Christ that is to be* (1903), p. 5. [56] *Ibid.*, p. 7.

[57] Percy Widdrington, 1873–1959; Vicar of St. Peter's, Coventry, 1906–18, Rector of Great Easton, Essex, 1918–55, Canon of Chelmsford 1939–55.

[58] B. F. Westcott, *The Incarnation, a Revelation of Human Duties.*

[59] Frederic Lewis Donaldson, 1860–1953; Vicar of St. Mark's, Leicester 1896–1918, Canon of Peterborough 1918–24, and of Westminster 1924–51, Chairman of the C.S.L. 1913–16; one of the leaders and organizers of the first march of the unemployed, from Leicester to London in 1905.

An important point which was disputed within the C.S.L. from its earliest days was whether it should be principally a political or a theological society. Widdrington saw the need for study and for the formulation of a Christian sociology,[61] but was unable to persuade the 1906 conference to include a reference to such objects in the League's official basis. Carried away by their enthusiasm for Socialism, most of the delegates failed to foresee the unwelcome limitations which a particular political loyalty might impose on them, and it was of course impossible to know the direction in which Labour Party policy would develop when political power came within its reach. The thoroughgoing Socialists in the C.S.L. became disillusioned with the Labour Alliance policy of the I.L.P., by which Socialism was pursued only in so far as the trade unions and labour movement could be induced to support it, and with the Fabian collectivism which the Labour Party adopted as its ideal. The drift away from support for the Labour Party, which later became apparent in the C.S.L., was not so much because the Labour Party was too radical as because it did not go far enough, seeming to lose its Socialist fervour. But at first the C.S.L. was united in its political enthusiasm, and its objects included: 'The establishment of a democratic commonwealth in which the community shall own the land and capital collectively, and use them co-operatively for the good of all.'[62]

In 1912 the C.S.L. began to publish a monthly magazine, the *Church Socialist*, and contributions to it during the first year of its life show that the original political enthusiasm quickly gave way to a much stronger emphasis on the duty of the League towards the Church and towards Christians who were not sympathetic towards

[61] 'Christian Sociology' was an expression much used by some Christian social thinkers between the wars, particularly those of the group which Widdrington continued to lead. See below, Chapter 6.

[62] See G. C. Binyon, *The Christian Socialist Movement in England*, pp. 190–200. The avowed principles and methods of the C.S.L. are set out in full in this source.

---

[60] From an article by Widdrington on the C.S.L., in the series 'Christian Socialism, Past and Present', in *Commonwealth*, April 1927, p. 119. The Guild of St. Matthew was still in existence in 1906, but was too emphatically Catholic and not sufficiently Socialist to appeal to the group which founded the C.S.L. Widdrington described the ecclesiastical flavour of the G.S.M. as L.B. and S.C. (a reference to the London, Brighton and South Coast Railway), and its political tone as that of the Metropolitan Radical Federation (*ibid.*, p. 120).

the theology of the League: 'Our concern . . . is not to compel them to join a political party, but to accept the social implications of the Faith'.[63] Widdrington was more than ever convinced that the League had been right to withstand the demand for its affiliation to the Labour Party, and, after an abortive attempt in 1912, he was finally successful, in September 1916, in persuading the League to lay greater emphasis on its theological work.[64]

A notable defection from the ranks of the C.S.L. was that of Conrad Noel, who had at first been one of its most enthusiastic supporters. He had described it as 'the most vigorous champion of Catholic democracy that has yet taken the field. Its power is already out of all proportion to its numbers; its growth has been phenomenal; its activities are numberless.'[65] But disillusion set in, he resigned from the C.S.L. in 1916, and two years later formed his own society, the Catholic Crusade. This, even more than Headlam's G.S.M., was dominated by its founder, and its activities were centred on Thaxted where Noel was vicar. He stood for a revolutionary attitude in politics and the establishment, if necessary by force, of a classless, co-operative society on communist lines. This ideal, which he derived from his reading of the Fathers, was combined with an extreme form of Anglo-Catholicism and a vigorous dislike of pacifism.[66] The C.S.U. in particular came under the lash of his disapproval: 'That mild and watery society for social reform', as he once called it,[67] 'glories in its indefiniteness, and seems to consider it a crime to arrive at any particular economic conclusion. . . . An unkind critic has described it as for ever learning but never coming to a knowledge of the truth.'[68] Strictures of this kind on the C.S.U. were not confined to those of Noel's extremist views; a common jibe was that the C.S.U. attitude was 'Here's a social evil; let's read a paper on it',[69] and indeed its days were numbered.

[63] The *Church Socialist,* November 1912, p. 4.

[64] M. B. Reckitt, *P. E. T. Widdrington,* pp. 55f. and 67. See also the *Church Socialist,* October 1916, pp. 186–8.

[65] Conrad Noel, *Socialism in Church History,* p. 283. This fulsome eulogy of the C.S.L. was written in 1910, when it was at the height of its popularity and had about 1200 members. Conrad Noel, 1869–1942, is chiefly remembered for his political and liturgical activities as Vicar of Thaxted 1910–42.

[66] The aims, rules and constitution of the Catholic Crusade may be found in the *Church Socialist,* October–November 1918, pp. 108–10.

[67] *Conrad Noel, An Autobiography,* p. 71.

[68] Conrad Noel, *Socialism in Church History,* p. 257.

[69] Quoted by F. G. Bettany, *Stewart Headlam,* p. 95.

When war broke out in 1914, the attitude of the Church of England towards social affairs was still confused. The vast majority of both clergy and laity were indifferent; the G.S.M. had expired; the C.S.U. was in a sad decline; the C.S.L. was still struggling to discover its true vocation. But, despite these uncertainties, there were encouraging practical developments. The work begun by Barnett at Toynbee Hall in 1884 was taken up by the University Settlements; Oxford House, Bethnal Green, was founded in 1885, and Cambridge House, Camberwell, developed out of the Trinity College Settlement in 1896. This work was further expanded, in a rather different form, by the Society of the Divine Compassion, founded at Plaistow in 1894 by J. G. Adderley, and based on the community which he outlined in his autobiographical novel, *Stephen Remarx* (1893).[70] Adderley was disappointed that no method of social reform had been evolved which embodied successfully both Christianity and Socialism, and the Society abandoned political theory in favour of imitating as nearly as possible the life of Christ, adopting the Franciscan rule and working in any way that seemed necessary among the poor of East London. The S.D.C. developed into a flourishing religious order and did much valuable work, but inevitably it could have no influence on political and public life.[71] Here again, however, it is to the settlements that one must look for an important source of Christian inspiration; although they did not in themselves stand for any particular theory of social reform, they enabled a succession of future economists, politicians and administrators to gain first-hand experience of some of the most pressing problems of industrial society.[72]

Meanwhile, growing public dissatisfaction with the state of society was reflected in the Liberal programme of social legislation,

[70] The Hon. James Granville Adderley, 1861–1942; Head of Oxford House 1885–6, Head of Christ Church Mission 1887–93, Curate of All Hallows, Barking, 1893–4 and of St. Andrew's, Plaistow, 1894–7, Minister of the Berkeley Chapel, Mayfair, 1897–1901, various livings in Birmingham and London 1901–35, Prebendary of St. Paul's, 1935–42. Adderley left the S.D.C. in 1897 to pursue what he regarded as his true vocation, a mission to the rich.

[71] See Peter Anson, *The Call of the Cloister*, pp. 148–60. The Franciscan tradition in the Church of England was continued with the foundation of the Society of St. Francis in Dorset in 1921, particularly to help vagrants.

[72] Lord Attlee, Lord Beveridge and R. H. Tawney all spent some time at Toynbee Hall.

culminating in the National Insurance Act of 1911, which laid the foundations of a more just and stable social order, and went some way towards removing the incentive to a literally revolutionary solution of social problems. There seemed to be a good chance of steady progress towards the elimination of the worst results of industrialism and the provision of a reasonable standard of living for the whole population, but whether this was, by itself, the sort of development with which a Christian could feel satisfied was not so certain. When the war ended in 1918 there were many social issues, including the hitherto largely neglected questions of the status of the worker and his share in the control of industry, which demanded urgent and far-reaching action, providing an outstanding opportunity for the application of Christian standards in the organization of society. Succeeding chapters describe how the Church of England, equipped with the experience, knowledge and opinions which have been outlined in this chapter, responded to these new demands.

Mr. and Mrs. George Lansbury

The Rev. and Mrs. G. A. Studdert Kennedy

2

Post-War Problems: The Peace

THE EFFECT of war on a combatant nation is both to ennoble and to brutalize, and the 1914–18 War, if only because it was war on an unprecedented scale, had these contradictory effects to a notable degree. On the one hand the task of defending freedom and maintaining justice appealed to men's highest instincts, demanding energy, initiative, self-sacrifice and a sense of social solidarity of an altogether remarkable kind, particularly during the early part of the war, before profiteering became a notorious temptation and an occasion of bitter resentment. The mood of idealism was reflected in the ambitious and imaginative plans which the govenment set in hand, before the war ended, for reconstruction at home and for the creation of the League of Nations, plans which received vigorous if not undivided support from the Church of England. The National Mission of Repentance and Hope, conducted throughout the country in 1916, was not a great evangelistic success, perhaps chiefly because it was so difficult to strike the note of repentance in a convincing way when the country was straining every muscle in the pursuit of what was inevitably upheld as a just and noble cause, but it did give birth to five important reports, commissioned by the Archbishops, of which the fifth, *Christianity and Industrial Problems*, can without exaggeration be described as one of the finest and most important expressions of Christian opinion on social and industrial affairs ever produced by the Church of England. The domestic sphere, however, is dealt with in the next chapter; the most pressing need in 1918 was to establish peace and international security, and here also the Church, particularly in the persons of Gore and Lord Robert Cecil,[1] made strenuous efforts to

[1] Lord Robert Cecil, 1864–1958; Conservative and Independent Conservative M.P. 1906–23, created Viscount Cecil of Chelwood 1923, Lord Privy Seal 1932, Chancellor of the Duchy of Lancaster 1924–7, President of the League of Nations Union 1923–45, Nobel Peace Prize 1937. From 1923 to 1927 Robert Cecil was responsible for the government's handling of League of Nations affairs, but he resigned in 1927 when he felt that Baldwin's Cabinet was not seriously interested in supporting the League. (To avoid confusion he is referred to throughout as (Lord) Robert Cecil.)

influence the course of events in the light of Christian principles.

On the other hand, in contrast to the optimism and idealism, there was the fact that the country was physically and spiritually exhausted, and the degrading and vulgarizing effect of the war was much in evidence, not least in the campaign leading up to the so-called 'coupon' election of December 1918.[2] Lloyd George, determined to exploit his reputation as the man who won the war, called for a general election immediately after the armistice. His first election manifesto, of November 22nd, promised a 'fit country for heroes to live in', emphasized the need for disarmament and support for the League, and echoed the widely held belief that the opportunity should be taken to make the world a better place. But his acute political instinct persuaded him that he would enlist greater support if he identified himself with the unsavoury and vindictive campaign, led by the Northcliffe newspapers,[3] for hanging the Kaiser and making Germany pay the full cost of the war. Both of these objects were unattainable, as Lloyd George must well have known, but he allowed himself to be carried along by the rising tide of malice until his final manifesto of December 11th—'this concoction of greed and sentiment, prejudice and deception', as Keynes described it[4]—demanded the trial of the Kaiser, the punishment of those responsible for atrocities, and the exaction of the fullest indemnities from Germany. 'A vote for a Coalition candidate meant the Crucifixion of Anti-Christ and the assumption by Germany of the British National Debt. It proved an irresistible combination. No candidate could safely denounce this programme, and none did so.'[5] So the coalition swept to an

[2] The name 'coupon' was a derisive reference by Asquith to the letter of endorsement, signed by Lloyd George and Bonar Law, which was required by all coalition candidates; these included most Conservatives, and such Liberals as accepted Lloyd George's leadership. The Liberal Party had been split since 1916, and the section led by Asquith did not receive the 'coupon'. For the purposes of the 1918 election the Labour Party withdrew from the coalition, although a few Labour M.P.s, notably G. N. Barnes, continued to support it.

[3] At that time *The Times*, *Daily Mail*, *Daily Mirror* and *Evening News*.

[4] J. M. Keynes, *The Economic Consequences of the Peace*, p. 131. John Maynard Keynes, 1883–1946; Fellow of King's College, Cambridge 1908–46, created Baron 1942. Keynes was a Treasury representative at the Paris Peace Conference in 1919, but resigned when he was unable to prevent what he regarded as the punitive folly of the provisions of the Peace Treaty. *The Economic Consequences of the Peace* (1919) is his classic exposition of the economic errors of the Treaty of Versailles. He was not a Christian.

[5] *Ibid.*, pp. 132f.

overwhelming victory,[6] and Stanley Baldwin confided in Keynes that the new Parliament was filled with 'a lot of hard-faced men, who look as if they had done very well out of the war'.[7]

From the Church there were few of the denunciations of the campaign which might have been expected, but this was partly due to the fact that in less than three weeks there was hardly time for Christian opinion to make itself felt. Nevertheless it cannot be claimed that very strenuous efforts were made, at least in some of the most obvious quarters, to attack and condemn the spirit of revenge. Archbishop Davidson,[8] although recording in his diary that the demands for vengeance were mischievous and harmful, did not make his views known.[9] The *Church Times* rejected as 'absolutely false' the argument that it was useless to insist on payment from a prostrate Germany, and went on, with complete disregard of economic facts, to speak of Germany's 'unlimited internal resources'.[10] A week later the same paper regretted that in the course of the election campaign the speeches had 'daily grown more and more personal and acrimonious', but ventured no criticism of the coalition's election manifesto.

There may have been many Christians, both clergy and laymen, who spoke out against the spirit of vengeance, but the record of their opposition has largely disappeared and its influence was

[6] The result was: Coalition 484, Labour 59, Independent Conservatives 48, Asquith Liberals 26, Independents 9, Irish Nationalists 7. (C. L. Mowat, *Britain Between the Wars*, pp. 6f.)

[7] Keynes, *op. cit.*, p. 133. He does not mention Baldwin by name.

[8] Randall Thomas Davidson, 1848–1930; Bishop of Rochester 1891–5, of Winchester 1895–1903, Archbishop of Canterbury 1903–28. Davidson was often in principle sympathetic with progressive thought, but his approach to social and industrial questions was always extremely cautious. In 1905 he refused to receive a delegation of the unemployed who had marched from Leicester, led by Lewis Donaldson, and he declined (unlike non-conformist leaders) to join in the agitation for old age pensions. In both cases he claimed to be avoiding the easy popularity which such a gesture would win, but which would not be justified, in his opinion, unless his intervention could make some real contribution to the cause in question. He perhaps underestimated the effect which the mere fact of his intervention would have had. (G. K. A. Bell, *Randall Davidson, Archbishop of Canterbury*, Vol. I, pp. 488–91 and 545f.)

[9] Bell, *op. cit.*, Vol. II, p. 942.

[10] The *Church Times*, December 6th, 1918. A similar opinion was expressed in the *Guardian*, which on December 5th and 12th supported both the trial of the Kaiser and the demand for very heavy indemnities. 'We trust that the clergy will lose no opportunity of impressing upon those who listen to them that, in this matter of indemnities, we are not taking revenge but are performing a great act of justice' (December 5th) is a sentence to delight the connoisseur of the religious press.

certainly slight. Studdert Kennedy[11] acknowledged that the 1918 election was 'one of the most shameful episodes in our history', and claimed that the Church tried to give a lead but received no support from the public at large; Lloyd George had exactly judged the political mood of the country, which got the government it deserved.[12] When the election results were made known, *Commonwealth* prophesied that the government would be seen to be an 'unrepresentative, heart-in-the-mouth affair, doomed to a speedy end. Its calamity will be that it is so palpably out of accord with the actual moral and intellectual forces that are at work in the country.'[13] In the event, despite some severe by-election setbacks for the coalition, this judgment proved too optimistic, and William Temple had occasion to write in 1921: 'Duty even more obviously than charity begins at home. The moral atmosphere of British political life has never been lower than it is just now. Opportunism is triumphant. Political life is directed according to no intelligible principles and towards no distinguishable goal.'[14]

In 1918, however, there was at least one important goal in view, and that was the Peace Treaty. Here in particular 'the mischief of the general election could not be undone; and the Government had not only to pretend to abuse its European victory as it had promised, but actually to do it by starving the enemies who had thrown down their arms. It had, in short, won the election by promising to be thriftlessly wicked, cruel and vindictive; and it did not find it as easy to escape from this pledge as it had from nobler ones.'[15] The terms of the Treaty of Versailles, which Germany was forced to sign on June 28th, 1919, chiefly by the pressure of the blockade, inflicted severe military and political punishment on her, fixed the war guilt exclusively on the Central Powers, and exacted

[11] Geoffrey Anketell Studdert Kennedy (Woodbine Willie) 1883–1929; Vicar of St. Paul's, Worcester, 1914–21, Chaplain to the Forces 1915–19, Rector of St. Edmund, Lombard St., 1922–9, Messenger of the Industrial Christian Fellowship 1921–9.

[12] Studdert Kennedy, *Democracy and the Dog Collar* (1921), p. 221.

[13] *Commonwealth*, January 1919, pp. 4f.

[14] *The Pilgrim*, January 1921, p. 126. *The Pilgrim* was a quarterly magazine, founded in 1920 by William Temple and edited by him throughout its life of seven years, which dealt from a Christian point of view with social and political questions.

[15] G. B. Shaw, from the Preface to *Heartbreak House* (1919), p. 25 in the Longman's edition of 1961.

heavy reparations from them. The final amount of reparations was left to be computed by a separate commission,[16] but the principles on which the question had been dealt with by the Allies were open to serious criticism. Keynes particularly objected to the inclusion in the demand for reparations of war pensions and separation allowances, in defiance of the armistice terms, and to the fact that so obviously spiteful and punitive a document should be hypocritically couched in the language of idealism and justice. Christian reaction was more in evidence than at the time of the general election, and Davidson wrote to Lloyd George on May 24th, 1919, complaining that the demands made on Germany, although individually plausible, were cumulatively intolerable. Lloyd George's reply, although conciliatory in tone, defended the imposition of severe terms on Germany and emphasized the need to balance the demands of justice with those of mercy. Lord Robert Cecil dissuaded Davidson from publicly attacking the Treaty, fearing that such a course might encourage the Germans to refuse to sign, and thereby increase the already very great suffering of the civilian population, which would last until the signing of the Treaty enabled the blockade to be lifted.[17]

The justice about which Lloyd George was so concerned is mentioned in much of the Christian comment on the Treaty, but it is not always understood in the same sense. The *Guardian* assured its readers on May 15th, 1919, that 'Germany is really escaping very easily'. The *Church Times* advised the Allies to ignore 'piteous stories of German suffering', and sternly preached the primacy of justice over mercy: 'The way of suffering is the only one by which she can be brought to repentance. We desire, as she does, a Peace of Right, but such a peace implies the satisfaction of the claims of justice.'[18] On June 20th the editorial condemned an appeal which was being made on behalf of the people of Oberammergau: 'Germany's part for the present is to make reparation, not to receive charity, and justice must be done before sentiment is

[16] It was finally fixed at the impossible sum of six thousand six hundred million pounds, but meanwhile, before this assessment was made, the Peace Treaty required payment by Germany of one thousand million pounds in two years. (C. L. Mowat, *Britain Between the Wars*, pp. 112f.)

[17] Bell, *op. cit.*, Vol. II, pp. 946–9.

[18] The *Church Times*, May 23rd and 30th, 1919.

indulged.' *Commonwealth*, on the other hand, was moved by an authentically Christian spirit. Starting from the conviction that 'justice is sterile which does not open out a way of redemption', it examined the terms of the Treaty, expressing concern in particular that the size and duration of the financial penalties seemed to be aimed at permanently crippling Germany rather than restoring her. It was also worried about the long period (fifteen years) envisaged for the occupation of the Rhineland, the confusion of a legitimate claim to the Saar coal with an illegitimate desire to annex German territory, and the concessions made to Poland which, being at the expense of East Prussia, were not likely to be permanently to Poland's advantage.[19] Among this intelligent and far-sighted comment the most important point was the recognition of the fact that plans to cripple Germany economically, in the interests of French security, were futile. This policy did in fact prove to be not only the most important cause of German poverty and financial instability, and consequently of German humiliation and resentment, but also one of the chief causes of economic depression in Britain in the ensuing decade, since a poverty-stricken Germany could not provide a market for British exports, and the enormous quantities of coal and manufactures exacted from Germany in the form of reparations considerably reduced the normal demand for these from Britain.[20]

The international scene was not, however, one of universal darkness. Lord Robert Cecil had submitted a memorandum to the Cabinet in 1916 outlining a plan for the prevention of war. This led to the publication in 1918 of the Phillimore Report, which favoured his ideas and included the first draft of the League of

[19] *Commonwealth*, June 1919, pp. 142f. The issue of February 1920 commends *The Economic Consequences of the Peace*, and speaks of the 'tremendous fiasco' and 'monumental folly' of the peace settlement (p. 34). The Church Socialist League, at its A.G.M. in May 1919, also voiced disapproval of the Peace Treaty, condemning it as a violation of the terms of the armistice and an indefensible breach of international morality. (The *Church Socialist*, June–July 1919, pp. 189f.)

[20] Before the terms of the Treaty of Versailles were settled Lloyd George did try to achieve some reduction in the demands made on Germany, but without success. The folly of the reparations clauses in the Treaty was far-reaching: 'They could not be enforced, and with their failure went other portions of the treaty, like disarmament, which ought to have been maintained.' (Lord Robert Cecil, *All the Way*, p. 157.)

Nations Covenant, but warned that in view of past attempts to achieve peace by means of treaties and alliances, any new system must enjoy the general support of all the major powers and be flexible enough to provide for future developments.[21] Following the lead given by President Wilson, the Allies incorporated the League Covenant in the Treaty of Versailles, but the need to make it generally acceptable prevented the development of a satisfactory and reliable system of mutual security. The Covenant made no provision for the enforcement of the decisions of the League Council, relying entirely on the principle that a dispute must be submitted to the League, a period of six months allowed for arbitration, and then, failing a satisfactory solution, a further three months must elapse, during which the issue would be exposed to the pressure of public opinion, before the country with a grievance might legitimately resort to the use of force. In practice these delaying tactics were never used, and this obligation of League membership did not deter Japan, Italy and Germany from the pursuit of their aggressive policies. The Covenant in this toothless form was a failure because it did nothing to curb the power of individual governments, but it was nevertheless attacked in Britain on the grounds that it involved a surrender of sovereignty.

Parliament was not enthusiastic: 'All or almost all the House professed support of the League; very, very few knew anything about it. Some of the Conservatives in their hearts disliked it, many disbelieved in it. Even the Labour members were at that time doubtful. The Liberals in the opposition were its best friends and they were powerless.'[22] In an attempt to arouse public interest in the League and support for it, the League of Nations Union was formed, to work through local branches, but this too was largely frustrated by the prevailing apathy and the feeling that, with the war over, such matters were best forgotten. A not unkind critic wrote at the time: 'While the "League of Nations Union" exists, and is run by passionate idealists, and holds great meetings, and has no reputable enemies, there is no general uprising in its defence or interest in its doings. The editor of a great newspaper told me that, in all his articles descriptive of the League's activities, he always had to put the headlines, and if possible the

[21] Lord Robert Cecil, *A Great Experiment*, p. 57. [22] *Ibid.*, p. 101.

first few sentences, without mention of the League. Otherwise he knew the article would go unread.'[23]

Responsibility for public indifference about the League cannot be pinned on the Church, for this was a matter in which a firm lead was given at almost every level. The League was discussed in both Convocations in 1918 and 1919, and by the Church Assembly at its first meeting in 1920. In the Upper House of Canterbury Convocation on February 7th, 1918, Gore's resolution welcoming the proposal to form the League was accepted without dissent,[24] and the Lower House of York Convocation, on July 9th, 1918, recorded its opinion that 'it is the duty of the Church at the present time to approve, and to use its best effort to promote, the inception of a League of Nations, as the first step to a better world-order', acknowledging in the course of the debate that there would be some loss of national sovereignty, but seeing it as the duty of the Church to help to educate public opinion to accept this.[25] On February 13th, 1919, the Upper House of York Convocation also welcomed and approved the idea of the League, accepting Lang's warning that it was likely to be opposed by 'vulgar and strident patriotism'.[26] The only serious opposition came from the Lower House of Canterbury Convocation when, on February 7th, 1918, the Archdeacon of Lewisham (C. E. Escreet) moved a resolution asking for the appointment of a committee to consider what the clergy might do to win support for the League. His speech was attacked by E. G. de S. Wood, of Ely, who claimed that the peace preached by Christ was interior peace, not political peace; indeed, Christ promised wars, commotions and tumults to precede his second coming. Preachers of the gospel should not concern themselves with political problems such as the League. A League of Peace might be a good idea, but as an ecclesiastic and minister of Christ he did not know whether it was or not, and indeed he had no means of knowing.[27] Wood was not unsupported in this curious point of view, and the Archdeacon was finally persuaded to accept

[23] C. F. G. Masterman, *England After War*, p. 21.
[24] The *Chronicle of Convocation*, 1918, pp. 169–77.
[25] *York Journal of Convocation*, 1918, pp. 254–9.
[26] *Ibid.*, 1919, pp. 93–7. Cosmo Gordon Lang, 1864–1945; Vicar of St. Mary's, Oxford, 1894–6 and of Portsea 1896–1901, Bishop of Stepney 1901–8, Archbishop of York 1908–28, of Canterbury 1928–42.
[27] The *Chronicle of Convocation*, 1918, pp. 195–8.

an amendment to his resolution expressed in the vaguest terms—so vague, in fact, that the League was not even mentioned.[28] There was some opposition, albeit of a less reactionary kind, to a resolution welcoming the League and calling on all churchmen to support it which was moved by Lord Hugh Cecil[29] in the Church Assembly on November 19th, 1920, but the resolution was finally passed.[30]

More important, perhaps, than these debates and resolutions was Gore's *The League of Nations, the Opportunity of the Church*, written in 1918 before the League actually came into being, and an elaboration of his Convocation speech. Significantly Gore found it necessary in this pamphlet to begin by pointing out that the League was not the brainchild of the 'peace at any price' group, and that its establishment depended on an Allied victory.[31] He went on to outline what he hoped would be the principles of the League, emphasizing that in his view the authority of the League should be backed up not only by economic pressure (which was suggested by the Covenant but not enforceable), but also in the last resort by armed force.[32] Gore acknowledged the need for a religious basis for any ideal scheme of international co-operation, but felt that the Covenant came near enough to providing such a basis for it to be fully acceptable to Christians. 'It will rest upon the idea of a fellowship of humanity, supreme in its interests over all separate national claims, a fellowship based on justice and the rights of weaker as well as stronger nations—an idea which has mainly had its origin in Christian thought or imagination.'[33] Moreover, Gore saw the promotion of the League as an opportunity for divided Christendom to act as though it were already one: 'I have long been persuaded that the best immediate way of promoting religious unity in our own country is for all the fragments of the Christian Church to act together, as if they were one, on the moral and social questions of the day.'[34]

[28] *Ibid.*, pp. 201f.

[29] Lord Hugh Cecil, 1869–1956; younger brother of Lord Robert Cecil, created Baron Quickswood 1941. He stood to the right of his brother, in both ecclesiastical and political affairs.

[30] *National Assembly of the Church of England, Report of Proceedings*, Vol. I, pp. 119–22.

[31] C. Gore, *The League of Nations, the Opportunity of the Church*, p. 3.

[32] *Ibid.*, p. 4. [33] *Ibid.*, p. 16.

Gore was thoroughly realistic about the difficulties facing the formation of the League, and many of his anxieties proved to be only too well founded. Among the dangers which he mentioned were the exclusion from the League of Germany, the chaotic state of Russia, the feebleness, as a deterrent system, of the delaying procedure of League arbitration, the lack of an effective international police force, the failure of the Allies to disarm, and the difficulty of achieving fair representation in the Assembly for nations of widely-differing size and influence.[35] Against these fears he set three grounds of hope: the increasing pressure of public opinion in the democratic countries in favour of peace, the awful fear of the future without the League of Nations, and the potential influence of the Church.[36]

Two important points emerge from this statement of Gore's beliefs about the League; his insistence on the need for sanctions to back up the moral pressure of the League's decisions, and the need for disarmament. In a speech in the House of Lords on June 26th, 1918, Gore criticized Curzon, then Foreign Secretary, for his lack of interest in these two matters; attention to both was essential if there were to be any real advance on old methods of establishing and maintaining peace.[37] But Gore's point of view, at least over sanctions and the use of force, was not shared by all Christian protagonists of the League. *Commonwealth* expressed the opinion that 'it will have to build itself surely on firmer stuff than earthly force. Its permanence, its appeal, its inspiration for the peoples, will depend upon something more than the mere fear of material and external pressures.'[38] Its comment otherwise followed very closely the lines laid down by Gore, including emphasis on the urgent need to admit Germany to the League and to pursue disarmament, thereby ending a state of affairs which was

[35] Gore, *op. cit.*, pp. 18–21. [36] *Ibid.*, pp. 21–4.
[37] H.L. Deb., 1918, Vol. 30, Cols. 407–12.
[38] *Commonwealth*, August 1918, p. 214.

---

[34] C. Gore, *The League of Nations, the Opportunity of the Church*, p. 17. Gore's idea of approaching Christian unity through practical action was very close to that of Nathan Söderblom, Archbishop of Uppsala, whose suggestion for an ecumenical conference on the Life and Work of the Church, originally put forward in 1919, was realized at Stockholm in 1925. (*The Stockholm Conference, 1925*, edited by G. K. A. Bell, p. 5.)

politically provocative and economically oppressive.[39] Another Christian expression of doubt about the use of force was that of Major-General Sir Frederick Maurice in the first issue of *The Pilgrim.* The opening words of the League Covenant, 'In order to promote international co-operation . . .', underlined for him the fact that it was a moral issue, dependent for its success not on the use of force, but on the moral climate of Europe.[40]

This dislike of the use of force was natural enough in those whose ideal of the League was a high one, and the most able and outspoken opponents of sanctions were in fact the thoroughgoing idealists, to whom the alternative policy of achieving security by means of maintaining large national armies was even more abhorrent and utterly discredited by the experience of the war. But the opponents of sanctions betrayed a naïve confidence in human nature, and Lord Robert Cecil, although passionately concerned for the success of the League, recognized the need in the absence of effective sanctions to maintain national armaments. He was always bitterly critical of Britain's half-heartedness in support of the League and in the pursuit of disarmament, but even he would have preferred security on the old terms to no security at all; as it was, the Laodicean attitude of successive governments 'hampered the preparation for war without doing anything efficient to guarantee peace'.[41]

General Maurice's article also dealt with another legacy of the war which the Allies were painfully slow to recognize, the desperate need for help in the war-devastated and economically dislocated countries of Europe. He pointed out that malnutrition, starvation, disease and despair were rife, and that even in Britain's own long-term interests, to provide markets for her industries, it was essential that former enemies should recover some measure of prosperity. As it was, 'unwillingness to support remedial measures which would benefit our late enemies, combined with readiness to profit from their distresses, places us in a position unworthy of

[39] *Ibid.*, June 1919, p. 143. Clemenceau had promised the German delegation at Versailles that the disarmament of Germany would be the first stage in a general international reduction and limitation of armaments, which it would be the duty of the League to bring about. Progress in disarmament was in fact resisted by the Allies, actively by France and passively by Britain.

[40] *The Pilgrim*, October 1920, p. 34.

[41] Lord Robert Cecil, *All the Way*, p. 171.

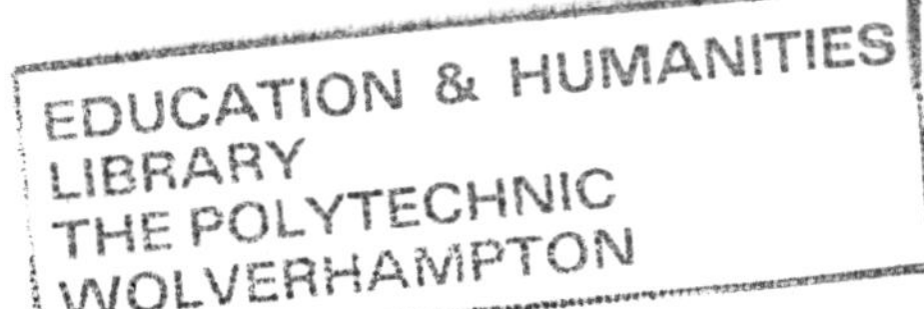
EDUCATION & HUMANITIES
LIBRARY
THE POLYTECHNIC
WOLVERHAMPTON

ourselves'.[42] Davidson contributed to the Lords' debate on this subject on February 18th, 1920, calling on the government to provide help, but, unlike some speakers, he refrained from attributing blame for the distress in Europe to the terms of the Peace Treaty.[43] The problem was also discussed in Convocation, when on February 11th and April 27th, 1920, the Upper House of Canterbury Convocation debated two official reports by Sir William Goode on economic conditions in central Europe.[44] On the first occasion Davidson opened the debate, laying great emphasis on the appalling conditions, of which the British public had virtually no knowledge. The devastation, starvation, and apparently invincible hopelessness and apathy had hardly been touched by the help so far provided by the British and American governments. He warned against the danger that familiarity with stories of horror and suffering could breed indifference,[45] and called for a tremendous effort by the whole of Christendom to help the victims of distress. He mentioned the wretched response of the British public, who had contributed a beggarly £100,000 when collections for European relief were made on Innocents' Day in every Christian church in the country, and Gore reflected bitterly on the attitude of determined indifference which must somehow be broken down. The Bishop of Exeter (Lord William Cecil) argued that, if no higher call evoked a response, the appeal to self-interest should be exploited; the chaos and despair in central Europe could not be contained, and would affect Britain in due course. By the time of the second debate in April, Gore had himself been to Geneva to a conference held to co-ordinate the use of voluntary relief funds, but he was pessimistic about what he had seen, partly because there was no will to co-operate among the governments of the afflicted countries.

[42] *The Pilgrim*, October 1920, p. 37. [43] H.L. Deb., 1920, Vol. 39, Cols. 80–3.

[44] The *Chronicle of Convocation*, 1920, pp. 53–63 and 235–41.

[45] The opinion that this was what had happened to Lloyd George, Wilson, Clemenceau and Orlando when they drew up the terms of the Treaty of Versailles is expressed by J. L. Hammond in a pessimistic article, 'The Next Revolution', in *The Pilgrim*, October 1921, p. 23: 'Pain and hunger had ceased to touch their pity sharply, because pain and hunger had been their weapons. They did not come upon a scene of desolation with a sense of shock and horror, because they had been living in a world in which desolation had been the lesser of two evils in all their deliberations. And so they took the measures that had the result of inflicting on a great part of Europe misery more acute and widespread than all the misery of the world war.'

Practical work to help deal with the distress in Europe was undertaken notably by the Society of Friends, and their magnificent achievement was contrasted pointedly with the attitude of governments which preferred to go on trying to squeeze impossible reparations out of devastated and hopeless nations.[46] An effort in which the Church of England did share was that made by the Student Christian Movement, through an organization called European Student Relief, which was set up in 1919 and eventually raised a total of £500,000 for destitute students, mainly in Austria.[47]

A disturbance of the peace much nearer home, and one of such a kind as to trouble the Christian conscience, was provided by the fighting in Ireland. The British government's unsympathetic handling of the situation had succeeded, by 1916, in throwing the leadership of the nationalist movement into the hands of the violent extremists of the new Sinn Fein party, which won seventy-three seats in the general election of 1918, but whose candidates refused to take their seats at Westminster. Instead they set up the Dail, an unofficial Irish parliament in Dublin, issued a declaration of independence on January 21st, 1919, and formed the I.R.A. Gradually a state of war developed between the I.R.A. and the British Forces, which consisted mainly of the armed, military-style Royal Irish Constabulary, reinforced from 1920 onwards by the notorious irregulars known as the Black and Tans. 'Thus did the British government equip itself to fight down Irish aspirations, by all means, fair and foul. This is the greatest blot on the record of the Coalition, and perhaps upon Britain's name in the twentieth century. . . .'[48] It was the methods adopted by the British forces, including cold-blooded murder and deliberate reprisals, albeit in response to almost equally unpleasant behaviour on the part of the I.R.A., which earned for the Black and Tans such an unenviable reputation, and provoked bitter and repeated denunciations of the government's policy by Church leaders. Even the *Church Times*, particularly during October and November, 1920, regularly attacked Lloyd George and his tactics: 'Short of formally sanc-

[46] *Commonwealth*, May 1921, p. 115.
[47] Tissington Tatlow, *op. cit.*, pp. 708–26.
[48] Mowat, *op. cit.*, p. 65. Mowat's clear and fair account of the events in Ireland will be found on pp. 57–108.

tioning a policy of reprisals, the Prime Minister has made it perfectly plain that such a policy can be safely pursued so far as the Government's connivance is concerned' (October 15th); 'To punish outrage not by lawful methods but by intensified imitation, is to confess failure to govern' (October 29th); 'The Government's refusal to institute inquiries into the true facts of the outrages alleged by either side is taken as an indication that they dare not expose their own recent record of organised terrorism' (November 5th). The *Church Times* of November 19th included a letter signed by seventeen bishops, deploring the government's Irish policy and calling for a truce. The editorial notes of *Commonwealth* repeatedly attacked the 'savagery and barbarism' of the methods employed by the British forces, and Temple, writing in *The Pilgrim* of January 1921, not only criticized the policy of reprisals, but called for an enlightened public opinion prepared to accept an independent southern Ireland.[49] Davidson spoke twice in the Lords; on November 2nd, 1920, he began by vigorously attacking the Sinn Fein atrocities and expressing sympathy with their victims, but went on to condemn in uncompromising terms the conduct of the Black and Tans—'terrible examples of the very kind of disorder which they are sent there to suppress.'[50] For the government Curzon remained indifferent, and 'in a speech compounded of annoyance and cynicism extolled the Government's measures in terms extravagant enough for the most perfect piece of statecraft'.[51] Davidson, supported by the Bishop of Winchester (Talbot), renewed the attack on February 22nd, 1921, indignant at the uninformed and indifferent attitude of the government: 'Not by calling in the aid of the devil will you cast out devils, or punish devilry.'[52]

[49] *The Pilgrim*, January 1921, pp. 128–30.

[50] H.L. Deb., 1920, Vol. 42, Cols. 142–8. Lord Robert Cecil expressed the opinion that public horror at the brutality and terrorism in Ireland helped to win support for the League of Nations (*A Great Experiment*, pp. 103f.).

[51] The *Church Times*, November 5th, 1920.

[52] H.L. Deb., 129, Vol. 441, Cols. 79–91. *Cf*. also a speech made by Lang as President of York Convocation on February 23rd, 1921: 'The sword of justice must be strong and sharp, but let it also be clean' (*York Journal of Convocation*, 1921, p. 17). When the British and Irish delegations finally reached agreement on the terms of peace, on December 6th, 1921, Davidson issued a message of thanksgiving for the nearer approach of peace and goodwill in Ireland; this provoked angry criticism on the grounds that he was condoning the brutal Irish tactics which had led to the British government's 'ignominious surrender'. (Bell, *op. cit.*, Vol. II, pp. 1060–6.)

It is impossible to make any accurate assessment of the influence of this concerted opposition by the Church to the government's conduct of the Irish affair, but it was no doubt considerable, both in informing public opinion and in bringing pressure to bear directly on Lloyd George and his colleagues to conclude the truce on June 11th, 1921.

The Church's thinking about international affairs and the maintenance of peace in the immediate post-war years was summed up by the committee of the 1920 Lambeth Conference appointed to report on Christianity and international relations, especially the League of Nations. 'The law of unselfish human neighbourliness is expressly declared as fundamental',[53] and must be applied in the international field in three ways. First, there is the duty and dignity of service, which means that a nation's claim to greatness can be measured only by the degree to which it is conscious of its mission to humanity; secondly, 'no national policy can be Christian which ignores the needs and rightful claims of other nations. . . . If we really want peace we must set our faces decisively against the vested interests which have so often in the past stood behind governments, and vitiated their action;'[53] finally, there is Christ's fierce emphasis against the misuse of strength: the stronger nations must not only safeguard the weaker against wrong, but actively encourage them to grow towards independence and a fuller life. The road to internationalism, as it has been well said, 'lies through nationalism. . . . True nationalism and a keen sense of international responsibility are in truth indispensable correlatives.'[54]

The report calls on all Christians to welcome and support the League of Nations as an instrument for the application of this threefold principle. At present its work is hampered by the prevalence of the spirit of hatred, which even colours the attitude of many Christians and is at its most dangerous when it masquerades as righteous indignation.[54] An example of Christian duty in repudiation of this spirit is the need to campaign for the admission to the League of Germany and former enemy countries as soon as possible, and support is badly needed for the work of the International Labour Organization in dealing with illegal traffic in

[53] *The Lambeth Conferences, 1867–1948: The Reports of the 1920, 1930 and 1948 Conferences*, p. 56.
[54] *Ibid.*, p. 57.

opium, arms and liquor.[55] But the League is still in its infancy, and there are manifest imperfections in the Covenant—weaknesses which can be overcome only by a world-wide campaign of education and propaganda through the organization of the League of Nations Union, 'which should have in every place the Church's active co-operation and support'.[56] The report also mentions with approval the World Alliance for Promoting International Friendship through the Churches,[57] and the S.C.M., describing the latter, with its membership of two hundred thousand students throughout the world, as 'a mighty instrument for propagating the spirit of peace.'[58] Support for the League is bound, in the committee's view, to meet with honourable opposition from both sceptics and passionate idealists, on the grounds that the League is either too ambitious or too timid, 'but we appeal to all those who are held back by these or kindred scruples, to view the matter in the Christian way, and to have the courage of faith'.[59]

The full Lambeth Conference endorsed the findings of this committee and embodied its acceptance of the report in a series of resolutions, adding an expression of grave concern about the disease and distress in Europe and Asia, and calling on Christians to support relief work of any kind.[60]

There was, therefore, strong support for the work of the League at all levels in the Church. It was widely accepted that the League had a more or less religious basis, and that support of it involved no compromise of Christian principle. Moreover, there was also the complementary World Alliance for those who preferred to work through what was 'essentially a religious thing'.[61] It is true

[55] *The Lambeth Conferences, 1867–1948.* [56] *Ibid.*, p. 59.

[57] The World Alliance came into being on the eve of the outbreak of war in 1914, and was unable to begin its active work until 1920, when a conference of twenty member-nations was held in Geneva.

[58] *Ibid.*, p. 60.

[59] *Ibid.*, p. 61. [60] *Ibid.*, p. 37.

[61] The distinction between the League and the World Alliance was drawn by Davidson in a debate in Canterbury Convocation on February 16th, 1923, when the Bishop of Oxford (Burge) asked for more vigorous support for the World Alliance. It was objected that such support was unnecessary in view of the existence of the League of Nations Union, and that it would be unwise to divide enthusiasm between the two bodies. Davidson held that there was room for both: the World Alliance should concentrate on the cultivation of a right attitude towards international affairs, while the League of Nations Union could properly work for the acceptance of specific political measures. (The *Chronicle of Convocation*, 1923, pp. 88–90.)

Ireland, 1920: a Black and Tan holds up a Sinn Feiner

that there was a small number of Christians whose determined opposition to the League was already in evidence;[62] this was particularly true of a dissident group in the Church Socialist League, and it was their outlook which dominated the attitude towards international affairs of the League of the Kingdom of God, into which the C.S.L. was transformed in 1923. For a time, from 1924 onwards, *Commonwealth* was the unofficial organ of the new L.K.G., and as such was sharply critical of the League, claiming that it was 'dominated by the mind and organisation of plutocracy', and that 'we cannot wholly commit ourselves or sacrifice our national responsibility to anything so essentially imperfect'.[63] But for the first few years of the League's existence, apart from the dangerous division of opinion over the use of sanctions and armed force to impose the will of the League on recalcitrant members, the Church was virtually united in its support and in the confident hope that it would grow in wisdom and authority.

[62] As early as 1915 P. E. T. Widdrington, writing in the *Church Socialist* (April 1915, p. 70) ridiculed the possibility of 'an artificial peace' which rested on 'Hague tribunals backed by an international gendarmerie'.
[63] *Commonwealth*, October 1924, p. 301.

3

Reconstruction at Home: Industry and Society; the Fifth Report; Copec

THE POST-WAR wave of idealism was not least apparent in the widespread belief that far-reaching steps should be taken to make life pleasanter for the least privileged members of society. The war had opened many people's eyes to social inequalities and hardships hitherto unquestioningly accepted, and had given to many of the poorest families a taste of higher living standards which they were naturally determined to maintain, and if possible improve still further. It was one of the ironies of the war that the full employment and high wages which it created gave to many people their first experience of real security, and it was a sad reflection on the British economy—and in some cases on the integrity of the British workman—that the separation allowances paid directly to soldiers' wives gave them for the first time in their lives a regular income, protected from the depredations of the bookie and the barmaid, the expenditure of which they could plan for themselves.[1]

It was expected that there would be difficulties and problems when the war ended, but the mood of exhaustion and scepticism was matched by a determination to meet them with bold and imaginative policies. The process of dismantling Victorian capitalism and replacing it by something more flexible and socially just, begun in earnest in 1906, seemed likely to be carried

[1] See Eleanor Rathbone, *The Disinherited Family*, pp. 59–61, for a description, on the basis of the author's experience during the war as a social worker in Liverpool, of the improvement in the health and well-being of children, and in the efficiency and responsibility of mothers, as a result of the system of separation allowances.

still further.[2] This would probably involve the nationalization of coal, power, railways and shipping, and would be accompanied by a vigorous campaign to provide, in Lloyd George's pathetically optimistic phrase, 'homes fit for heroes'. Education was to be dealt with by H. A. L. Fisher's Education Act of 1918, which provided for school-leaving at fifteen, compulsory part-time education up to the age of eighteen, an extension of secondary education, and the establishment of nursery schools.

Of the ambitious schemes which the government evolved, some at least were begun. To deal with the shortage of six hundred thousand houses, the Housing and Town Planning Act of 1919, the work of Christopher Addison as Minister of Health, made it obligatory for local authorities to survey the housing needs of their areas and, subject to Ministry approval, carry out both the replacement of slums and new house-building—an acknowledgment that it was no longer possible to leave the job to private enterprise. Apart from the product of a penny rate, the Treasury had to meet the difference between building costs and the rent which could actually be charged, the latter calculated on the basis of the level fixed by the Rent Restriction Act of 1915, and by 1919 bearing little relation to the economic rent. It was hoped that costs would eventually fall, and that from 1927 onwards rents could be adjusted in most cases to an economic level, but meanwhile houses were urgently needed and the government must be prepared to bear a heavy loss which it could not hope to recover.[3]

This pattern of ambitious plans impetuously undertaken and then peremptorily abandoned, of which housing was the classic example, was repeated in other spheres. There seems to have been an element of deliberate calculation on the part of the government to concede, or appear to concede, just enough to avert serious discontent. Industrial unrest was widespread, and there was even talk of revolution, particularly on Clydeside, where there was an

[2] The optimistic expectation that far-reaching social changes would take place after the war is expressed in an extreme form in an article by H. Hutchinson, 'The Passing of "Property" ', in *Commonwealth*, January 1918, pp. 8–10. See also F. W. Bussell, *The National Church and the Social Crisis*, pp. 86–150, for a more balanced, but distinctly pessimistic, attitude towards the possibilities of post-war social reconstruction.

[3] In fact the scheme was abandoned in 1921 on grounds of expense; Marion Bowley, *Housing and the State*, pp. 15–35.

ugly strike from January 27th to February 11th, 1919. Arthur Henderson, a leading Labour politician, warned that 'the temper of the workmen is dangerous, and the unyielding attitude of the government is bringing the country to the verge of industrial revolution'.[4] There were strikes during 1919 by cotton-operatives, ironmoulders and railwaymen, and even among a section of the police force in London and Manchester. The serious threat of a coal strike in January 1919 compelled Lloyd George to appoint a commission to investigate wages and hours in the industry and report on the question of nationalization. The commission consisted of three coal-owners, three industrialists, three leaders of the mining unions, and three economists approved by the unions;[5] the chairman was Sir John Sankey. Three interim reports were issued on March 20th, of which the compromise worked out by Sankey was finally accepted by both the miners and the government. This recommended a seven-hour working day, an increase in wages of two shillings a day, and a levy of a penny a ton on output to help to provide better housing and amenities for miners. On June 20th the reports on nationalization appeared. This time there were four, but all agreed in recommending the nationalization of the mineral, the improvement of retail distribution, and the appointment of a Minister of Mines. The mine-owners and two of the industrialists were wholly opposed to the nationalization of the industry; the third industrialist, Sir Arthur Duckham, recommended a compromise arrangement of amalgamation, while the miners, economists and Sankey himself—a majority of seven out of thirteen—were in favour of full nationalization.[6] In the end Lloyd George, skilfully exploiting these disagreements, public apathy, an un-

[4] Quoted by the Bishop of Peterborough, F. T. Woods, in a speech in the Upper House of Canterbury Convocation, February 8th, 1918. (The *Chronicle of Convocation*, 1918, p. 215.) Frank Theodore Woods, 1874–1932; Bishop of Peterborough 1916–24, and of Winchester 1924–32, and a leading episcopal spokesman on social issues.

[5] The economists were R. H. Tawney, Sidney Webb and Sir Leo Chiozza Money. Richard Henry Tawney, 1880–1962; Fellow of Balliol College, Oxford, 1918–21, Lecturer in economic history, University of London, 1921–31, Professor 1931–49, President of the Workers' Educational Association 1928–44. Tawney's work in the spheres of education and industrial welfare was very extensive, and he was perhaps the leading lay exponent in his time of Christian social thought. See below, Chapter 5.

[6] The miners and economists also recommended some form of workers' control, to which the miners' leaders, if not the rank and file, attached great importance. See A. Hutt, *The Post-war History of the British Working-class*, p. 11.

timely strike in the Yorkshire coalfield, and the miners' refusal to consider the Duckham plan, contrived to concede only the seven-hour day, a miners' welfare fund, and a Mines Department inside the Board of Trade. Whatever the validity of some of his pretexts, it seems undeniable that his final refusal on August 18th to accept the majority recommendation of nationalization was a breach of the government's undertaking, given on March 21st in response to a request from the miners' representatives, to 'carry out in the spirit and in the letter the recommendations of Sir John Sankey's Report'.[7]

The affair of the coal dispute of 1919 has been mentioned in some detail, not only because it was an outstanding example of Lloyd George's policy of using delaying tactics to avert the need for radical social change, but also because it was productive of much ill-will among the miners, and in this way a contributory cause of the general strike of 1926.[8]

By 1921 the impetus had gone out of the campaign for reconstruction, and the brief burst of post-war prosperity, during which it might have been possible to carry through extensive changes, had given way to the first bout of the chronic depression which was to bedevil the British economy for the whole of the inter-war period. It was the boom, even more than Lloyd George, which was the undoing of idealism; ambitious plans for social reconstruction could be carried out only with the help of sustained political pressure by the labour movement, but the temptation to cash in on the short-term benefits offered by booming industry proved in fact to be irresistible, and the energy which might have been devoted to pressing relentlessly for nationalization and a share by the workers in the control of industry, or at the very least for the further development of Whitley Councils,[9] was diverted to the

[7] Quoted by Hutt, *op. cit.*, p. 19. The account of the work of the Coal Commission is based on Mowat, *op. cit.*, pp. 30–6.

[8] The National Industrial Conference, ostensibly the fore-runner of a permanent parliament of employers and workers, also failed for lack of government support; Mowat, *op. cit.*, pp. 36f.; G. D. H. Cole and R. Postgate, *The Common People, 1746–1946*, pp. 548–50.

[9] A committee under J. H. Whitley recommended in 1917, as part of the government's plans for reconstruction, the formation of national and local industrial councils, including representatives of both management and labour, to improve relations in industry. By 1920 there were fifty-six national councils, covering three and a quarter million workers. The fact that Whitley Councils were intended to make the status quo more tolerable, and not to inaugurate a radical reconstruction of industry, led to some harsh criticism by Christian social thinkers. See, e.g. Egerton Swann, 'Reconstruction—on Rock or Sand?', in *Commonwealth*, March 1918, pp. 80–2.

pursuit of higher wages and shorter hours, benefits which were largely to be lost again when the boom came to an end.[10] Prosperity also reinforced the reluctance of industrialists to contemplate concessions to labour; not only could they interpret the fact that the traditional economic processes had weathered the storms of war as a vindication of them, but they could also point to the success which they were enjoying in the immediate post-war period. The conditions in which industry was flourishing were, however, artificially favourable, and it was not long before the first signs of trade depression were apparent.

Unemployment, which had been less serious than most people expected, increased sharply at the end of 1920[11], and the government was compelled to extend the period of unemployment benefit and to increase the rates, both of contributions and benefits. The Unemployment Insurance Act of 1920, which greatly enlarged the provisions of the original act of 1911, met little opposition; it had an apparently sound actuarial basis, and unemployment was not yet serious. When it did begin to rise, it was impossible to restrict payment of benefits to those who were entitled to them on the basis of their contributions, particularly in view of the precedent set by the non-contributory Out-of-Work Donations granted to ex-servicemen on demobilization. By an act of March, 1921, the principle of uncovenanted benefit, the dole, was inaugurated, although the rates of relief to which the unemployed were entitled were often not high enough to make them independent of recourse to the Poor Law Guardians.

As a cure for the industrial depression the government, following what were commonly thought to be sound financial principles, prescribed an economy drive. The Agricultural Wages Board and minimum wages for farm workers, which had been introduced during the war and had done much to revive the agricultural

[10] Widdrington, as organizing secretary of the C.S.L., made a tour of Yorkshire and Lancashire in March 1920; writing of his impressions in the *Church Socialist*, May–June 1920, p. 57, he remarked ominously that 'the masses of the workers are content to bask in precarious prosperity. Never have fortunes been made more rapidly than during the present boom.'

[11] Yearly mean percentages of unemployment were: 1918, 0·8; 1919, 2·4; 1920, 2·4; 1921, 14·8; 1922, 15·2. Unemployment then fell to 8·1 % in 1924, before rising again steadily to a peak in 1933. (From the Board of Trade's *18th Abstract of Labour Statistics*, 1926, p. 95.)

industry and the morale of countrymen, were abolished in 1921, and in February 1922 a committee under Sir Eric Geddes recommended cuts in government expenditure of seventy-five million pounds, mostly on the service estimates, but also on education, by means of cutting teachers' salaries, raising the minimum school age to six and suspending the provision of nursery schools and day continuation classes, and on health services, by means of reducing expenditure on the treatment of tuberculosis and on maternity and child welfare work.

The post-war years were a critical period; opportunities were short-lived, and idealism was quickly frustrated as determination to reconstruct society competed unsuccessfully with the lure of selfish advantage. The chance for the Church to influence the course of events by pressure on public opinion was perhaps unprecedented; certainly it was not likely to recur. It was eagerly seized by many Christians, and if they seem to have had little immediate success it was partly because of the way in which their effort was dispersed over a wide field and channelled into so many different and sometimes contradictory schemes. Before the end of the war Lang had distinguished, in a speech in the Lords, between the temporary causes of unrest—the strains and difficulties of the war, and the more serious underlying causes which would remain to be tackled after the war. These included the unequal distribution of the rewards of industry, and the dehumanizing way in which industry was organized; it was essential, he felt, that labour should have a share in the control of industry as well as in its profits.[12] The same problem was debated at great length in the Upper House of Canterbury Convocation in 1918,[13] when the speeches showed how seriously the bishops viewed the situation which the end of the war would create, and how radical were the measures which many of them were prepared to envisage for dealing with it. The Bishop of Peterborough, Woods, introduced the debate, calling for 'a spirit of adventure which would prefer bold schemes of real reconstruction to the patchy palliatives which had often enough done duty in the great cause of social reform', for both the spirit of the age and

[12] H.L. Deb., 1917, Vol. 26, Cols. 914–26.
[13] The *Chronicle of Convocation*, 1918, pp. 215–26, 265–81, 303–21.

the spirit of Christianity were urging him, he said, to support the radical reorganization of society.[14] The Bishop of Lichfield, Kempthorne, emphasized that the working classes rightly wanted real liberty—industrial and economic freedom to complement their political freedom. There was growing opposition to the organization of industry for private profit, and discontent with conditions of sordid poverty and bad housing; it was useless to expect a new spirit of fellowship unless these grievances were removed. He maintained that workers should enjoy some share in the control of industry, a living wage, reasonable leisure and protection against unemployment; he called for the nationalization of vital industries, for better housing and town-planning, regeneration of rural life, and better education for all children, irrespective of ability. Christ's victory, he said, was won in the spiritual sphere, but its fruits must be manifest in the whole life of man, and redemption made visible in society as well as in individuals.[15]

The Bishop of Hereford, Hensley Henson,[16] not unexpectedly struck a less enthusiastic note, and was particularly concerned about reconciling the Christian desire to emphasize the importance of the individual and the value of private property, with the advocacy of policies which would strengthen the system of public control under which people lived. This doubt was well answered by the Bishop of Chelmsford, Watts-Ditchfield, who pointed out that personal liberty and the virtues of property would most probably be better preserved by a reconstructed social system, since for nine-tenths of the population they were already effectively abolished by the tyranny of the existing form of freedom; the situation was so unsatisfactory that great changes and sacrifices were necessary.[17]

[14] The *Chronicle of Convocation*, 1918, p. 216. Woods specifically declined to label himself a 'socialist', although he acknowledged that the form of social reorganization which he outlined, including nationalization and some form of co-partnership, would be attacked as such. It is hard to see what meaning socialism can have if not something similar to what Woods had in mind, but it was a dangerous and much-feared word, particularly after the Russian Revolution of 1917, and he was not alone in preferring not to use it.

[15] *Ibid.*, pp. 265–8. John Augustine Kempthorne, 1864–1946; Bishop of Hull 1910–13, and of Lichfield 1913–37, Chairman of the Industrial Christian Fellowship 1924–37.

[16] Herbert Hensley Henson, 1863–1947; Canon of Westminster 1900–12 and 1940–1, Dean of Durham 1912–18, Bishop of Hereford 1918–20, and of Durham 1920–39.

Kempthorne's speech was, however, open to more fundamental and damaging criticism, and raised the problem of the validity of Christian comment on social affairs in its most acute form. Should Christians, and especially Church leaders speaking in an authoritative capacity, suggest practical measures for the improvement of society? If not, how far is it possible to go in the permitted sphere of principle without encroaching on the forbidden ground of technicality? If a bishop is justified in calling for better housing —as few would deny—is he also justified, or even perhaps under an obligation, to explain how it might be financed? May it not sometimes be the duty of a Church leader to make practical, detailed suggestions, if only to undermine vested interests and compel effective action when it would otherwise be resisted for lack of energy or imagination?

The charge that the subject lay outside the sphere of his competence was levelled at Canon C. F. Garbett,[18] when he moved a resolution in the Lower House of Canterbury Convocation on May 1st, 1918, expressing the conviction of the House that 'the demands of labour for a national minimum wage, for state provision against unemployment, and for the recognition of the status of the workers in the industries in which they are engaged, are in accordance with the principles of Christianity'.[19] This was particularly controversial, because so specific, but it was vigorously supported by Temple, speaking, as he said, as a member of the Labour Party of one week's standing; he condemned as nonsense the argument that the principles of economics lie outside the range of moral or ethical concern, since all economic theory, as soon as it begins to be applied, makes ethical presuppositions.[20] By Temple's criterion, if by no other, a number of later speakers treated the House to a display of the utmost nonsense; the Dean

[18] Cyril Forster Garbett, 1875–1955; Vicar of Portsea 1909–19, Bishop of Southwark 1919–32, and of Winchester 1932–42, Archbishop of York 1942–55.

[19] The *Chronicle of Convocation*, 1918, p. 344.

[20] *Ibid.*, pp. 349–53.

---

[17] The *Chronicle of Convocation*, 1918, pp. 269–72 and 310–3. Christian support for the government's reconstruction plans was not undivided; the Church Socialist League, at a conference in April 1918, condemned any form of reconstruction which involved a continuation of the capitalist system, and called on the Church to demand the redemption of society and the emancipation of the workers from the wage system. (The *Church Socialist*, April–May 1918, p. 53; June–July 1918, pp. 66–70.)

of Canterbury (H. Wace) was 'not at all prepared to pronounce any opinion' on the desirability of a minimum wage and security against unemployment,[21] and the Dean of St. Paul's (W. R. Inge) asserted that they had no right to mix up politics with religion: there was in any case much to be said against a minimum wage, and almost all economists agreed that a system of unemployment insurance was highly dangerous. 'They did not want, and they did not need, the contemptuous patronage of the hard-headed Labour leaders',[22] an echo of his overwhelming scorn for those clergy whom he regarded as the 'Court Chaplains of King Demos'.[23]

There was, therefore, no general agreement about whether the Church should be concerned with social issues at all, and this was a point about which controversy continued to rage for many years. But it was not the only occasion of disagreement among Christians. Even those who gladly acknowledged, with Gore, Talbot, Kempthorne, Woods and Temple, that it was both a right and duty to criticize society in the light of Christian beliefs and standards, disagreed profoundly in their judgment of the sickness of society and about the remedy which should be applied. Was the existing structure of society basically sound, so that an infusion of the Christian spirit would suffice to remove its abuses and rectify its faults, or was it so thoroughly incompatible with Christian standards that it must give way to something radically different? And if Christians were bound to work for a new social order, where were they to find its outline? Failure to resolve these differences of opinion was responsible for much of the feebleness of Christian social witness, since any expression of opinion which was to secure wide and representative support was inevitably, in view of these disagreements, either confined to pious platitudes or compelled to compromise on some of the most important issues.

The Report of the Archbishops' Fifth Committee of Inquiry, *Christianity and Industrial Problems*, the famous Fifth Report,[24] was

[21] The *Chronicle of Convocation*, 1918, p. 354. [22] *Ibid.*, pp. 355f.

[23] The phrase was first used by Canon Knox Little about 1890, and it was one of which Inge and Hensley Henson were particularly fond. See an article by J. G. Adderley in the *Church Socialist*, January 1912, which welcomes the role.

[24] Published in 1918. The committee included three C.S.U. bishops—Gore, Kempthorne and Woods—as well as the chairman, the Bishop of Winchester (E. S. Talbot). Among the other members were R. H. Tawney, Albert Mansbridge, George Lansbury and two Conservative M.P.s, Lord Henry Bentinck and W. C. Bridgeman.

the outstanding expression of Christian thought about post-war society but even here, although they are largely hidden by skilful presentation, there are unresolved differences of opinion. The Report begins by acknowledging the 'lamentable failure in the Church's recent witness' and its preference for the ambulance work of charity rather than an attack on the systems and principles which work havoc in social life.[25] Five main points are listed as relevant to the application of the Christian faith to economic and industrial problems: Christian moral teaching applies as much to society, industry and economics as to the individual; N.T. teaching about the dangers of wealth and its legitimate use must be emphasized; since Christ taught the supreme importance of personality, men must never be regarded as mere instruments of production;[26] the high regard of Christianity for the individual is complemented by its insistence on the duty of service in man's corporate life; and society must accept responsibility for the welfare of its members.[27] The Report then deals with three common objections to the application of Christian principles in industrial and social affairs, and surveys the history of Christian social ethics from the teaching of Christ to the present day.[28]

On the crucial issue of whether Christian principles can be applied to the social order in its present form or whether it must be changed, the Report comes down clearly on the radical side: 'The system itself makes it exceedingly difficult to carry into practice the principles of Christianity. Its faults are not the accidental or

[25] *Christianity and Industrial Problems*, p. 2 (page references are to the 1926 edition).

[26] There is no attack in this context on the existing organization of industry, but it is claimed that 'the welfare of human beings, including . . . freedom to take part in the control of industrial organization and direction of economic conditions and policy, must be the first condition of any industry carried on by Christians' (p. 24).

[27] The five points are expounded on pp. 13–32.

[28] The treatment of the three objections is particularly vigorous. They are: (i) that Christian ethics concern the individual, not society; (ii) that they were worked out for Galilean peasants and therefore cannot be relevant for modern society; (iii) that to express a Christian view on social and industrial matters is to play wrongly for popularity. The Report answers that the first is just not true. The second is prima facie plausible; humanly speaking it is improbable that what was taught to Galilean peasants should be relevant today, but Christianity itself is humanly speaking improbable, and if one accepts it at all one must accept the social gospel which is an integral part of it. Lastly, the Church is bound to condemn social evils simply because they are evil; if it thereby gains popularity, that is its good fortune; it is certainly not always the case (pp. 34–8).

occasional maladjustments of a social order the general spirit and tendency of which can be accepted as satisfactory by Christians. They are the expressions of certain deficiencies deeply rooted in the nature of that order itself.'[29] The most serious of these deficiencies are held to be the treatment of men as hands, involving their subjection to casual labour, arbitrary piece-rates and wholesale dismissal without compensation; an over-emphasis on the motive of self-interest, and the business morality which drives as hard a bargain as it can within the limits of the law; the co-existence of poverty and riches in extreme forms;[30] the evil of insecurity and unemployment; and antagonism between employers and workers—still the rule rather than the exception.[31]

Turning to constructive suggestions, the Report defines the function of industry as service and its method as association, and goes on to give an outline of what will be involved in the realization of these ideals: the establishment of a living wage and of adequate leisure, both generously defined;[32] provision for, and if possible prevention of, unemployment; the elimination of blind-alley jobs and casual labour.[33] Other desirable developments include further legal protection for young people, and for women, whose industrial status is very low; better co-operation between

[29] *Christianity and Industrial Problems*, p. 80.

[30] To help alleviate the burden of poverty, of which there is a moving and sensitive account on p. 100, the Report favours the principle of redistributive taxation, and dismisses the theory that the problem can be solved by an all-round increase in prosperity: 'A mere increase in the amount, which left the proportions unaltered, would not solve that problem' (p. 94). This point of view is precisely that expounded by Tawney in *The Acquisitive Society*, and its expression here in such uncompromising terms is one of the reasons why Tawney was credibly rumoured to have been the effective author of the Report.

[31] *Christianity and Industrial Problems*, pp. 82–110. The last section (pp. 105–10) is particularly favourable towards the workers' interests, and stresses the importance of preserving the right to strike.

[32] 'By a living wage we mean not merely a wage which is sufficient for physical existence, but a wage adequate to maintain the worker, his wife and family, in health and honour, and to enable him to dispense with the subsidiary earnings of his children up to the age of sixteen years. By reasonable hours we mean hours sufficiently short not merely to leave him unexhausted, but to allow him sufficient leisure and energy for home life, for recreation, for the development through study of his mind and spirit, and for participation in the affairs of the community. We hold that the payment of such a wage in return for such hours of work ought to be the first charge upon every industry' (p. 116).

[33] Casual labour had been recognized as an outstanding industrial evil since 1880 at least. A good study of it, by a Christian investigator, is H. A. Mess, *Casual Labour at the Docks* (1916).

employers and workers; the restriction of profits; the extension of non-profit-making municipal services; a vigorous and adequate housing programme.[34] It is in the section on co-operation between employers and workers that the basic divergence of opinion within the committee becomes apparent; some feel that, in the interests of economic progress and efficiency, the ultimate responsibility for decisions on questions of industrial policy and organization must always remain 'in the hands of individuals who are unfettered by subordination to any superior authority', while others want to see the workers themselves assuming an increasingly responsible role in the organization of their industry, so that eventually the employer and manager would be reduced to the status of ordinary workers in the industry, fellow-servants of the community, with the other workers, in a form of producers' co-operative.[35] The alternatives are not worked out, but the cleavage is plainly between those who are prepared to envisage some radical revision of the oligarchic government of industry which capitalism requires, and those who are not.[36]

The Report makes four suggestions for increasing the helpfulness and influence of the parish priest in industrial society: there should be more working-class clergy; the training of the clergy should include some grounding in economic and social science; the clergy should be more active in campaigning against social evils, and encourage the laity to be so, particularly by taking part in local government; and, to make time for this social concern, the clergy should delegate much of their administrative work to lay helpers.[37]

The Report ends by dealing with the need for a great increase in the provision of education, to help to create useful citizens and to break the vicious circle of ignorance and poverty. Christians must

[34] Figures are quoted from the 1911 Census to show the alarmingly high levels of overcrowding, and, associated with it, infant mortality (pp. 152–8).

[35] *Ibid.*, p. 138.

[36] The issue was more complicated than a straightforward choice between capitalism and syndicalism, and various suggestions were made for different degrees of workers' control, co-partnership and profit-sharing. Basically, however, the division within the committee was an important one. See Egerton Swann, 'The Sin of Society and the Way of Wisdom', parts 2 and 3, in *Commonwealth*, August and September 1920, pp. 228–31 and 262–6, where this disagreement is examined from the radical point of view.

[37] *Christianity and Industrial Problems*, pp. 159–62.

defend and promote expenditure on education in the face of the materialism which would subordinate it to the exigencies of industrial activity. There must be better medical services for schoolchildren to enable them to benefit by the education they are given, more practical work to bridge the gap between art and labour, and an educational 'highway' to replace the existing educational 'ladder'. To achieve all this, much greater public expenditure on education will be necessary, even to the point of extravagance, and the medieval expenditure on great churches is suggested as an analogy. The whole status of education and the teaching profession must be raised.[38]

The Fifth Report as a whole was an ambitious and imaginative document, of great range, and representing the best of the Christian social thought which was paradoxically inspired by the horrors of the war: 'The stern teaching of the war has undoubtedly had a tremendous effect in awakening the social conscience of Christians. All are resolved that the sacrifice of our best men shall not have been in vain, and that among the fruits of it must be a new and better order in which justice and friendship shall reign.'[39]

In view of the division of opinion in Convocation, already noticed, it was not to be expected that the Fifth Report would be accorded a rapturous welcome on all sides. Hensley Henson lugubriously observed in his diary that it was 'a matter of surprise and regret that the Archbishop should commend this dangerous pamphlet in a "Foreword" conceived in a very exalted strain',[40] and it was sharply attacked by the Regius Professor of Divinity at Oxford, A. C. Headlam, and the Archdeacon of Ely, W. Cunningham. Headlam accepts 'all that it says about the moral duties of Christians, of the ideal of service, of true citizenship, of brotherhood among mankind, of the right use of wealth and of the danger of luxury', but he objects to 'much doubtful economic history, confused thinking and hazardous politics'.[41] He distrusts the

[38] *Christianity and Industrial Problems*, pp. 169–209. [39] *Ibid.*, p. 75.

[40] H. Hensley Henson, *Retrospect of an Unimportant Life*, Vol. I, p. 318. In an article in the *Edinburgh Review*, January 1920, Henson described the Report as 'eloquent, interesting, full of irrelevant learning, and in substance and effect a Socialist tract' (p. 6).

[41] A. C. Headlam, *The Church and Industrial Questions*, p. 11. Headlam, who later became Bishop of Gloucester, held some remarkable views on economics. See the *Chronicle of Convocation*, 1933, pp. 128–30.

Report's attack on the old political economy, and disputes the suggestions which it makes for the embodiment of its principles, drawing the unjustifiable conclusion that the Report 'would have us believe that State Socialism is an integral part of Christian teaching'.[42] Headlam condemns what he describes as the Report's attempt to 'create Christian political and social doctrines', but a few pages later he exhorts the Church 'to strive to substitute the conception of brotherhood for a spirit of competition and rivalry'.[43]

Cunningham also begins by praising some aspects of the Report, and he is happy about the Church's right in principle to consider social questions, taking issue chiefly with the practical suggestions made in the Report.[44] He accuses it, unfairly it would seem, of 'contrasting the material progress of the country with moral progress', and, more justifiably, of paying too little attention to the need for material progress as a pre-requisite of the social welfare services which it recommends. The existing competitive system, says Cunningham, works quite well: 'There is no need of a revolution, and of reconstituting society on a moral rather than on a material basis, if pains are taken that material progress shall be directed to public interests, and so moralized.'[45] A fair criticism is that the Report neglects to discuss agriculture, and even seems to acquiesce in the depressed state of that industry, not appreciating that its revival is essential if the rural standard of living is to be raised. But Cunningham's repudiation of the Report's attack on the classical political economy, and his assertion that a proper distinction can be made between the sphere of religion, which deals with ends, and that of economics, which deals with ways and means,[46] is a measure of his failure to understand the Report's fundamental belief that all economic theory and practice must be judged in the

[42] Headlam, *op. cit.*, p. 16.

[43] *Ibid.*, pp. 18f. and 21f. The contradictions in *The Church and Industrial Questions* are well exposed in a review in *Commonwealth*, April 1920, pp. 112–14.

[44] W. Cunningham, *Personal Ideals and Social Principles*, pp. 5f. Cunningham died in 1919, and this was one of his last works.

[45] Cunningham, *op. cit.*, p. 8. In favour of private enterprise he points out that it can flourish only if it is meeting a public demand, and that it is in this sense a servant of the community. He ignores the qualifications and limitations of this half-truth, such as are set out, e.g. in *Competition* (see Chapter 1), and which led the authors of the Fifth Report to look in some cases for alternative means of meeting the needs of the community.

[46] Cunningham, *op. cit.*, p. 19.

light of Christian ethical standards. Cunningham disagrees with the Report's interpretation of the social implication of Christ's teaching, and maintains that social improvements should be brought about by the gradual operation of a sense of personal duty working on social institutions, as in the case of slavery. He is apparently indifferent to the slowness of this method, and he does not explain why he accepts the individual application of Christian principles in a social situation, and yet rejects the translation of such action into terms of social ideals which can be preached and taught.[47]

The most serious weakness of the Fifth Report, which neither Headlam nor Cunningham attacks with the vigour it deserves, is the fact that it makes far-reaching claims for a living wage and adequate leisure, without suggesting how these demands might in fact be met. The failure of the Archbishops' committee, or any other representative and authoritative Christian body, to produce an economic vindication of the feasibility of these ideals exposed the ardent but defenceless champions of the Fifth Report to the contemptuous hostility of industrialists. This was particularly true in 1922, when the Federation of British Industries, in the course of a campaign to reduce wages, issued a memorandum which laid down that in the matter of wages 'the real and ultimate test must always be what industry can bear'; workers must be prepared, 'where efficiency may make it desirable, to extend the existing working hours', and if necessary 'to accept a money-wage which may, until business revives, give them a lower standard of living . . . even than their pre-war standard'.[48] This pronouncement seemed to be a direct challenge to the principle of the living wage as the first charge on industry, originally laid down by the Convocation committee of 1907, reaffirmed in the Fifth Report, and, most recently, endorsed by the 1920 Lambeth Conference. The Church Socialist League issued an appeal to the bishops, clergy and laity,

[47] Cunningham, *op. cit.*, pp. 24–36. The hostility to the Fifth Report expressed by Headlam and Cunningham was representative of right-wing dissatisfaction, but the Report was also attacked by those on the left wing of Christian social thought, who felt that it did not go far enough. Widdrington praised its expressions of principle, but denounced its conclusions, using the word 'reconstructionist' as a term of abuse. (The *Church Socialist*, February–March 1919, p. 152.)

[48] Published in *The Times*, February 10th, 1922.

protesting against the F.B.I. memorandum and demanding that, if under the present economic and financial system it was 'economically impossible' to meet the Christian claims, then the Church must insist that the existing system be changed for one which could provide a living wage.[49] The bishops, who had no cut-and-dried alternative order of society in mind, not unnaturally failed to respond to the C.S.L. appeal.

Although the authors of the Fifth Report should have considered more seriously whether their demands could in fact be met, they could reasonably claim that it was not their business to work out economic details, and the Report contained in any case a great deal that was valuable and practical. The report to the 1920 Lambeth Conference of the committee appointed to consider the opportunity and duty of the Church in the industrial and social sphere expressed substantial agreement with the Fifth Report, but also qualified or modified some of its conclusions. In particular the Lambeth committee felt that the Church should concern itself with political questions only when they involve a clear moral issue.[50] Its report emphasizes the need for more production, and although it endorses the 1897 Lambeth judgment that moral responsibility must be exercised in controlling economic conditions, it recognizes that the Church must co-operate with economists and accept the conclusions of scientific investigation into the processes which govern the production and distribution of wealth.[50] It echoes what the Fifth Report has to say about human value, human brotherhood and human responsibility, and about the practical implications of accepting these principles. Individual Christians must show a keen sense of honour in all business dealings, take care in choosing investments, and avoid vulgar and ostentatious expenditure. The Church corporately must eliminate class distinctions from its worship and organizations, recruit its clergy from all classes, and

[49] The appeal, whose signatories included Widdrington, Reckitt, Egerton Swann, Fred Hughes (a member of the committee which produced the Fifth Report), A. J. Penty and Henry Slesser, was distributed as a broadsheet and inserted in the magazine *Commonwealth*. The demand for a living wage was repeated even by as distinguished an economist as Sir William Ashley, e.g. in his article 'The Ethics of Commerce', in *The Pilgrim*, January 1921, but again without any demonstration of how it could in practice be achieved.

[50] *The Lambeth Conferences 1867–1948*, p. 68. The Chairman of the committee was Kempthorne.

organize social studies and practical social work.[51] The full Lambeth Conference adopted a series of resolutions on the basis of this committee's report, of which one asserted, rather more cautiously than the Fifth Report, that there must be 'a fundamental change in the spirit and working of our economic life',[52] and another emphasized the duty of the Church to work for the removal of 'inhuman or oppressive conditions of labour in all parts of the world, especially among the weaker races'.[53]

Another report, complementary to *Christianity and Industrial Questions*, appeared in 1920, entitled *The Church and Social Service*.[54] This enlarges on the practical duties of Christians, and points to the danger of bureaucratic methods being used if responsibility for all social service is assumed by the State. There will always be much social work which is performed most satisfactorily and sympathetically on a voluntary basis, and this provides an important opportunity for Christian service.[55] The clergy's approach to social service should be more knowledgeable and imaginative, and they should be fully conversant with all the statutory and voluntary services which exist to help people. To achieve this, the report suggests a compulsory study course of two terms for all ordination candidates.[56] The laity should take part in local interdenominational social councils and in local government work, and 'the workman must be made to feel that work for the Church and work in the Labour movement are not incompatible'[57]—a somewhat archaic and paternalist note in an otherwise sensible and realistic report. If a choice exists between setting up independent Church organizations, and throwing the weight of the Church behind the social work carried out by the State, the report recommends the latter course, but it calls also for the strengthening of

[51] *The Lambeth Conferences 1867–1948*, pp. 73–5. [52] *Ibid.*, p. 51. [53] *Ibid.*, p. 52.

[54] The report was commissioned by the Archbishop of Canterbury, and its terms of reference were: 'To consider and report upon the ways in which the clergy, churchworkers, and churchpeople generally can best co-operate with the State in all matters concerning the social life of the community.'

[55] *The Church and Social Service*, pp. 5–13.

[56] *Ibid.*, pp. 13–26. An outline of such a course is given in an appendix, pp. 56f. *Cf.* an examination paper set for candidates for a priest's orders and reproduced (with editorial commendation) in the *Modern Churchman*, February 1921, pp. 553–5; this included a number of detailed and searching questions about social welfare, poor relief, medical services, and club work—presupposing a diaconate much concerned with such matters.

[57] *The Church and Social Service*, p. 29.

the rural deanery as an ecclesiastical unit responsible for the social welfare of the people.[58]

During the post-war years several attempts were made to put into practice the principles of the Fifth Report, and although few could claim any obvious or striking success, they were at least signs that its message had gone home to many leading churchmen. The railway strike of 1919 provoked Davidson to offer his services as mediator; Lloyd George and the railwaymen's leader, J. H. Thomas, replied in friendly terms, and although Davidson's intervention was not necessary, his offer was welcomed.[59] In a speech in the Lords on February 25th, 1919, Lang referred again to the problem of industrial unrest: 'The utmost possible goodwill, personal regard, gratitude, even in some cases affection, between masters and men does not in the least blunt the determination of the men to do what they can to change a system which is quite independent of those kindlier personal relations.'[60] He welcomed the establishment of Whitley Councils, but wanted to see them formed into a permanent Industrial Council, on which employers, workers and the government would be represented. Resolutions welcoming the Fifth Report were passed by the Lower Houses of Convocation,[61] and debates in the Upper Houses were also pervaded by its spirit.[62]

A more serious test of the social faith of churchmen was provided by the coal strike of 1921. The increasingly unprofitable character of the coal industry, due to the recovery of the continental coal-fields and the influence of Germany's reparations payments in coal, persuaded the government to accelerate the process of decontrol of the mines, bringing forward the date of their restoration to private enterprise to March 31st, 1921. When the government de-

[58] *Ibid.*, pp. 43–7.

[59] Bell, *op. cit.*, Vol. II, pp. 951f. A letter to *The Times* by Woods, published on October 4th and expressing sympathy with the railwaymen, provoked Hensley Henson to write: 'The wheel has gone full circle; and the clerical toadies of this age do not flatter princes but mobs. And the reason is the same. *They worship the possessors of power.*' (*Retrospect*, Vol. I, p. 316.)

[60] H.L. Deb., 1919, Vol. 33, Col. 308.

[61] The *Chronicle of Convocation*, 1919, pp. 233–9; *York Journal of Convocation*, 1919, pp. 50–6.

[62] The *Chronicle of Convocation*, 1919, pp. 134–60; *York Journal of Convocation*, 1919, pp. 178–86.

cision on decontrol was announced, negotiations had already begun between the owners and miners on the miners' objectives of a national wages settlement under a National Wages Board, and a system of pooling profits so that the same wages could be paid in unprofitable mines as in the most prosperous. Left to themselves, the owners were prepared to offer only district agreements, in many cases involving heavy reductions in existing wages—in South Wales as much as 49%—which the miners refused to accept, and a strike began on April 1st. The Transport Workers' Federation and the National Union of Railwaymen, which with the Mining Federation constituted the so-called triple alliance of the trade union movement, agreed to support the miners, and a general strike call was issued for midnight on Friday, April 15th. This general strike never took place, as the railwaymen's and transport workers' leaders, who felt that the miners should have accepted an invitation from Lloyd George to discuss the question of wages independently of the matter of a national profits pool, withdrew their support on the day the strike was due to begin. In the end, after the miners' strike had lasted until July 1st, a National Wages Board was set up, but the miners had to accept defeat in the shape of district wage agreements.[63]

The miners' case for a national pool was a good one. In a Convocation debate on April 27th, 1921, Kempthorne welcomed it as a praiseworthy way of sharing the burden of unprofitable pits—'an entirely Christian outlook'—and if such an arrangement were incompatible with private ownership, that was a very strong indictment of private ownership. The motion was seconded by Woods, who referred in some detail to technical aspects of the dispute and quoted the judgment of Sir Richard Redmayne, the Chief Inspector of Mines, that the existing system of ownership was extravagant and wasteful. In view of the reactionary attitude of the government and owners it was the patience of the miners, he thought, not their impatience, which was remarkable. Talbot bitterly attacked the government for neglecting to prepare for the decontrol of the mines by any constructive changes in the organiza-

[63] Friday, April 15th, became known in trade union circles as Black Friday, since working-class solidarity had been broken on the first occasion on which it was put to the test.

tion of the industry, and Garbett, now Bishop of Southwark, deplored the mentality of those who wanted to beat the miners in a 'fight to the finish'.[64] The government was angered by such outspoken criticism from the bishops, and the Secretary for Mines, W. C. Bridgeman, wrote to Davidson complaining of the one-sidedness of the speeches. Davidson agreed that there had been some partisan speaking, and explained this on the grounds that, by a swing of the pendulum, the episcopal favour which had previously been denied to the working classes was now bestowed too lavishly upon them. He also blamed the sensational and unbalanced press coverage of the debate.[65]

The government economy drive of 1922, the so-called 'Geddes Axe', was the occasion of further vigorous Christian protest, particularly in so far as the ambitious plans of the 1918 Fisher Education Act were drastically curtailed. In the Church Assembly on February 9th, 1922, Miss G. B. Ayre moved a resolution viewing 'with deep concern the recent suggestions made for increased economy in education', and calling on the government 'to increase rather than diminish educational facilities in this time of unrest and unemployment'.[66] She was supported by Lang and Temple,[67] but there was strong opposition to the motion from several laymen. Athelstan Riley, urging a broad view of the nation's calamitous financial state and the withdrawal of selfish pressure for particular exemptions from the general drive for economy, moved the previous question. Other speakers supported him, arguing that unemployment was rife because of high taxation, that any further expenditure on education would involve even higher taxation, and that this would cause yet more unemployment. Finally Lord Hugh Cecil opposed the discussion of any matter not

[64] The *Chronicle of Convocation*, February and April 1921, pp. 241–63 and 281–96; Temple's editorial notes in *The Pilgrim* (July 1921, pp. 365f.) were less complimentary to the miners.

[65] Bell, *op cit.*, Vol. II, pp. 1045–8. Convocation evidently took fright at the criticisms expressed about this debate on the coal strike, and on July 7th, 1921, Woods withdrew his motion expressing concern at the state of the agricultural industry before a vote was taken, alluding to the unpleasant memory of the coal debate. (The *Chronicle of Convocation*, July, 1921, pp. 117–41.)

[66] *The National Assembly of the Church of England, Report of Proceedings*, Vol. III, No. 1, p. 82.

[67] *Ibid.*, pp. 83–5. Temple's views on the projected economies in educational expenditure are set out more fully in *The Pilgrim*, April 1922, pp. 334–43.

financial or legislative, and Miss Ayre was obliged to withdraw the motion.[68] The Church Assembly's handling of this debate was denounced in *Commonwealth* as a confirmation of the public suspicion that the Assembly was more interested in discussing ecclesiastical futilities, and Lord Burnham's judgment on the Geddes economies in education was repeated with relish—'the greatest stupidity—rank, gross and palpable'.[69]

On the other hand, the diehards of the Church Assembly were not alone in their views. A resolution was introduced by Canon Sorby in the Lower House of York Convocation on February 24th, 1921, expressing the House's support for the government's curtailment and postponement of the implementation of the Fisher Act, and indeed encouraging further postponement. This was, he said, in the interests of sound finance, but it would involve no serious hardship; nursery schools were an extravagance which 'would be taken advantage of by many mothers standing at their doors with arms akimbo, doing nothing', and since the mental ability of thousands of children was strictly limited, 'money spent on higher education would be thrown into the gutter'. Another speaker thought that educational activities were often unsound: 'In the evenings a lot of money was wasted upon having organized games in unhealthy buildings, and all initiative was taken out of our future men and women.'[70] These speeches were not, however, representative of majority opinion, and the previous question was carried, but even *The Pilgrim* was not unsympathetic towards the Geddes Report; the fact that the proposed economies in education, Temple's particular interest, were reduced from eighteen million to six and a half million pounds perhaps explains this lenient attitude towards the principles of the Report.[71]

The work of propagating the message of the Fifth Report was undertaken chiefly by the Industrial Christian Fellowship, an Anglican organization created in January 1919, out of the moribund

[68] *The National Assembly of the Church of England, Report of Proceedings*, Vol. III, No. 1, pp. 84 and 87f.

[69] *Commonwealth*, March 1922, pp. 61f.

[70] *York Journal of Convocation*, 1921, pp. 118–23. Sorby wanted the thousands of children whom he regarded as incapable of benefiting from higher education to become 'an asset in the labour market'. By a fine stroke of irony this debate on education was immediately followed by one on the distress of the unemployed. (*Ibid.*, pp. 123–6.)

[71] *The Pilgrim*, April 1922, pp. 243f.

Navvy Mission, which had been concerned with the evangelization of a narrow section of the working population. The I.C.F. widened its scope to include the whole of industry, and later in 1919 it absorbed what remained of the C.S.U., with the idea that the intellectual work and research of the C.S.U. should be carried on by a department within the predominantly evangelistic I.C.F.[72] The I.C.F. enjoyed lavish episcopal support and the dedicated services of its General Director, P. T. R. Kirk,[73] but its most successful work was probably done through the crusades, missions and lecture-tours of Studdert Kennedy, who was described by Temple as 'a prophet of social righteousness in the true succession of Henry Scott Holland'.[74] Kennedy's experience as a war chaplain in France profoundly affected his theology; it convinced him of God's intimate involvement in all suffering, but it also convinced him of the horror and futility of violence, in an industrial no less than a military context.[75] His passionate concern was that men should become 'God-determined', and an economic or social philosophy which rested on any other kind of determinism, whether Marxist socialism or Manchester capitalism, was abhorrent to him.[76] Seeing all problems as ultimately moral and spiritual, he was reluctant to lend his support to practical theories of social reform, and deeply suspicious of any which failed to take account of man's need of redemption.[77] Although he frequently sympathized with the radical point of view, and agreed for example that wealth was badly—even wickedly—distributed, and that the existing social system must ultimately give way to a better, he also maintained that these judgments by themselves were incomplete and futile; redistribution of existing wealth would have to be

[72] The I.C.F. Report for the year 1919–20 records the amalgamation, and the official objects of the I.C.F., printed in the annual report but subsequently revised in various ways, reflected its dual nature.

[73] There is a generous tribute to Kirk by Sir William Cash in the Annual Report of the I.C.F. for 1962.

[74] W. Temple, *The Man and his Message*, in the symposium *G. A. Studdert Kennedy, by his Friends*, p. 209.

[75] 'The very first thing that any true friend of Labour has got to make quite clear to the workers today is that there is just as little to be got out of industrial war in the long run as there is out of international war, and that little is considerably less than nothing.' (Studdert Kennedy, *Democracy and the Dog-Collar*, p. 43.)

[76] *Ibid.*, pp. 66 and 92.

[77] *Cf.* the essay by P. T. R. Kirk in *G. A. Studdert Kennedy, by his Friends*, (pp. 165–91) on his work as I.C.F. Crusader, which is entirely devoted, not to a description of his social philosophy, but to personal reminiscences and an emphasis on his preaching of the gospel.

accompanied by a great increase in production if the country's economic problems were to be solved, and any movement to 'smash the system' would have to be inspired by a higher motive than self-interest if it were to succeed.[78] He described material poverty as the 'sacrament of sin, the outward and visible sign of an inward and spiritual disgrace',[79] but he believed that a moralized form of capitalism was most likely to abolish poverty without offending against Christian principles, and he consistently refused to align himself with the Labour Party.[80]

The movement in Christian circles away from support for the Labour Party and Fabian collectivism, foreshadowed by the disagreements within the C.S.L. from 1912 onwards,[81] grew in strength during the post-war years, helped by the development of an alternative to state socialism which seemed to many people to be more in accord with Christian principles. This was guild socialism, originally expounded in 1912 in the *New Age*, a periodical edited by A. R. Orage, and soon supported by G. D. H. Cole and the National Guilds League which he founded. Guild socialism had a complex genealogy, including William Morris's emphasis on the value of craftsmanship, Hilaire Belloc's warning that collectivism would create the 'servile state',[82] G. K. Chesterton's emphasis on the need for private property as an expression of personality, A. J. Penty's hatred of the large-scale organization of industrial life, and syndicalism's offer of a better status for the producer.[83] A consideration which attracted much Christian

[78] Studdert Kennedy, *Lies!*, p. 49, and *Democracy and the Dog-Collar*, pp. 58–92.

[79] Studdert Kennedy, *The Wicket-Gate*, p. 166.

[80] 'Socialism is no more Christian than capitalism; apart from a higher level of social power, which can only be got through divine grace, Socialism is a dream, and a bad dream at that.' (Kennedy's words, quoted by F. A. Iremonger in *Men and Movements in the Church*, p. 39.)

[81] See Chapter 1.

[82] Hilaire Belloc, *The Servile State* (1912) was one of the most powerful influences behind the enthusiasm for guild socialism. It is an analysis of what Belloc claims to be the inherent instability of capitalism, and an examination of the three possible alternatives to it—distributism, collectivism and slavery.

[83] See M. B. Reckitt and C. E. Bechhofer, *The Meaning of National Guilds*, 2nd revised edition of 1920. The introduction, pp. ix–xiv, traces the origin of the movement. The book is an exposition, from the Christian point of view, of the form of guild socialism which advocated the establishment of national guilds. For an exposure of some of the inherent weaknesses of guild socialism, see H. Reynard, 'The Guild Socialists', in the *Economic Journal*, September 1920, pp. 321–30. See also S. T. Glass, *The Responsible Society*.

support for a guild organization of industry was its medieval origin, and associations with the whole idea of Christendom and the glorious ages of faith.[84]

Although guild socialists agreed in repudiating the doctrine of state sovereignty preached by the Fabian Society and the Labour Party, in favour of a pluralist view of society as a 'communitas communitatum',[85] the ideals behind the movement were so diverse that, not surprisingly, it split. There were basically three schools of thought: one, led by A. J. Penty, was strongly medievalist in character and advocated in the most unrealistic terms the dismantling of much of the existing industrial order, the restoration of craftsmanship, and a great revival of rural life.[86] At the opposite extreme was a left-wing group led by William Mellor, subsequently editor of the *Daily Herald*, and G. D. H. Cole, who were suspicious of religious tendencies in the movement; between the two, and the only one to stand for a programme which was both informed by Christian principles and could conceivably have been put into practice, was the National Guilds movement, of which M. B. Reckitt was a prominent member and propagandist.[87] The theory of this group was that the change to a guild system could be brought about by using the existing trade union principle, but replacing craft unions by industrial unions covering all the workers in an industry. The ownership of plant and capital would be vested in the State, but full responsibility for the management and conduct of the industry would be in the hands of the democratic self-governing guilds.[88] Unlike such palliatives of the existing system as a fixed minimum wage or profit-sharing, the guilds would offer the workers a fully satisfactory status, and a share in management and control without the 'taint of co-partnership or

[84] The medievalism of some Christian social thought is discussed in Chapter 6. S. L. Greenslade, *The Church and Social Order*, p. 67, puts the guild idea in perspective; although praised too highly by 'romantic medievalists of the Bellocian order', and of economic rather than religious origin, the medieval guilds did embody one particularly valuable principle, that of the just price, which compared favourably with the Roman Law principle of 'caveat emptor'.

[85] M. B. Reckitt, 'Industry and Democracy: the Evolution of an Ideal', in *The World and the Faith*, pp. 102–5.

[86] See Chapter 6 for a discussion of Penty's thought.

[87] The split in the guild socialist movement is recorded in Henry Slesser, *Judgment Reserved*, pp. 120–2.

[88] This variant of the guild system was related to collectivism in that it involved a partnership between guild and State: the idea that the State should own the plant and capital would not have satisfied Belloc.

complicity in profiteering',[89] the assumption being that it would be against their own interests and those of society as a whole for employees to become small-scale capitalists, as in most co-partnership schemes.

In *The Meaning of National Guilds*, Reckitt and Bechhofer envisage a strong trade union organization, like the triple alliance on a much larger scale, with militant local trades councils, using the workshop as the natural unit—on the lines of the shop stewards' movement. On this basis, assuming the principle of the 'closed shop', it would be possible to begin the process of encroaching control, by which the workers would gradually assume full responsibility. The authors are conveniently vague about how this would actually come about, but they do emphasize the need for financial independence; nationalization, with financial control still in government hands, is at the most only a possible stepping-stone to full workers' control.[90] The authors significantly point out that the Bolshevik regime in Russia, so far from realizing the ideals of the National Guilds movement, repudiates them all both in theory and practice.[91]

The last section of the book is devoted to a description of the one industrial guild which was actually set up, in the building industry. In 1919 a body known as the Building Trades Parliament produced the Foster Report, which outlined the possibility of creating 'one great self-governing democracy of organized public service', controlled by workers representing all grades.[92] Local guilds were formed in Manchester in January, 1920, and the system spread rapidly, helped by the offer of the C.W.S. to accept responsibility for providing materials needed by the guilds. In view of this flourishing embodiment of the guild principle, Reckitt and Bechhofer end on a note of high optimism about its future.

In fact the building guild movement collapsed in 1922, when the effect of economies in local authority housing programmes under the Addison Act began to be felt, and the guilds' lack of financial reserves prevented them from surviving a period of trade depres-

[89] Reckitt and Bechhofer, *op. cit.*, p. 126.

[90] *Ibid.*, pp. 250–71. This section includes a brief exposition of the financial theory known as Social Credit which, from 1920 onwards, became an increasingly prominent element in some Christian social thought. See Chapter 6.

[91] Reckitt and Bechhofer, *op. cit.*, pp. 212–30.

[92] *Ibid.*, pp. 274f.

sion. But the idea of guild socialism, in one form or another, remained an important one in Christian social thought. There was a growing feeling in some quarters that Christian attempts to moralize the existing social order, postponing indefinitely its radical transformation, were not only meeting with conspicuously little success, but were also bound to compromise essential Christian principles. So began the quest for an authentically Christian sociology, which some have seen as the distinctive feature of Christian social thought between the wars,[93] and which, because it did not take the existing state of society as its starting-point, was able to make free use of new ideas such as guild socialism. Meanwhile, despite the frustration of economic misfortune and political ineptitude, the spirit of the Fifth Report was shortly to enjoy a final flowering.

Despite the demoralizing effect of high unemployment and economic depression, and the increasing preoccupation of Convocation and the Church Assembly with questions of a narrowly ecclesiastical nature, particularly the revision of the Prayer Book, Christian interest in social and economic affairs continued to grow. The I.C.F. preached the Fifth Report, although it seemed uncertain whether it stood firmly for all that was in it, or merely for getting it widely read,[94] and there were individual attempts to elaborate and develop the ideas contained in the Report. An example of independent initiative was H. A. Mess's *Studies in the Christian Gospel for Society* (1923),[95] which illuminated various aspects of Christian social duty, and studied in greater detail the motives which govern men in industry. An important sign of the growth of official social concern in the Church of England was the decision of the Church Assembly in February 1923 to set up a permanent Social and Industrial Committee, while another small but significant indication of the climate of opinion was the fact that

[93] See M. B. Reckitt, *Maurice to Temple*, pp. 168f. and 197; and G. C. Binyon, *The Christian Socialist Movement in England*, pp. 207–10.

[94] See M. B. Reckitt, *Faith and Society*, pp. 118f. The I.C.F. was always torn between loyalty to the views of its many conservative supporters, and to those of the working men for whose benefit it chiefly existed.

[95] Mess had previously produced a penetrating survey of poverty in East London, *The Facts of Poverty* (1920), which was particularly valuable for its emphasis on the inter-relation and cumulative effect of the various aspects of poverty, notably bad housing, drunkenness and ill-health.

in March 1923 Davidson contemplated resignation, doubting whether he was enough in sympathy with the increasingly popular social interpretation of Christianity.[96]

It seems almost certain that the particular occasion of Davidson's doubt was the movement known as Copec, from the initial letters of its full title—the Conference on Christian Politics, Economics and Citizenship—which was to culminate in a great gathering at Birmingham in April 1924. The inspiration for this came originally in 1919 from the Interdenominational Conference of Social Service Unions, in which Gore took a leading part, and the preparatory work, which was spread over four years, began with the creation in 1920 of a council of three hundred and fifty members, presided over by Temple.[97] All the important Christian denominations were represented, and helped to prepare the reports, but the Roman Catholic delegates withdrew from the movement a few weeks before the conference itself took place.[98] The Basis adopted by the movement expressed the conviction that 'the Christian faith, rightly interpreted and consistently followed, gives the vision and the power essential for solving the problems of today'. It deplored the disastrous consequences of the neglect of Christian social ethics, and affirmed that in Christ's teaching there are 'certain fundamental principles . . . which, if accepted, not only condemn much in the present organization of society, but show the way of regeneration. Christianity has proved itself to possess also a motive power for the transformation of the individual, without which no change of policy or method can succeed.'[99] The Church press on the whole supported the movement, but there were some misgivings: *Commonwealth* remarked in

[96] Bell, *op. cit.*, Vol. II, p. 1154.

[97] The leaders of the Copec movement were, from the Church of England, Gore, Temple (chairman of the conference), and C. E. Raven (joint secretary); from the Free Churches, A. E. Garvie, Will Reason and Malcolm Spencer. The secretary of the movement, who was largely responsible for the organization of the conference, was Lucy Gardner, of the Society of Friends.

[98] This was apparently at the instigation of those British Roman Catholics who were suspicious of the attitude of Cardinal Mercier and the spirit of the Malines conversations, and wished to prevent further fraternization. See C. E. Raven, 'C.O.P.E.C. Then and Now', part 2, in *Crucible* (the organ of the Church Assembly Board for Social Responsibility), January 1963, p. 11.

[99] *The Proceedings of Copec*, edited by Will Reason, p. xi. The clear implication of the last sentence, that the transformation of the individual must precede the transformation of society, is an important one. Failure to appreciate it led to unfair and unjustified criticism of Copec. See below.

November 1922: 'Copec is in its Galilean phase, and the multitudes are thronging to hear its message. But if it is true to its calling, presently there must come a testing and a sifting. It must challenge the world; and when that challenge is understood, will it be multitudes who follow?' The question was not misplaced, as subsequent events were to show.

Writing of the preparations for Copec, Temple expressed the hope that the Conference would approach its work neither from the conservative nor from the idealist point of view, but from that of principle. He maintained that Christianity pointed to certain basic principles, the most important being the sacredness of personality, the brotherhood of men, the duty of service, and the way of sacrifice. Most Christians accepted these principles in theory, but the task of translating them into policies for action—the task of Copec—was, he said, highly controversial.[100]

On the basis of information and opinion supplied by study groups throughout the country, twelve commissions prepared reports on particular social issues, and these reports were available to the 1,400 delegates before they assembled at Birmingham from April 5th to 12th, 1924—a mere week in which they had to listen to speeches introducing each report, debate the reports and agree on resolutions based on their findings. Inevitably the account of the conference proceedings does not make a very striking impression; there was little opportunity for real debate, and in only one or two instances was the wording of suggested resolutions changed at the conference itself. In his opening address as chairman, Temple emphasized the comprehensive range of the reports, and the inter-relation of many important social issues. He also pointed out that the conference was representative of a movement which was being felt all over the world, in all branches of Christendom.[101]

The reports of the twelve commissions vary in their approach to the subjects with which they deal, both in depth and seriousness of treatment, and in the degree of unanimity which they achieve. In some cases a formula or conclusion was found to which all the members of a commission could assent, while in others—notably

[100] *The Pilgrim*, January 1923, pp. 218–25.
[101] *The Proceedings of Copec*, pp. 18–21.

over the questions of contraception and pacifism—there were deep cleavages of opinion which no compromise could conceal. Most reports have a theological introduction, usually including a collection of N.T. quotations or dominical sayings to justify a Christian treatment of the subject and supply a basis for the commission's discussion.

The reader is referred to the commission's reports for a full account of the thought of the Copec movement; here it is possible to do no more than indicate a few of the more important points. The first report, *The Nature of God and his Purpose for the World*, laid a sound theological foundation for the practical suggestions of later reports, and warded off the common criticism that the social gospel lacked a theological basis. It was remarkable that such a wide measure of agreement could be achieved on the theological level,[102] but, as Raven has pointed out, Copec came at a particularly favourable moment for such agreement—between the fall of fundamentalism, and the rise of Barthianism and the theology of crisis. It was possible, as it had not been previously and would not have been subsequently, to 'formulate a coherent interpretation of a creative–redemptive theology and a consequently Christ-centred ethic'.[103]

The second report, *Education*, shows clearly how different social problems react on each other; the value of education is much reduced by the crippling effect on many children of their environment. The report deplores class-distinction in education, but is more concerned with the gap between those who receive only primary education and those who go on to some form of secondary school, than with the divisive social effect of fee-paying schools. It calls for a great expansion of adult education, and vastly increased public expenditure over the whole educational field, claiming that the nation would thereby in the long run gain financially, as well as morally and spiritually.[104] The same combination of realism with

[102] This commission included the Bishop of Oxford (H. M. Burge), the Jesuit theologian A. J. Day, John Oman and Charles Raven; the chairman was Walter Moberly.

[103] Raven, *op. cit.*, p. 11. He is less than fair to Barthianism, but this does not invalidate his argument.

[104] *Education*, p. 187. It is interesting to compare the Copec proposals with what was actually achieved; for a good, brief survey of progress in education between 1920 and 1930 see Basil Yeaxlee's article in the *Torch*, August 1930.

idealism lies behind the passionate indignation of the next report, *The Home*, over housing conditions, and there are extensive references to the research work of Booth, Bowley and Rowntree in its analysis of the appalling effects of poverty. Public provision of medical and welfare services, particularly to eliminate preventable illness and ease the burden which falls on the working-class mother, is accepted as a worthy principle, as well as being abundantly justified by existing circumstances.

The fourth report, *The Relation of the Sexes*, reveals the apparently irreconcilable differences which existed between Christians of varying schools of thought about the question of contraception, and its contribution to this debate is dealt with later, in Chapter 7.

One of the most remarkable reports, not so much for its contents, but for the fact that it was produced at all, is the fifth, *Leisure*. Copec was one of the first movements to recognize the importance of working out a Christian view of leisure, and although the conference debate was largely confined to the traditional problems of drink and gambling,[105] the report itself was a notable venture into a largely uncharted area. It welcomes the fact that an increasing number of people have leisure to enjoy, and sees an important opportunity for the Church in the sphere of guiding those for whom leisure is a new experience into a right use of their time. Once again there is emphasis on the essential prerequisites of a satisfying life, notably decent housing.

The Treatment of Crime was another relatively neglected subject, and this report criticizes two prevalent theories of punishment, the retributive and the deterrent, on the grounds that they are largely unsuccessful. The members of the commission were divided over the principle of capital punishment, but the full conference passed by a large majority a resolution calling for the abolition of the death penalty.[106]

The report on *International Relations* is distinguished by its optimistic and confident view of the League of Nations, and by its unquestioning assumption of the desirability of helping backward countries to develop. Apart from a short section, added at the

[105] *The Proceedings of Copec*, pp. 133–5.
[106] *Ibid.*, p. 148.

instigation of M. B. Reckitt, which contrasts the League with the true Christian ideal of the restoration of Christendom, there is no trace of the opinion that the League was a sub-Christian organization which it would be dangerous to trust too far, or the conviction that the burdens of civilization should not be inflicted on the simple life of backward peoples—ideas which were becoming increasingly popular with a certain school of Christian social thought.[107] The commission which produced the companion volume, *Christianity and War*, was deeply divided between the thorough-going pacifists and those who accepted that war, although fundamentally incompatible with the Christian gospel, might be necessary at that particular stage in man's ethical evolution.[108]

Industry and Property is one of the longest and most interesting reports.[109] Based on the conclusions reached by the Fifth Report, and by the authors of *Property* in 1913, it makes a wide range of practical suggestions for reform in financial and industrial practice and in the laws of property and inheritance. Noticing that periods of unemployment and so-called over-production are in fact also periods of great want, the report suggests that some defect in the distributive system might be responsible for the fact that the demand for goods was not financially effective.[110] It is non-committal about collective ownership,[111] but surprisingly radical about the rights of inheritance and bequest, a system which perpetuates 'the privilege of receiving income without discharging equivalent responsibilities'.[112] In conclusion the report follows the conviction of the Fifth Report that the existing industrial and

[107] See *International Relations*, pp. 114–24, and *The Life of the Church and the Order of Society* (the report of the Malvern Conference of 1941), in which Reckitt's description of his differences with the other members of the Copec commission is to be found on p. 50. For a discussion of the Christendom Group's attitude to international affairs and the League, see below, Chapter 6.

[108] *Christianity and War*, pp. 51–73.

[109] The commission included Sir Henry Slesser, R. H. Tawney, Ben Turner (a leading trade unionist), and Will Reason; there is a particularly good article on its work by Tawney in *The Pilgrim*, October 1924, pp. 72–85. (This issue of *The Pilgrim* is devoted almost entirely to a survey of the conference.)

[110] *Industry and Property*, p. 87.

[111] *Ibid.*, pp. 153–7. For a more able exposition of this functional, empirical approach to the whole problem of public and private ownership see J. M. Keynes, *The End of Laissez-faire*, pp. 44–54 (originally delivered as the Sidney Ball lecture at Oxford in 1924).

[112] *Industry and Property*, p. 158.

economic order is 'not merely defective, but vicious and radically unchristian'.[113]

The report on *Politics and Citizenship* is, by contrast, notably more conservative than the Fifth Report, limiting the legitimate sphere of Christian concern in politics to the ultimate ends of political activity, not the means by which they may be achieved.[114] Indeed, the political role of the Church is more satisfactorily dealt with in the penultimate report, *The Social Function of the Church.*[115] It was this report which was to have the strongest influence on the subsequent development of Christian social thought, in particular with its recommendation that an interdenominational Christian council should be established to carry on the work of Copec on a permanent basis, by co-ordinating Christian work in the field of social studies, providing a central office of information, and pioneering social research.[116] The report follows *The Church and Social Service* in its preference for co-operation in practical social work between Christian and civic bodies, rather than independent Church activity: it commends the interdenominational study schools which discuss social issues, and it expresses limited sympathy with Gore's desire to see the Church provide authoritative guidance and discipline in social matters, but doubts the feasibility of building up a comprehensive Christian social casuistry.[117]

The final report was an uncontroversial survey of *Historical Illustrations of the Social Effects of Christianity.*

At the final meeting of the Copec assembly, Raven promised the formation of a Continuation Committee and urged the delegates to carry on the work of Copec by taking its message into the local life of the Church, by further detailed study of the reports, and by the transformation of their own lives. Lucy Gardner announced plans for thirteen regional conferences to be held during 1924, and Temple read the final message of the conference, which singled out the need to solve the unemployment and housing problems, to improve education and to seek international peace as the issues to

[113] *Ibid.*, p. 186.
[114] *Politics and Citizenship*, p. 45.
[115] The chairman of the commission was Kempthorne, and the members included Fred Hughes, P. T. R. Kirk, H. A. Mess and Malcolm Spencer.
[116] *The Social Function of the Church*, pp. 154–9.
[117] *Ibid.*, pp. 83–96.

which, above all others, Christians must devote their energies.[118]

Both Raven and Temple emphasized the need for sacrifice, and Gore, summing up the debate on Industry and Property, spoke of the courage which the delegates needed to ask themselves whether they were really prepared to accept and apply the fundamental principles which the report outlined.[119] But in the enthusiastic atmosphere of the conference such warnings went largely unheeded, and this failure to count the cost, even on the part of some of those most devoted to the cause of Copec, was partly responsible for the rapid disintegration of the movement and the fact that it left behind so little evidence of its scale and scope. It is, however, only fair to acknowledge its long-term influence in helping to prepare the way for the coming of the Welfare State and the establishment of the World Council of Churches,[120] and even in the short run it could claim some success.

The regional conferences mentioned by Lucy Gardner were the first sign of Copec's continuing activity. The Newcastle conference led to the formation in 1925 of a Bureau of Social Research for Tyneside, with H. A. Mess as director. As a preliminary to united Christian action it made a thorough survey of the area, published in 1928 under the title *Industrial Tyneside*. The Tyneside Christian Social Council, set up as a result of the survey, concentrated largely on housing, health, unemployment relief and provision for recreation.[121] Another notable local result of Copec, this time of the main conference, was the establishment of the Birmingham House Improvement Society, which bought up and renovated old property and made it available at low rents. This was one of the earliest specifically Christian undertakings of its kind, and depended on money being given for the work, or lent at interest rates as low as 2 or 2½%.

The Copec reports formed the British contribution to the ecumenical Life and Work Conference at Stockholm in 1925, and in 1928 the Continuation Committee arranged a conference on the Welfare of Youth, which called for legislation further to control

[118] *The Proceedings of Copec*, pp. 265–7 and 273–6. [119] *Ibid.*, p. 212.

[120] C. E. Raven, 'C.O.P.E.C. Then and Now', part 1, in *Crucible*, October, 1962, p. 108.

[121] See A. C. C. Firmin, 'On Tyneside', in *Commonwealth*, August 1930, pp. 235f., for a description of the Council's work.

hours of work and to prohibit blind alley jobs for juveniles, and recommended that vocational training and advice should be given to children while they were still at school.[122] The literary achievements of Copec included an additional report, *Rural Life*, which appeared in 1927. This makes some sensible suggestions for a revival of rural morale; higher wages and rents; cheap credit for small farmers; the establishment of commodity marketing boards and the replacement of tied cottages by local authority housing. But parts of the report are remarkably inept, and some scarcely coherent. Its ideal of rural education is not exactly exalted, since fourteen is accepted as a satisfactory school-leaving age for many country children, and it is suggested that infant and junior classes could be entrusted to 'village women who would train them to be clean and obedient, kind to each other and to animals, and to be happy with games and singing and handwork'.[123]

Copec also inspired three volumes of essays, *Christianity and the Present Moral Unrest*, edited by A. D. Lindsay, and *Social Discipline in the Christian Community* and *The Kingdom of God in Industry*, both edited by Malcolm Spencer.[124] *The Kingdom of God in Industry* claims to be unique in providing a critical introduction to the various efforts being made to evolve a Christian order of industry—'lines of progress which might be pursued simultaneously if they were judged to be promising'.[125] In fact it is a sketchy and unco-ordinated collection of conflicting points of view; some are constructive, like Malcolm Sparkes' imaginative industrial ideal of high wages and output coupled with low prices, and the anonymous discussion of the advantages and disadvantages of co-partnership schemes,[126] but others are quite unrealistic.

The undistinguished nature of this attempt to continue and develop the work of Copec showed how urgent was the need to set up a permanent Christian council to deal with social affairs,

[122] See Constance Smith, 'The Welfare of Youth', in *Stockholm*, 1928, Vol. 1, pp. 154–8, and F. S. Livie-Noble, 'Youth in Britain', in *Stockholm*, 1929, Vol. 2, pp. 170–4.

[123] *Rural Life*, p. 30.

[124] The first two were published in 1926, the third in 1927. *Social Discipline in the Christian Community* was the work of the commission which had produced *The Social Function of the Church*, and which continued to meet for an annual conference under Malcolm Spencer's leadership.

[125] *The Kingdom of God in Industry*, p. 7.

[126] *Ibid.*, pp. 18–20 and 21–7.

made up of fully qualified experts rather than interested amateurs. *The Social Function of the Church* had called for such a body, and *Social Discipline in the Christian Community* provided a possible outline of its function and method in the formulation of a distinctively Christian sociology,[127] but it was not until January 1929 that the Council of Christian Churches in England for Social Questions, commonly known as the Christian Social Council, was set up, and the Copec movement officially disbanded. The C.S.C. boasted seventy-two members, thirty of them from the Church of England, of whom half were nominated by the I.C.F. and half by the Social and Industrial Commission of the Church Assembly.[128] It worked through five committees, concerned with international affairs, local co-operation (the work of the old Christian Social Crusade), the welfare of youth, social education, and research. This last committee, under the direction of V. A. Demant,[129] and financed by the Halley Stewart Trust, was potentially the most influential, but the technical competence of its members proved inadequate for the task which it attempted to undertake. Its disappointing history is told in a later chapter.

Although these achievements of Copec were not particularly remarkable, the movement met with some stiff opposition, notably from Hensley Henson, who devoted part of his visitation charge in 1924 to an attack on Copec.[130] His criticism was partly justified, particularly in his accusation that the conference never really

[127] 'If the Church is not for ever to be open to the charge of "taking sides" in this issue or that, or (much worse) of being too spiritless to take them, she must step out into the open and make a "side" of her own.' M. B. Reckitt, 'The Present Phase of the Problem', in *Social Discipline in the Christian Community*, p. 102. See also Malcolm Spencer's essay, 'The Way Forward', *ibid.*, pp. 104–17.

[128] The object of the C.S.C. was: 'To apply the Christian faith to Social, Industrial and Economic questions, and as far as possible to co-ordinate all the various agencies existing for that purpose, and to promote and encourage the work of research relative thereto.' At Gore's suggestion the C.S.C. undertook to limit the sphere of its concern to questions of principle and to the education of the Christian social conscience, leaving it to other bodies to combat particular vices. (M. B. Reckitt, *Faith and Society*, p. 134. The distinction was not rigorously maintained).

[129] Vigo Auguste Demant, born 1893; curacies in Oxford and London 1919–33, Director of Research, C.S.C., 1929–33, Vicar of St John the Divine, Richmond 1933–42, Canon of St. Paul's 1942–9 and of Christ Church, Oxford, from 1949, Regius Professor of Moral and Pastoral Theology, Oxford, from 1949.

[130] Hensley Henson, *Quo Tendimus? The Primary Charge delivered at his Visitation to the Clergy of his Diocese in November 1924.*

decided what it was supposed to be doing, and by what authority: 'The orators seemed to oscillate between the oracular pronouncements of the prophet, and the argued reasoning of the student'.[131] He deplored their neglect of precise study, factual information and argued reasoning, and he accused them of expecting a largely non-Christian society to accept their Christian conclusions on political matters. In some ways, however, he was grossly unfair to Copec; he wrongly accused it of putting the transformation of the individual second to the transformation of society;[132] he asserted that 'Christianity is part, a vital part, of a larger thing', and although the N.T. is supreme within its own sphere, 'there are other spheres in which the attempt to assert its supremacy can only lead to disaster'[133]—thus showing his complete lack of sympathy with what was most valuable in the spirit of Copec. A staunch supporter of the movement assured him that 'Christianity is emphatically not "a part" of anything. It is rather a spirit, an outlook, a scale of values, an estimate of God, Man and the meaning of existence, by which the individual's attitude to all so-called secular problems, from the simplest to the most complex, is regulated at every turn.'[134] Finally, Henson claimed that Copec was pursuing mutually incompatible objects in desiring to improve living standards by appropriating for that purpose wealth created by industry, and at the same time advocating the replacement of the existing industrial system by some other, which, 'however in other respects superior, would confessedly be lacking in precisely those elements which have most stimulated the creation of wealth'.[135] The clear implication of this sentence, that only the motives of fear and greed would suffice to maintain industrial output at its existing low level, was economically implausible as well as disagreeably cynical.

[131] *Ibid.*, p. 80.
[132] The *Church Times* published an enlightened leading article on Copec on April 11th, 1924: 'It would be lamentable if the Church's proper interest in social reform should induce her to forget her primary duty. She must put first things first, and keep them there.' But, it goes on, 'because we put first things first it does not follow that we neglect their necessary corollaries and consequences. We are, therefore, glad to know that many zealous Anglo-Catholics are among the most ardent supporters of this conference.'
[133] Hensley Henson, *Quo Tendimus?*, p. 88.
[134] W. M. Pryke, 'Dr. Henson and C.O.P.E.C.', in the *Modern Churchman*, January 1925, p. 562.
[135] Hensley Henson, *Quo Tendimus?*, p. 98.

There were other, less harsh, criticisms of Copec. *Crockford's* was afraid that the message of the conference might be interpreted as being that 'the primary function of religion is to produce an economic paradise of short hours and high wages, and that on its own showing the Church of England stands or falls by its power of ushering in a Golden Age of this nature'.[136] There were inevitably some people who were disappointed at Copec's failure to express their own idiosyncratic points of view: contributors to *Commonwealth* bemoaned the failure of the *International Relations* report to warn against the danger that the League of Nations might degenerate into the tool of international high finance, and the failure of the *Industry and Property* report, having singled out the distributive system for criticism, to recommend Social Credit as an economic panacea.[137] There were even passionate radicals who ridiculed the name Copec as standing for Conventional Official Platitudes Expressing Caution.[138]

The valid criticisms which can be levelled against Copec are not conspicuously damaging, and in view of the enthusiasm generated by the conference, the considerable amount of good material in the reports, and the official support which the movement enjoyed,[139] its lack of success is not immediately understandable. The failure of most delegates to appreciate the full implications of their resolutions has already been mentioned. The delay in setting up the C.S.C. meant that there was a lack of continuity in research and discussion. There was by no means unanimous support for the more radical suggestions made by the reports, and even Temple must have had some misgivings about the degree to which Copec had involved itself with politics, for, in a preface which he contributed to the account of the proceedings of the Sheffield regional Copec conference, he described as 'one of the considerations which gives me most hope' the fact that 'the movement steadily tends to lay greater stress on the spiritual roots of progress in comparison with the political methods to be followed'.[140] It is fair to say that

[136] *Crockford's*, 1925, Preface, p. xvii.

[137] *Commonwealth*, June 1924, pp. 188f., and September 1924, pp. 282–5.

[138] *Ibid.*, November 1925, p. 349.

[139] See the *Chronicle of Convocation*, 1924, pp. 227–31.

[140] *The Fourfold Challenge of Today*, edited by Henry Cecil. Preface by W. Temple, p. 5.

Copec was not quite sure where it stood, what it wanted, or what its next move should be, and the quest of an authentically Christian sociology, eventually undertaken by the C.S.C. and the Christendom Group, was fraught with difficulty and controversy.

But there was also a larger reason for the collapse of the movement, quite beyond the power of Copec itself to influence or control, although it might perhaps have been foreseen. This was the calamitous course of economic and political events during the next decade: 'We thought—and all history seemed to vindicate our faith—that no second war could possibly come for half a century, till a full new generation had been bred up. We thought we could afford to go slow. . . . The economic slump of 1930 and Hitler's advent to power three years later fell upon us before we had begun to realize that we had been too late.'[141]

[141] C. E. Raven, 'C.O.P.E.C. Then and Now', part 2, in *Crucible*, January 1963, p. 12.

4
The General Strike

HENSLEY HENSON'S attack on Copec showed that the right and duty of the Church to concern itself with social, political and economic affairs was still not universally accepted, but his attitude was not representative of Church opinion as a whole. In a debate in the Upper House of Canterbury Convocation on May 7th, 1924, Copec was welcomed as a sign of the acceptance by the whole Church of an attitude previously confined to small groups of enthusiastic propagandists, and as the answer to all who criticized the Church for ignorance or lack of interest in social affairs.[1] An article in the *Torch* in June 1925, although bemoaning the persistent absence of Christian standards from the conduct of international affairs, claimed that the lordship of Christ over social and industrial life was slowly coming to be acknowledged.[2] The most critical test during the twenties of the interest and competence of the Church in such matters, and of the degree to which that interest and competence were approved by churchmen, was provided by the so-called general strike of 1926.

Since the strike of 1921 the coal industry had enjoyed relative prosperity, thanks chiefly to the follies and misfortunes of other coal-producing countries—the destruction of the French mines, the occupation of the Ruhr coalfield in Germany, and labour disputes in America. On the strength of this prosperity, the Miners' Federation negotiated with the coal-owners a new wage agreement in May 1924, which guaranteed the miners a uniform national minimum addition to the basic rate of $33\frac{1}{3}\%$, in place of the 20% which they had won in 1921. Because the basic rate itself was still determined by district agreements, there were wide variations from one coalfield to another in wages for the same job, but there was in each area a subsistence minimum below which the

[1] The *Chronicle of Convocation*, 1924, pp. 227–31.
[2] W. M. Pryke, 'The Church and International Relationships', in the *Torch*, June 1925, p. 89.

basic rate plus minimum percentage addition of the lowest paid workers was not allowed to fall.[3] Unfortunately the prosperity of the industry which had made possible this new wage agreement was only temporary, and the owners almost immediately proposed new terms involving wage reductions. These were naturally unacceptable to the Miners' Federation, and a strike was called for July 31st, 1925, supported by an embargo on the movement of coal by rail or sea. At the last moment, to avoid a disastrous strike, the government offered a subsidy of ten million pounds to maintain existing wages for a period of nine months, during which a Royal Commission, under the chairmanship of Sir Herbert Samuel, would examine the industry's problems and recommend measures to put it on a permanently satisfactory basis. Temple saw that Baldwin's offer of a subsidy was a dangerous precedent, but he welcomed it as the only right course in the circumstances; the alternative was a general strike, of which 'the social and political consequences are past calculation. Certainly the volume of distress would have been immense; probably some sort of revolution would have followed'.[4] *Commonwealth* welcomed the postponement of the crisis, without perhaps appreciating the seriousness of the coal industry's plight: 'For any fundamental reconstruction public opinion is not prepared, and neither are the necessary principles and plans worked out.'[5]

A fundamental change of some kind was in fact urgently necessary if the industry's problems were to be solved. The owners saw the answer in increased exports of coal, and to achieve more competitive export prices they were demanding a reduction in wages and an extension of the working day from seven hours (established on the recommendation of the Sankey commission in 1919) to eight. This would have increased production at no extra cost, and, provided the additional output could have been sold, enabled the industry to maintain its existing labour force. It was hard to see how any plan could be devised which neither reduced

[3] Weekly wages in the coal-mining industry ranged from four pounds ten for the highest-paid hewers to two pounds five as the minimum subsistence rate, taking into account allowances and privileges; *Report of the Royal Commission on the Coal Industry (1925)*, pp. 158f. The wages structure of the industry is explained on pp. 131–5.

[4] *The Pilgrim*, October 1925, p. 3.

[5] *Commonwealth*, August 1925, p. 233.

the miners' living standard nor increased unemployment in the industry,[6] but the Miners' Federation emphasized the inefficient and unco-ordinated management of the industry under private ownership, and demanded nationalization.

On March 6th, 1926, the Samuel Commission completed its work, and on March 11th the Report was published. It recognized a twofold problem, both temporary and permanent; it rejected nationalization, but it also rejected the owners' point of view. As long-term solutions it proposed state ownership of royalties, and of unworked or undiscovered coal; large-scale amalgamation of mines; co-operation with allied industries, particularly electricity; State-supported research; better retail distribution systems; and a number of measures to improve labour relations, including joint pit committees, family allowances (to be paid from a pool to avoid discrimination against the employment of men with families), profit-sharing schemes, the provision of better housing and pit-head baths, and, when prosperity returned, holidays with pay. There should be no increase in the working day, but the closure of a number of small, unprofitable mines was considered inevitable.

To deal with the short-term financial crisis in the industry, the Report recommended some reduction of the national minimum percentage addition to the basic rate, but not of the existing subsistence rates of the lowest-paid men. The subsidy 'should stop at the end of its authorized term, and should never be repeated,' and, on the controversial issue of national or district wage settlements, it was suggested that 'the representatives of the employers and employed should meet together, first nationally and then in the districts, in order to arrive at a settlement'.[7]

The Report had a mixed reception in the Church press. *Commonwealth* rejected it as 'hopelessly academic' and 'worse than useless' compared with the practical suggestions of the Sankey commission, reflecting its disappointment at the Report's rejection of nationalization.[8] A manifesto to the archbishops and bishops issued by the

[6] Unemployment in coal-mining was already a serious problem; in December 1925, 11·4% were unemployed out of a total labour-force of about 1,120,000; Ministry of Labour, *19th Abstract of Labour Statistics, July 1928*, pp. 25 and 49.

[7] *Report of the Royal Commission on the Coal Industry (1925)*, Summary of Recommendations, pp. 235f.

[8] *Commonwealth*, April 1926, pp. 98 and 101.

League of the Kingdom of God was even more outspoken,[9] demanding that wages be maintained regardless of cost, in accordance with the Lambeth Conference principle of the living wage, implying that any reduction of the 1924 wage rates would mean an end to the living wage for miners. The manifesto urged a continuation of the subsidy to enable the recommendations of the Report to be carried out, but conveniently forgot that one of the recommendations was a reduction in wages.[10] The *Church Times* welcomed the reorganization proposals and the rejection of longer hours, but viewed with grave misgivings the recommendation of wage reductions, not only because the miners' leaders had made it plain that they would oppose such a course, but because miners' wages were already so low that it would be contrary to the principle of the living wage embodied in the Fifth Report.[11] An article in the *Guardian* professed both sympathy with the miners and satisfaction with the Report, apart from its recommendation of profit-sharing—a hollow suggestion at a time of low or non-existent profits, and in any case likely to take the form of an unwelcome system of compulsory saving.[12]

On March 24th Baldwin announced that the government, although opposed to certain parts of the Report, was prepared to accept it in its entirety provided both parties to the dispute also did so; indeed, the government was prepared to go beyond the provisions of the Report and offer an additional subsidy of three million pounds to soften the blow of wage reductions, tapering off as reorganization was carried through. The necessary agreement from owners and miners was not forthcoming; the miners,

[9] The Church Socialist League was disbanded in 1923, and most of its members joined the League of the Kingdom of God which was founded to replace it, but with significantly different ideals. This process is described in Chapter 6.

[10] The manifesto is among a collection of documents concerned with the general strike in the possession of the I.C.F.

[11] The *Church Times*, March 12th and 19th, April 9th and 16th, 1926. On March 19th the paper included a surprisingly radical leading article which attacked in effect the whole capitalist system, but in particular the organization of the coal industry. It welcomed what it described as the Samuel Commission's suggestions for making the miner 'a real partner in the industry', but in fact the joint pit committees recommended by the Report were only those provided for, but never actually set up, under the Mining Industry Act of 1920; diminution of managerial responsibility by any form of workers' control was specifically excluded by the Samuel Report from the functions of the pit committees.

[12] The *Guardian*, March 19th, 1926.

clumsily led by A. J. Cook and Herbert Smith, stuck to their slogan 'Not a penny off the pay, not a minute on the day',[13] while the owners, who were opposed to a national wages agreement, provocatively announced their intention of inviting negotiations on new district agreements. Baldwin declined to play a decisive part in the negotiations during April, but did finally persuade the owners to submit their terms for a national wage agreement. These were not made known to the Miners' Federation until 1.15 p.m. on April 30th, the day on which the old agreement expired, and by that time two-thirds of the miners were already locked out. Moreover, the owners' terms involved not only the wage reductions recommended by the Report, but also an extension of the working day, to which the Report was firmly opposed.

A conference of trade union leaders on April 29th had pledged support for the miners in their struggle, but it was still by no means certain that there would be a general strike. The tone of the *Church Times* and *Guardian* on April 30th was optimistic; disaster had been averted in the past, and it seemed incredible that it would not somehow be averted again. The general feeling was that the owners were largely to blame, and to a less extent the government for failing to bring pressure to bear on them. The miners were understandably adamant about both wages and hours, 'not only because they are naturally opposed to any worsening of their position, but even more because they need assurance that the reorganization of the industry demanded by the Commission will be undertaken'.[14] This was the crux of the matter; if the government had acted, independently of agreement by the owners, to put into effect the reorganization, or had undertaken to maintain existing wages until the reorganization was actually in hand, it seems that the General Council of the T.U.C., to which the conduct of the dispute on behalf of the mining unions was handed over on the afternoon of May 1st, would have been satisfied.[15] The

[13] A variant of the slogan was 'Not a cent off the pay, not a second on the day.'
[14] The *Guardian*, April 30th, 1926.
[15] The miners' most conciliatory mood is represented by their reply to the owners' terms issued at 8.50 p.m. on April 30th: 'The miners state that they are not prepared to accept a reduction in wages as a preliminary to the reorganization of the industry, but they reiterate that they will be prepared to give full consideration to all the difficulties connected with the industry when the schemes for such reorganization will have been initiated by the Government.' At

government's final offer came near to meeting these requirements, and negotiations with the T.U.C. seem to have been at the point of success on the evening of May 2nd, when Baldwin unexpectedly broke them off on the pretext that 'overt acts' had already taken place which involved a 'challenge to the constitutional rights and freedom of the nation'. He referred to the refusal, on their own initiative, of the *Daily Mail* machine-men to print the issue of the paper for Monday, May 3rd, unless a biased and provocative leading article were altered. The T.U.C. delegates immediately left to investigate the printers' action, but when they returned to tell Baldwin that they repudiated it, the members of the Cabinet had dispersed and the Prime Minister was in bed. As Temple pointed out in retrospect, responsibility for breaking off the negotiations rested entirely with Baldwin,[16] and to that extent it was his fault that the T.U.C. leaders, against the inclination of the more moderate of their number, were compelled to go through with the ill-fated general strike.[17]

Church leaders were deeply divided in their attitude towards the strike. The note of conciliation and sympathy with the miners was struck in a letter from Woods and Garbett, written before the negotiations broke down and published in *The Times* on May 3rd. This acknowledged that the principle of subsidizing an industry was unsatisfactory, but pointed out that it was unfair to place the financial burden on the miners, who could least afford to bear it,

[16] *The Pilgrim*, July 1926, p. 365.

[17] The strike did not by any means involve all trade unionists, and to this extent the name 'general strike' is misleading. The T.U.C.'s instructions involved calling out only the 'first-line' workers on May 3rd—railwaymen, dockers, road transport workers, printers, and workers in the iron and steel, heavy chemical, building, electricity and gas industries. The sources used in this account of the negotiations and of the strike itself are *The Times*, the *British Worker* (the emergency newspaper produced by the T.U.C.), the *British Gazette* (the emergency newspaper produced by the government, and edited by Winston Churchill); Bell, *op. cit.*, Vol. II, pp. 1304–18; Mowat, *op. cit.*, pp. 298–335 (this includes a good bibliography); F. A. Iremonger, *William Temple*, pp. 336–44. For a fair and comprehensive account of the whole strike, including a perceptive summary of its social significance, see Julian Symons, *The General Strike*.

this point the slogan seems to have been temporarily abandoned, but the miners carefully avoided pledging themselves to acceptance of wage reductions, and it is possible that, in subsequent negotiations, the General Council to some extent deluded itself over the attitude of the miners, underestimating their intransigence.

and unreasonable to ask them for a definite sacrifice in return for the inadequately guaranteed prospect of reorganization: 'There are moments in a nation's life when the sacrifice of strict economic principles to higher considerations of justice, mercy and humanity is at once worldly wisdom and spiritual duty.' On May 7th two letters appeared in the abridged edition of *The Times* taking issue with Woods and Garbett; one was from the Archdeacon of Chester, W. Paige Cox, who claimed that there could be no opposition between moral and economic law, and the other from an Honorary Canon of Christ Church, W. la Trobe Bateman, who wrote in glowing terms of Baldwin's 'eminent example of what the true Christian spirit means'.

The most influential, and also perhaps the most controversial, Christian action during the nine days of the strike involved Archbishop Davidson. Speaking in the Lords on May 5th, he had expressed his strong disapproval of the strike, but also called on the government to take the initiative—even if it were illogical or apparently inconsistent—to avert the growth of a spirit of bitterness and real hatred, and the fear of the poorest classes that their standard of living was to be even further depressed.[18] On May 7th he met a group of churchmen and non-conformists, including Garbett, the Bishop of Ripon (E. A. Burroughs), and P. T. R. Kirk, to discuss a conciliatory appeal. A message was issued, headed *The Crisis. Appeal from the Churches*, which spoke of the growth of suffering and loss with the prolongation of the dispute, and called for a resumption of negotiations in a spirit of fellowship and co-operation for the common good. As the basis of a possible concordat it was suggested that there should be a return to the status quo of April 30th, involving 'simultaneously and concurrently':

1. The cancellation on the part of the T.U.C. of the general strike.
2. Renewal by the government of its offer of assistance to the coal industry for a short, definite period.
3. The withdrawal on the part of the mine owners of the new wage scales recently issued.[19]

The message in this form had the approval of Ramsay MacDonald, leader of the Labour Party, of the President of the Free

[18] H.L. Deb., 1926, Vol. 64, Cols. 49–51.

[19] Bell, *op. cit.*, Vol. II, p. 1308.

Church Council, and of Cardinal Bourne, Roman Catholic Archbishop of Westminster. Baldwin disliked the words 'simultaneously and concurrently', believing that the cancellation of the strike must precede any other action, but otherwise accepted the terms of the message.

Davidson was to broadcast the appeal, but at the last moment the Director-General of the B.B.C., John Reith, withdrew his permission. He acted on his own initiative, motivated by his fear that to broadcast the message might prejudice the independence of the B.B.C. and provide the government with an excuse for requisitioning it—a proposal already made by some ministers but hitherto resisted by Baldwin. In effect Reith was preserving his freedom by refusing to exercise it, and although he seems to have acted in good faith, his refusal to broadcast so cautious, pacific and impartial an appeal virtually reduced the B.B.C. to the status of a government agency. Churchill refused to publish the message in the *British Gazette*, but it did appear in *The Times* and the *British Worker* on May 8th and it was eventually broadcast on May 11th. The difference of opinion between Davidson and Baldwin was not over the fact that the general strike was an attack on the community —Davidson had already said as much in the Lords—but over the action which should be taken to bring it to an end. Davidson saw the Prime Minister on May 11th to make his position plain, and he expressed his distrust of the truculent and fighting attitude of some members of the Cabinet, who seemed to want the defeat of the trade unions rather than a fair settlement.[20]

In general there was welcome and support from churchmen for Davidson's action, although he was also sharply criticized. Support was canvassed in Oxford for the terms of the appeal, but not all were prepared to signify their approval; H. D. A. Major, Principal of Ripon Hall and a leading modernist, explained in a

[20] Lord Birkenhead was one of the most belligerent ministers. He rejoiced that the miners had rejected the government's most conciliatory offers, since they thereby contributed to their own ultimate defeat. Of the T.U.C. delegation's announcement that the strike was over he wrote: 'It was so humiliating that some instinctive breeding made one unwilling even to look at them'; Baldwin, by contrast, wrote to the King that the statement by Arthur Pugh, Chairman of the T.U.C., was 'short, simple, dignified and courageous'. See *Frederick Edwin, Earl of Birkenhead: The Last Phase*, by his son, the Earl of Birkenhead, pp. 274f. and 287–9; H. Nicolson, *King George V*, p. 419.

letter to *The Times*, published on May 12th, why he could not add his signature to the Archbishop's appeal: first, the appeal involved only the conditional cancellation of the strike, but it was in fact important that the principle of lightning and sympathetic strikes should be utterly discredited by its unconditional abandonment; secondly, the appeal presumed to give advice to the Prime Minister, and to do so was 'to stab him in the back'. Hensley Henson foresaw 'practical mischiefs' as a result of the appeal, and considered it grotesque that it should fall to Cardinal Bourne (who had denounced the strike in a sermon on May 9th as 'a sin against the obedience which we owe to God . . . and against the charity and brotherly love which are due to our brethren') to act as the 'mouthpiece of national sentiment and civic duty'; it was regrettable that a great impetus had been given by the appeal to the tendency 'to substitute for religious teaching a declamatory, sentimental socialism as far removed from sound economics as from Christian morality'[21] Inge also thought that the bishops had come out of it very badly, 'bleating for a compromise while the nation was fighting for its life'.[22]

The Archbishop's appeal was clearly not 'bleating', but that would have been a not wholly inaccurate description of the contribution made by the Copec movement. The Continuation Committee wrote on May 6th to all clergy and ministers, calling on them to hold 'religious meetings', and to bring to bear 'a spiritual pressure on the contending parties and on the Government that would be more potent even than the material pressure of resolutions and postcards', while Raven sent a letter on May 3rd to all the 'Companions of Copec' which ignored the actual issues of the strike, but saw it as a sign of man's inability to fulfil God's purposes, and of the fact that 'we are out of touch with God . . . [Christ] bade us lift up our hearts, for through cloud and thick darkness redemption drew nigh. And His great apostle, outcast and persecuted, lonely and toil-worn and bruised and burdened, could proclaim in His name a profession of faith more magnificent than any uttered by mortal lips: "We know that all things work together for good to them that love God" '. True as this was, it

[21] Bell, *op. cit.*, Vol. II, p. 1316.
[22] W. R. Inge, *The Diary of a Dean*, p. 111.

The General Strike: Newsprint for the British Gazette *arrives under police protection*

The General Strike: Armoured cars and troops at Hyde Park Corner, before escorting the food convoy from the London Docks

must have left the Companions in some uncertainty about what they should do in the prevailing circumstances.[23]

The strike came to an end on May 12th, as unsatisfactorily as it had begun. Its abandonment by the T.U.C. was unconditional, but there were five conditioning factors:[24] most important was the intervention of Sir Herbert Samuel, who independently drew up a memorandum outlining a possible basis for negotiations. This included a renewal of the subsidy for the negotiating period, a National Wages Board with an independent chairman, and no reduction in wages without sufficient assurances that reorganization would be carried out. The T.U.C. leaders, who were becoming increasingly apprehensive about the constitutional and legal implications of the strike, clutched at this straw, and although there was no reason to suppose that the government would endorse Samuel's terms, they decided to call off the strike on the strength of the memorandum. The other factors which influenced them were Baldwin's conciliatory mood and his offer of a further brief subsidy, Sir John Simon's judgment that a general strike was illegal and the unions liable for damages, and the Archbishop's appeal. The miners' leaders, on the other hand, not unreasonably regarding the T.U.C. decision as betrayal, refused to accept the terms of the memorandum, and the coal stoppage went on.

On May 14th Baldwin repeated the government's terms, based faithfully on the recommendations of the Commission, but still including also the offer of a further three million pounds subsidy. This offer was conditional on acceptance of the terms by both owners and miners, but on May 20th both parties rejected them, the owners rudely expressing their resentment of what they described as political interference.[25] In an attempt to conciliate them,

[23] These two letters were published in the *Guardian* on May 14th. On May 21st the paper published a letter from the Vicar of Grimsby, who could not imagine any course 'more mischievous and unpatriotic' than that suggested in the Copec letter. On May 28th, however, two correspondents expressed their gratitude for the action of the Copec Committee.

[24] See Temple's analysis of these factors in *The Pilgrim*, July 1926, pp. 361–72.

[25] Temple did not spare the owners in his comment on their complaint: 'For people whose industry has just received from the Government (that is, from the public) £23,000,000 to say that all they want is freedom from interference by the Government (that is, by the public) is gross impertinence; for people who supply a public necessity to say that the public must go without while they settle their own quarrel is constructive treason.' (*The Pilgrim*, July

Baldwin announced legislation for a permissive eight-hour day, in the hope that on such a basis they would be prepared to go on paying wages at the 1924 level. This same solution was suggested by a contributor to the *Guardian* on June 4th, who called for a referendum over the heads of the owners' and miners' leaders to decide its acceptability, but both the *Guardian* and the *Church Times* attacked the proposal for longer hours in their editorial comment, particularly in view of the commissioners' words: 'We do not recommend the State, of its own motion, to make any change of working hours or to endeavour to force upon the miners a longer working day than at present.'[26]

Controversy continued to rage over the general strike. The *Church Times* tried to face both ways, agreeing with Cardinal Bourne that despite all the mitigating circumstances the strike was a sin, and yet also justifying as 'entirely defensible' the miners' refusal to accept the wage reductions recommended by the Report.[27] This denunciation of the strike as a sin was answered by a letter from Tawney and Lansbury, published on June 4th, which claimed that it was fully justified in view of the 'far graver sin of inhumanity and oppression by which it was provoked', and warned that there would be no permanent industrial peace until 'the wage-earners have gained some measure of real control over the industry by which they live'.

Disagreement over the strike itself was, however, trivial compared with the torrent of criticism and abuse occasioned by the action of a group of Christian leaders, including Gore, Temple, Woods, six other bishops and eleven non-conformists, which assumed the title of the Standing Conference of the Christian Churches on the Coal Dispute, and attempted to mediate between the owners and miners. There had been strong but unsuccessful pressure on the government to act independently and proceed with

[26] *Report of the Royal Commission on the Coal Industry* (*1925*), p. 178.
[27] The *Church Times*, May 14th, 1926.

1926, p. 372.) Even Lord Birkenhead was appalled at the owners' behaviour; he wrote to Lord Irwin on May 20th: 'It would be possible to say without exaggeration of the miners' leaders that they were the stupidest men in England if we had not frequent occasion to meet the owners.' (*Frederick Edwin, Earl of Birkenhead: The Last Phase*, p. 275.)

the reorganization of the industry, and the *Church Times* and *Commonwealth*, both previously opposed to any wage reductions, came to see that decisive government action on reorganization might justify some temporary wage cuts.[28] The Standing Conference, concerned at the increasing bitterness and apparent deadlock, approached both owners and miners in an attempt to bring them back to the terms of the Report. The owners would neither accept the Report nor make any constructive suggestions of their own, but on July 15th agreement was reached with the miners' leaders on several important points, notably that the commissioners should interpret certain ambiguities in the Report, and that points of difference should be referred to a joint committee, or if necessary to the final decision of an independent chairman. On this basis, the miners were prepared to abandon the slogan. The abandonment of the slogan was seen as an important concession, and a memorandum was prepared and submitted to the government by a delegation from the Standing Conference on July 19th. This proposed a continuation of the subsidy for not more than four months, to enable existing (i.e. 1924) wage rates to be maintained while negotiations took place and reorganization was put in hand; if a subsidy were unacceptable to the government, the delegation suggested that it might be replaced by a private loan, which they had been assured could be made available.

These terms were certainly optimistic, but this was no justification for the fact that Baldwin discourteously published and rejected them on the morning of July 19th, before he had even met the delegation.[29] A valid criticism of the work of the Standing Conference which did not come to light until much later, and of which the Conference members were at the time unaware, was that Cook had used his invitation to a final meeting with the secretaries of the Standing Conference as an excuse for cancelling a meeting already arranged with another negotiating group, B. S. Rowntree, W. T. Layton and Frank Stuart. Cook had been in touch with this group for some weeks, and on July 3rd he had

[28] *Commonwealth*, July 1926, pp. 200f. The *Church Times*, May 21st and 28th and June 18th, 1926.

[29] Baldwin himself compared the intervention of the Standing Conference with an attempt by the F.B.I. to bring about reunion between the Particular Baptists and the Anglo-Catholics. (Quoted in the *Guardian*, July 23rd, 1926.)

signed a draft settlement, which the group had drawn up, involving abandonment of the slogan. The Rowntree group arranged a further meeting for July 13th, hoping to persuade Cook to submit the draft terms for ratification by the Executive Committee of the Miners' Federation, and it was this meeting which Cook cancelled. A plausible hypothesis, which Rowntree himself put forward, is that Cook hoped for better terms from the Standing Conference, and so withdrew from what might have been the way towards a satisfactory solution. To this extent it may be true that the intervention of the Standing Conference prolonged the coal stoppage, but there can be no certainty about this. The miners themselves, in a district ballot on August 11th, rejected the favourable terms of the Standing Conference memorandum which their own leaders had accepted, and it is highly unlikely that the terms proposed by the Rowntree group would have been any more welcome to the rank and file.

The hostile onslaught on the work of the Standing Conference began in *The Times* of July 21st and 22nd, with letters from Presbyterian and Methodist sources deploring the involvement of prominent Church leaders in a particular secular issue. On July 23rd a reply from Woods admitted that the Conference was not officially representative of the Christian denominations, but claimed that it rightly took its mandate from the authority by which Christian ministers are appointed to promote peace and goodwill: 'Our critics cannot have it both ways. We preach justice and fellowship: immediately we are reminded of the futility of these excellent platitudes apart from any definite suggestions for their embodiment. We make such definite suggestions, and immediately we are lectured for stepping on to ground where economists, if not angels, fear to tread.' The matter, he claimed, was one of confidence; mindful of the government's handling of the Sankey Report in 1919, the miners were understandably suspicious, and would remain so until they saw some earnest of the government's intentions over reorganization.

The correspondence in *The Times* included hostile letters from Lord Hugh Cecil and Sir Ernest Benn, both Anglican laymen, and from the Archdeacon of Chester, who mistakenly attributed the initiative for the Standing Conference to the I.C.F.[30] A letter from Headlam showed that he had misread the manifesto of the Standing Conference, published in *The Times* on July 24th, since he wrongly accused the delegates who met Baldwin of claiming to be representatives of the Churches; they had in fact merely claimed to represent the Conference.[31] The Dean of Durham (J. E. C. Welldon) was non-committal, and the Dean of Worcester (W. Moore Ede) supported the intervention,[32] but most of the letters were hostile, and included such phrases as 'the sentimental imaginings of well-meaning but uninformed enthusiasts', and 'a few misguided prelates and dignitaries', while on August 11th one correspondent asserted that 'a few Bishops have been decoyed into the Communist trap'. A no less absurd and even more offensive contribution to the debate was an article written by Inge for the *Sunday Express*, in which he identified as two of the classes of supporters for the work of the Standing Conference 'obvious time-servers, who will have their reward when the Socialists come into power', and 'the new type of parson, sprung from the ranks and soured by poverty and thwarted social ambition'.[33]

A letter from Canon S. J. Sykes of Liverpool, published in *The Times* of August 12th, more reasonably pointed to a danger in the commonly-heard argument that a continuation of the subsidy would be cheaper than a continuation of the strike. This, he pointed out, was to sacrifice principle to expediency—'an attractive process, but not on that account wise, moral or Christian'. On August 13th a letter appeared from Hensley Henson, who attributed ecclesiastical meddling in economic affairs to an obsolete

[30] There was some justification for the widespread assumption that the I.C.F. had organized the Standing Conference, since the Conference's chairman was Kempthorne (who was also Chairman of the I.C.F.), one of its secretaries was P. T. R. Kirk (who was General Director of the I.C.F.), and its meetings were held at the offices of the I.C.F. In fact all of this was fortuitous, as Kempthorne pointed out in a letter which appeared in *The Times* on August 12th, 1926.

[31] Headlam's letter was published in *The Times* on July 27th. He was bitterly attacked by *Commonwealth* in October 1926, p. 296: 'Bishop Headlam . . . writes of "economic laws" for all the world as though Professor Marshall had never lived, the London School of Economics had never been set up, and Lambeth Conferences, Committees of Convocation, and Archbishops' Committees had never reported. . . . It is simply incomprehensible that a man in such a position, at this time of day, should take the line he does as to the irrelevance of ethical considerations in economic practice.'

[32] *The Times*, August 5th and 10th, 1926.

[33] W. R. Inge, 'Interfering Parsons', in the *Sunday Express*, August 1st, 1926.

WOLVERHAMPTON TEACHERS
COLLEGE LIBRARY

conception of 'the masses', involving forgetfulness of the fact that they can now protect themselves by political action, to misunderstanding about the bearing of morality on economic processes, and to a medieval notion of episcopal responsibility. Henson was answered on August 16th by Slesser and John Burnaby, and on August 17th at greater length by Talbot, who pointed out that the claim that moral considerations must not dominate economics was condemned by history, that labour did still *de facto* regard itself as the underdog, and that it was the workers, not the employers, who felt the pinch of penury. The *Guardian*, which had welcomed the move by the Standing Conference, contrasted Talbot's 'broad, human and kindly sympathy' with Henson's 'hard, acrid and academic' tone and attacked the attitude of those who invariably interpreted sympathy with the working classes as an expression of loyalty to the political programme of the Labour Party.[34] The last important contribution to the debate about the work of the Standing Conference was a letter from Temple, published in *The Times* on August 21st, which explained and justified at some length the intervention.[35]

By the end of August the miners' position had become very weak, as destitution caused mounting pressure in many districts for a return to work on any terms. Cook and Herbert Smith found it difficult to maintain solidarity, and the owners, sensing victory, were more than ever reluctant to make concessions. They were rebuked by Baldwin for being stupid and discourteous in declining the government's invitation to a conference at the beginning of September,[36] but no further pressure was put upon them, and

[34] The *Guardian*, August 20th, 1926.

[35] A letter written by Temple to Kempthorne on July 18th, expressing the fear that he might not be able to be present at the meeting with Baldwin the following day, made many of the same points as his letter to *The Times*, but emphasized in particular two things: first, the nationalization of royalties, although financially insignificant, was psychologically important; secondly, the ultimate rejection of the Report of the Royal Commission by the government and the owners would be very dangerous; there was already the precedent of the Sankey Report, and if the same thing happened again the miners would be 'alienated from constitutional ways of acting and driven into the arms of the extremists'. (This unpublished letter is in the possession of the I.C.F. In fact Temple did travel to London, and was a member of the delegation which presented the Conference's memorandum to Baldwin.)

[36] H.C. Deb. 1926, Vol. 199, Col. 275. Churchill also attacked the owners for showing 'so little respect for the lawfully constituted authorities of the country'; *ibid.*, Col. 318.

gradually the men trickled back to work, for an eight-hour day, on district agreements, and at reduced wages. It was a bitter and humiliating defeat.

Could Church leaders have done more to avert such an end to the coal stoppage? In May, Kempthorne had asked Davidson whether the Ecclesiastical Commissioners might forgo their income from mining royalties, amounting to about £250,000 a year, as a token of the Church's willingness to accept the Commissioners' recommendations that royalties should be nationalized. Davidson replied that, although the Church would not in any way oppose a government measure to nationalize royalties, he was not prepared to support unilateral action such as Kempthorne suggested.[37] Indeed, as the work of the Standing Conference proceeded Davidson became increasingly unhappy about episcopal participation in the search for particular economic remedies, and although, apart from the idea of a loan, the discussions of the Standing Conference were based entirely on the Report and Sir Herbert Samuel's later proposals, he was afraid that a situation might develop in which the Church and the miners would be united in opposition to the government.[38] The only way out of the deadlock would have been independent government action on the basis of the Report, and it is this which Christian opinion might perhaps have urged more vigorously, rather than the feeble hope of voluntary agreement between owners and miners. The Church press did its best, but could not overcome Baldwin's chronic inertia and the active hostility of a section of the government.

It is not easy to assess the significance of the contribution made by Church leaders to the ending of the general strike, or the efforts of the Standing Conference to end the coal stoppage. The sympathy shown by influential churchmen towards the strikers probably succeeded in some small measure in moderating the traditional working-class suspicion and dislike of the Established Church, but the failure of their counsels to prevail may have tended to substantiate the popular feeling that the Church was

[37] Davidson's unpublished reply is in the possession of the I.C.F.

[38] This fear was expressed by Davidson in a letter to Kempthorne written on August 9th, 1926; see Bell, *op. cit.*, Vol. II, p. 1318.

irrelevant.[39] There was, moreover, a deep cleavage of opinion among churchmen, and a vocal minority spared no effort to discredit and disown the work of Davidson's group and of the Standing Conference. Temple's final verdict on the general strike was that it was wrong, not because there can be admitted no authority within the State but the government, nor because there was in any sense a treasonous usurpation of power by the T.U.C., but simply because it did more harm than good.[40] On the other hand there were many Christians who continued to regard it as a sin, and made sure that their opinion was heard.

Needless to say, the owners' victory failed to restore prosperity to the coal industry; only a vigorous policy of modernization, extensive pit closures and massive schemes for industrial transference and retraining could have achieved this. Unemployment remained a serious problem in mining districts, poor relief was a constant drain on the rates, and high rates strangled already depressed industries. The plight of the coalfields continued to cause concern among many Christians who were familiar with the facts,[41] and two attempts were made to examine the problem from a Christian point of view. In 1927 Alan Porter edited *Coal: A Challenge to the National Conscience*,[42] which attacked the collective irresponsibility of the middle classes towards the coal industry, but fastened the blame for its troubles chiefly on a false financial system, and made none of the right practical suggestions. In 1929, as one of the first results of the foundation of the C.S.C., Demant produced *The Miners' Distress and the Coal Problem*. This was a clear and capable analysis of the difficulties facing the industry and the steps necessary to overcome them, but Demant betrayed an astonishing lack of imagination in his cautious estimate of the

[39] See *Theology*, September 1926, p. 164, where the Vicar of Mansfield (in the Nottinghamshire coalfield) remarks on the very favourable impression made on the local miners by the intervention of the Standing Conference.

[40] W. Temple, *Industry and the Community*, in *The Pilgrim*, October 1926, p. 98.

[41] See G. Burden, 'The Miners' Plight', in the *Torch*, July 1927, pp. if.; also a letter from the Rural Dean of Aberdare published in the *Church Times* on March 23rd, 1928, and an appeal from ten South Wales clergy published in the *Church Times* and the *Guardian* on November 30th, 1928. There are editorial notes in the *Guardian* of April 5th and November 30th, 1928.

[42] The contributors were Demant, Reckitt, Philip Mairet, Albert Newsome, Egerton Swann and W. T. Symons.

chances of absorbing redundant miners in new or expanding industries, and his sensible call for a flexible use of government credit to stimulate trade and provide employment was compromised by his reiteration of the fallacious theory that society was suffering from a chronic insufficiency of purchasing power.[43]

Industrial action was discredited, trade union funds exhausted, and the morale of the workers in most cases very low; these were inevitable results of the strike and the prolonged coal stoppage. But the decline in the membership, resources and prestige of the unions was also a deliberate aim of government policy, or at least of a number of the more belligerent ministers. In March 1925, Baldwin had opposed a private member's bill which would have required trade union members to contract in to paying a political levy to the Labour Party, instead of the existing arrangement by which the levy was paid unless a member specifically contracted out, but the general strike revived interest in curbing the power and political influence of the unions, and as early as June 25th, 1926, Lord Birkenhead was reprimanded by the *Church Times* for threatening punitive legislation against the unions. The government finally gave way to its own right wing, and introduced the Trade Disputes and Trade Unions Bill of 1927, by which sympathetic strikes, or strikes 'designed or calculated to coerce the government either directly or by inflicting hardship on the community' (i.e. general strikes) were declared illegal; intimidation and picketing were forbidden; trade union members were required to contract in to the political levy; and civil servants were not allowed to join a union connected with the T.U.C. or the Labour Party.[44]

These limitations of trade union freedom were immediately attacked, not only by the Labour Party and the T.U.C., but also by some Christian social thinkers. The opposition to the bill in the Commons was led by Sir Henry Slesser,[45] who later described it as 'the re-introduction of servile labour into the State', and 'an

[43] V. A. Demant, *The Miners' Distress and the Coal Problem*, pp. 60–8.

[44] Mowat, *op. cit.*, p. 336.

[45] Sir Henry Slesser had been Solicitor-General in the first Labour government of 1924. He was a prominent member of the League of the Kingdom of God, but was later received into the Roman Catholic Church, whence he bitterly attacked the Church of England. (See Rose Macaulay, *Letters to a Friend*, p. 312.)

unqualified attack by plutocracy'.[46] This was extravagant language, but during the debate on the second reading of the bill he made some important criticisms of it. In particular he pointed out that it imposed criminal penalties which public morality would not endorse, that if a strike were declared to be illegal it would also be illegal in some circumstances for an employee to leave his work, even after giving the required notice, and that it was so intolerably vague in its wording that nobody who helped a trade unionist or his family during a dispute could be certain that his action might not be construed as a criminal furtherance of the dispute. The League of the Kingdom of God issued a manifesto which reproduced most of Slesser's arguments and particularly deplored the fact that the bill might deprive a man of the right to enter into or terminate a contract of service.[47] The Copec Continuation Committee met on June 14th, and passed a resolution attacking the bill as a measure bound to check the growth of the spirit of goodwill in social and political life, and to hinder the establishment of good industrial relations.[48]

The Bill was not, however, without its supporters, either in the ranks of labour or in the hierarchy of the Church. A contributor to *Commonwealth* pointed out that the implications of the general strike had worried working-class people, and many had been thrown out of work by it; it was understandable that some should therefore support the Bill, believing that it would control the sometimes excessive power of the unions.[49] This point of view was expressed more vigorously by Hensley Henson, who attacked the L.K.G. appeal as 'one more illustration of that moral obliquity which is the Nemesis pursuing every attempt to bind Christianity to the service of partisan politics'.[50] He denounced the power of the

[46] H. H. Slesser, *Judgment Reserved*, p. 206. The important speech which Slesser made during the second reading of the Bill is set out in full on pp. 210–24. The Bill was eventually amended to include illegal lock-outs as well as strikes, and in this form became law. It was finally repealed by the Labour government in 1946.

[47] *The Trade Unions Bill: An Appeal for Christian Justice and Liberty*. The manifesto is reproduced in *Commonwealth*, June 1927, p. 165.

[48] The resolution is quoted in *Commonwealth*, July 1927, p. 196.

[49] *Ibid*., pp. 213f.

[50] In a letter to *The Times*, published on June 18th, 1927, Henson recounts that a workman, whose opinion about the bill he had sought, had told him: 'It seems to give us more freedom than we've had for a long time past.'

unions as 'a ubiquitous, cruel and continuing tyranny, degrading to the character of their members and very perilous to the State'; the bill would open to 'men bound under a harsh yoke of oppression a promise of liberty—liberty to think and act as self-respecting men and inheritors of all that makes British citizenship a proud possession'.[51]

The possibility that the trade union movement might exercise a tyrannous rather than a liberating power was something new. Scott Holland had seen that trade union membership could provide the worker with 'something of the worth and the dignity with which a man of property is endowed . . . the moral stability of ownership'.[52] J. N. Figgis had praised the expression of the principle of brotherhood in the trade union movement, which he described as 'ethically considered, the most thoroughgoing Christian movement of the last century'.[53] Immediately after the war, Sir William Ashley had seen industrial organization as the best way to improve industrial relations, and expressed the hope that all workers would be loyal members of a union.[54] A good analysis of the conflict between freedom and security, and the temporary inevitability of some degree of tyranny in trade union membership, is to be found in an essay by the Bishop of Plymouth, J. H. B. Masterman, *The Church and Political and Economic Problems.* He points out that the Church should direct its efforts to the creation of 'such conditions of life as shall make self-determination not the privilege of the few but the common right of all. Under existing economic conditions, the worker is constantly obliged to surrender his freedom in return for a measure of security. . . . It is vain to protest against the tyranny of Trade Unions or Employers' Federations till Christian influence has been able so to moralize industry as to make such tyranny unnecessary.'[55]

[51] From a speech by Henson in the Lords on July 5th, 1927; H.L. Deb., Vol. 68, Cols. 135 and 137. At the time of the general strike Henson had speculated in his diary whether the tyranny of the trade unions might 'perish as that of the Popes perished under the disgrace of its own excesses'; *Retrospect of an Unimportant Life*, Vol. II, p. 118.

[52] H. Scott Holland, *Property and Personality*, in the symposium *Property*, p.189.

[53] J. N. Figgis, *Hopes for English Religion*, p. 53. The quotation is from a sermon preached at the Grosvenor Chapel in 1917.

[54] Sir William Ashley, *The Christian Outlook*, pp. 27–37; a sermon on Combination, preached at Bristol in 1919.

[55] J. H. B. Masterman, *The Church and Political and Economic Problems*, in *The Future of the Church of England*, edited by Sir James Marchant (1926), p. 162.

Between 1918 and 1926 the trade unions consolidated their power, but failed to decide which path they should pursue. They could either follow the advice of their more militant leaders, working for the overthrow of the existing industrial order and the establishment of workers' control, or they could support enthusiastically the system of Whitley Councils and the method of joint consultation between management and workers, without prejudice to the ultimate introduction of democratic control in industry. The general strike was the first and last attempt to use the naked pressure of united industrial force, although ironically enough there was in this case no revolutionary intention on the part of the T.U.C. leaders. Lack of conviction and weakness in leadership destroyed the possibility that the unions might openly challenge capitalism in an industrial duel. The following year, however, there was an important development which might have gone far towards achieving, by peaceful means, that moralization of the industrial order to which Masterman looked forward.

In November, 1927, union leaders accepted with some misgivings an invitation from a group of industrialists, led by Sir Alfred Mond,[56] to a conference to discuss industrial relations and organization; this was a genuinely conciliatory move by the employers, intended to draw the T.U.C. into positive support for a policy of co-operation with capital. The so-called Mond–Turner Conference produced elaborate plans, in March 1929, for a joint council of employers and trade unionists, not merely to prevent industrial disputes, but to work out an agreed economic policy and press its acceptance on the government. After a dramatic debate, with Cook leading the opposition, the 1928 T.U.C. Conference had accepted the principle of Mondism, so committing the movement to an evolutionary policy and to the principle of coming to terms with capitalism, but in the event circumstances were to kill this promising sign of progress towards better industrial relations. Mond was unable to win the full support of the F.B.I. and the Employers' Confederation for his policies, and the economic and

[56] Mond was chairman of I.C.I., and was created Baron Melchett in 1928. The leader of the T.U.C. delegation, and joint chairman with Mond of the conference, was Ben Turner, the textile trade unionist. The discussions are variously referred to as the Mond–Turner or Melchett–Turner Talks or Conference, and the principle of union co-operation in exchange for concessions by employers came to be known as Mondism.

political crises of 1929–31 added to the difficulties of setting up the projected National Industrial Council.[57]

Despite its failure to bear immediate fruit Mondism was a significant development, and it is both regrettable and surprising that it was not more warmly supported by Christian social thinkers. It could well have led to a gradual but steady change in the balance of power in industry, and so to the eventual reorganization of the industrial order envisaged by the Fifth Report and Copec. By putting his finger on the need for more flexible and imaginative financial policies, Mond was himself moving in the same direction as the more radical Christian social thinkers, although in a more realistically Keynesian fashion than those enthusiasts of the L.K.G. who continued to canvass entirely fanciful and unrealistic ideas of currency reform.[58] *Commonwealth*, still strongly influenced by L.K.G. ideas, in fact sympathized to some extent with the militant concept of trade unionism, and rather unconstructively suggested that the trade union movement, faced with the need to decide its attitude towards Mondism, should merely continue to oppose the capitalist system and to beware of conferences.[59] The *Church Times*, however, described the report of the Mond Conference as a 'highly important document . . . indicating the way to permanent peace and fruitful co-operation,'[60] and denounced the refusal of some employers to accept its recommendations as 'stupid, selfish and intensely unpatriotic'.[61] Although criticized by correspondents for supporting by implication a policy of industrial rationalization,

[57] See Alan Bullock, *The Life and Times of Ernest Bevin*, Vol. I, pp. 392–405; Trevor Evans, *Bevin*, pp. 126–139; G. D. H. Cole, *British Trade Unionism Today* (1939 edition), pp. 75–7; the chapter in H. Bolitho, *Alfred Mond, First Lord Melchett*, pp. 306–18, is very inadequate.

[58] See M. B. Reckitt, 'The Potentialities of the Mond Committee', in *Commonwealth*, April 1928, pp. 124f. Mond's economic ideas may conveniently be found in a letter from him, published in *The Times* of April 25th, 1928, to clarify the points made in the first report of the Mond–Turner Conference. He attributed the general strike largely to the way in which Churchill managed Britain's return to the gold standard in 1925, a move which sacrificed internal price stability to a stable international exchange rate and made it unnecessarily difficult to finance industrial expansion. His view of Churchill's performance in 1925 was supported by J. M. Keynes, *The Economic Consequences of Mr. Churchill*. For a discussion of the economic and financial theories which were popular in L.K.G. circles, see Chapter 6.

[59] *Commonwealth*, September 1928, pp. 257f.

[60] The *Church Times*, July 6th, 1928. The *Guardian* had given a cautious welcome to the discussions on March 30th, 1928.

[61] The *Church Times*, December 28th, 1928.

which would cause even higher unemployment, the *Church Times* adhered to its view that a more just and Christian society could be built up only by means of goodwill and co-operation. Significantly, however, it pinned its faith in protective tariffs and large-scale emigration as solutions to the unemployment problem, sharing in the dismal Christian failure either to support the economic policies advocated by Keynes and Mond, or to understand the almost unlimited scope for expansion of both production and consumption.[62]

The three years between the general strike and the onset of the great depression were the last opportunity between the wars for Britain to change her economic policies for the better, and although it would be absurd to attach any blame to the Church for the failure of both Conservative and Labour governments to act boldly and imaginatively in the economic sphere, it was a pity that the energies and enthusiasms of Christian social thinkers during this period were not in general directed to more fruitful and constructive ends. The next four chapters give some account of what was in fact said and done in the name of the Church about social and economic matters.

[62] The *Church Times*, August 17th, 24th and 31st, 1928.

5

Leaders of Christian Social Thought

CHRISTIAN CONCERN with social issues between the wars does not fall readily into neat divisions or categories. Only those thinkers who came to be known as the Christendom Group naturally demand to be considered together and they, together with the Anglo-Catholic movement with which they were associated, are discussed in the next chapter. But there were many individuals, representing between them a wide range of ecclesiastical and political persuasion, who made important contributions to the social thought of the Church of England. Of these the doyen was undoubtedly Gore, the only survivor from the early days of the C.S.U., whose interest in social affairs and comment on them continued unabated throughout the twenties. Talbot, his friend and colleague since the time of *Lux Mundi*, outlived him by two years, but, apart from his contribution to the discussion of the ecclesiastical intervention in the coal stoppage of 1926, he ceased to play an active part in Church life after he relinquished the bishopric of Winchester in 1924. Gore, however, continued his support of the League of Nations Union and the I.C.F., and after the intervention of the Standing Conference he became chairman of the executive committee of the Council of Christian Ministers on Social Questions, which was formed to provide the same kind of Christian comment and witness as the Standing Conference whenever the need for it should arise. He continued to write on social questions, and was generous with forewords to the efforts of other writers.

Gore's social thought in its most mature form is summed up in his Halley Stewart lectures for 1927, *Christ and Society*. These are built round four main theses: the present state of society gives ground for deep dissatisfaction and alarm, demanding so thorough a reformation as to amount to a revolution, but one which can be achieved only by gradual and peaceful means; social evils are not inevitable, but result from human blindness, wilfulness, selfishness and avarice, and their removal therefore demands a real change of heart as well as legislation; this change of heart will begin with small groups of dedicated and visionary individuals, and will not be achieved suddenly by mass conversions; underlying all this, Christ is the saviour and redeemer of mankind in its social as well as its individual life, in this world as well as the next.[1] These principles lead to Gore's conviction that the Church is bound to concern itself actively with human relationships in whatever form, including their political and economic aspects.[2] There must be radical social change and greater social equality, but this must not take the form of levelling-down: 'The ultimate test of any democracy is to be found in the demand that in its organization of human society it shall so truly grant equality of opportunity to all who are born into its citizenship as to encourage and enable them freely to develop the fullest richness of personality of which they are capable.'[3]

Gore's survey of the existing state of society is perceptive and highly critical; he deplores the impersonal and irresponsible nature of capitalist industry, and the great contrasts of wealth and poverty which it encourages. He refers with interest to a possible plan for the reformation of the structure of industry, the Harty–Valder scheme, which had been worked out in New Zealand and authorized by the New Zealand parliament in 1924; under the scheme the workers in an industry would enjoy a status equal to that of the shareholders, but on the basis of work done instead of money invested. Labour shares would receive, as dividend, a share of the firm's profits, while capital shares would receive only a fixed interest rate, calculated according to the risk involved.[4]

[1] C. Gore, *Christ and Society*, pp. 15–18. After the introductory chapter, in which these principles are expounded, the main body of the book is devoted to a historical survey of Christian social ethics.

[2] *Ibid.*, pp. 130f.

[3] *Ibid.*, pp. 135f. This idea is taken up in much present-day Christian concern with social developments, *cf.* Daniel Jenkins, *Equality and Excellence* (1961). Gore did not himself join the Labour Party, and saw the possible dangers of its policies, but he was convinced that the social ideals of Christianity, as he saw them, had much in common with those of Labour. See his Essex Hall lecture for 1920, *Christianity applied to the Life of Men and of Nations*, esp. p. 28 of the 1940 reprint.

[4] Details of the Harty–Valder scheme are set out in *Christ and Society*, appendix A, pp. 181f. Gore made its advocacy a particular concern of his own, and supported it at a meeting of the I.C.F. Council in January 1927.

The General Strike: An omnibus, disabled by strikers in Southwark, is towed away; May 6th, 1926

The General Strike: A volunteer driver at Paddington Station

Gore's social thinking is clearly in the tradition of the Fifth Report and Copec, which is what one would expect. It is disappointing, although not perhaps surprising, to find that his last chapter offers no new ideas for bringing the teaching and influence of the Church to bear on social problems. A mark of the elder statesman, to some extent out of touch and out of sympathy with recent developments, is his fear that Christianity is being undermined not only by doctrinal revolt, but also by 'modern novel literature', by 'the movement called euphemistically Birth Control', and by 'an important section of the feminist movement'.[5] To arrest this disintegration of Christianity, Gore suggests a reconstruction of the Copec movement, with ecumenical action at all levels from the local to the international, and the preparation of a comprehensive treatment of Christian social ethics, both theoretical and practical, and involving a whole new casuistry—a course, it will be remembered, which Copec wisely rejected.

One of the books to which Gore contributed a prefatory note, and one to which he refers in *Christ and Society*, is Paul Bull's *The Economics of the Kingdom of God.* Bull was a member of the Community of the Resurrection, and his theological background was much like Gore's, but his book is less concerned with history and theology than with the existing economic situation in relation to the Christian ideal. Once again the Fifth Report is held up as a definitive expression of Christian social policy, but Bull draws widely on quotations from other Christian sources and shows that the point of view of the Fifth Report is not confined to the Church of England. In particular he mentions an American report, published in 1920, *The Church and Industrial Reconstruction.* He draws a fair distinction between pure political economics and social economics, the former dealing only with facts and relations which result from the nature of things, while the latter embraces also those which are dependent on man's intelligence and will,[6]

[5] *Ibid.*, p. 160.

[6] P. Bull, *The Economics of the Kingdom of God*, pp. 52f. *Cf.* Temple's expression of this distinction: 'Economics is a science based, like any other science, on observation of facts. It generalises from those facts, and its generalisations constitute the laws of political economy. But the facts which it studies are the facts of human behaviour, which is at least to some extent affected by the human will'; quoted in F. A. Iremonger, *Men and Movements in the Church*, p. 25.

but there is an element of exaggeration in his criticism of capitalism, to which he attributes responsibility for gross waste, for the destruction of a sense of truth and beauty, and for the spoliation of the countryside. This ignores both the possibility that a moralized and disciplined capitalism might avoid these results, and that similar evils might stem from Socialism, which is seen as the more Christian way.

Unlike Gore, who is always careful to point out that a change of system is of little value without a change of heart, Bull seems to place too much trust in political and economic measures by themselves. His attack on class distinctions is fiercely uncompromising, and again rather too passionate to be altogether convincing. He sees the vested interests of capital actively backed up by the shareholders in whose interest it is to maintain the status quo, and passively assisted by the expanding but subservient salariat, and by 'the deadly influence of caste which is nourished in our great public schools'.[7] He does, however, acknowledge certain hopeful signs, and believes that some Conservative politicians and industrialists are beginning to see the importance of the element of service in industry, and the virtues of co-partnership.[8]

Bull looks forward to the development of some form of industrial self-government, and judges the Harty–Valder scheme to be more satisfactory than anything hitherto attempted in Britain, but he also examines the merits of other co-partnership schemes, and of the paternalist method of humanizing and improving industrial relations. He sees a particular danger in paternalism, as practised in Britain by the firms of Rowntree, Cadbury and Lever Brothers, in that it may easily sap the initiative of the workers and seriously weaken the position of the trade unions, tending to reinforce the existing structure of industry.[9] In conclusion there is a conventional assessment of the role of the Church in bearing social witness, and of its relation to the State. Bull holds that loyalty to the Church

[7] Bull, *op. cit.*, p. 122. He complains of the 'habitual insolence' with which the rich still tend to speak of the poor: 'I am not referring to occasional spiteful outbreaks such as the venomous vulgarities of Dean Inge, but to the habit of some who are otherwise gentlemen in referring to the poor as "the lower orders" ' (p. 123).

[8] Bull refers in particular to Lord Robert Cecil, and to W. L. Hichens, chairman of Cammell Laird and a prominent Christian layman; pp. 137–9.

[9] *Ibid.*, pp. 158–63.

must always take precedence over loyalty to the State, but every churchman is also a citizen and therefore, as far as his Christian conscience permits, owes allegiance to the State in all temporal matters. It is his duty to use what political power he has in such a way as to promote God's glory and the good of mankind.[10]

The Christian attitude towards the State is dealt with more fully in Temple's 1928 Scott Holland lectures, *Christianity and the State*. These trace various stages in the recovery of a Christian concern with the problems of society, beginning as straightforward sympathy with distress, branching out into an attack on certain elements in the accepted social order, and finally, since the war and the general strike, subjecting the whole structure of society to critical examination.[11] Although it is true, as Temple says, that the Church was assuming an increasingly ambitious and radical role in its study of society, there is an important point which he fails to make, but which has a direct bearing on any estimate of the Church's social thought; this is that movements for radical social reform did not coincide in the ecclesiastical and secular spheres. The agitation for revolutionary political action was probably at its height in 1919, and with the onset of the depression in 1920 began to grow weak and confused, until by 1926, as the outcome of the general strike showed, it was to all intents and purposes dead. But the idea that the whole social structure should be subjected to radical criticism in the light of Christian principles was, in the early twenties, still confined to a small and fairly uninfluential group of churchmen. The Fifth Report was gradualist and evolutionary in its approach, and the full implications of what it said were grasped at first only by those to whom they were immediately congenial. Disappointment with Socialism as a political remedy was only gradually replaced by the ideal of developing a specifically Christian sociology, and this was in any case a policy which appealed only to a minority of those who had been enthused by the Fifth Report. The situation was a good deal

[10] *Ibid.*, pp. 180–5. This section is interesting for the use which Bull makes (pp. 180–3) of quotations from Reinhold Niebuhr. This is one of the earliest references to him by an English writer on Christian social ethics.

[11] W. Temple, *Christianity and the State*, pp. 2f. There is a more detailed account of the earlier stages of this process in 'The Church and Social Questions', an article which Temple contributed to *Stockholm*, 1928, Vol. 1, pp. 21f.

more complicated than Temple suggests, and by 1928 the chance of an alliance between radical Christian social thought and revolutionary secular political aspiration was long past.

In *Christianity and the State* Temple maintains that the Church should not commit itself to any particular political programme or identify itself with a political party, but should instead emphasize 'the utterly fundamental realities—God and Immortality. . . . The first effect of connecting our political thought with our faith in God is to destroy the ultimate or absolute character which has so often been attributed to the State. For that character belongs to God alone.'[12] Temple's own political attitude during this period was non-committal; many years previously he had written: 'The alternative stands before us—Socialism or Heresy', and he had warned his readers that to stand aside from supporting the Labour Movement 'would be to incur the guilt of final and complete apostasy, of renunciation of Christ, and of blasphemy against his Holy Spirit'.[13] But this crusading zeal in politics, and indeed the whole mood of ethico-social idealism which was the counterpart of Temple's early metaphysical idealism, and was still perhaps to be seen at the time of Copec, gave way during the twenties to a greater realism, both in politics and philosophy.[14] There is a misleading reference in his biography to a 'gradual movement to the Right during his later years';[15] in fact, although it is true that he gave up his membership of the Labour Party in 1925, and that the political comment in *The Pilgrim* (which he edited from 1920 to 1927) is not marked by any discernible party bias, it was perhaps Temple's greatest achievement as a social thinker that he was able to find his way back, towards the end of his life, to a position scarcely less radical than that of his early Socialist enthusiasms. In *Christianity and the Social Order* (1941) he works out in some detail, and in a manner fully relevant to the changed circumstances, a Christian policy for society, and it is interesting to see that this still has much in common with the political objectives of the Labour Party. During the twenties, however, and particularly in

[12] *Christianity and the State*, pp. 6 and 27.

[13] W. Temple, 'The Church and the Labour Party', in the *Economic Review*, April 1908, pp. 199 and 195 respectively.

[14] See R. Craig, *Social Concern in the Thought of William Temple*, pp. 19–22.

[15] F. A. Iremonger, *William Temple*, p. 512.

Christianity and the State and *Essays in Christian Politics* (1927),[16] he was above all concerned to emphasize that the authority of the Church in the political sphere is different in kind from the authority of any secular institution: 'The Church has a great concern with the spirit in men which shapes the economic system',[17] but this does not mean that it is the job of the Church itself to do such shaping. On the contrary, it was the Church's mistaken claim to authority over political and economic life, and its assumption of functions which did not properly belong to it, which created the need for a Reformation: 'So it lost the spiritual kind of control which belonged to it, without even successfully usurping the political kind of control which did not. This brought discredit on the whole notion of the authority of religion in commercial and political affairs.'[18]

It was clearly valuable to point to the lessons of history, and necessary to assert the duty of the Church to exercise the right kind of spiritual control over society, but it could with some justification be argued that, during the inter-war period, Temple paid disappointingly little attention to the pressing need to discuss the economic implications of Christian ethical principles, and to advise bewildered Christians in matters of practical politics. His contribution to such discussion and advice is chiefly embodied in his later book, *Christianity and the Social Order*, and it is this, rather than his earlier writings, which is more directly comparable in scope and function with the other points of view which are examined in this chapter.

There are, however, several points in Temple's earlier books which are of interest, although they do not form part of a clear pattern of thought about society, and seem merely to add cogency to the claim that during this period he was eclectic and even idiosyncratic in his social opinions.[19] For example, in a speech to the Anglo-Catholic Summer School of Sociology in 1927, and again in *Christianity and the State*, Temple showed his unusually

[16] *The Essays in Christian Politics and Kindred Subjects* consist chiefly of articles which originally appeared in *The Pilgrim*.

[17] W. Temple, 'Christianity and Politics', in *Essays in Christian Politics*, p. 29.

[18] *Ibid.*, p. 30.

[19] For this view of Temple's social thought see W. G. Peck, 'William Temple as a Social Thinker', in *William Temple, an Estimate and an Appreciation*, pp. 66f.

high regard for private property. Gore and Scott Holland had previously urged that the benefits of property-holding should be widely shared, but Temple went further: 'There can be no doubt about the Christian hope, however difficult it may be to reach it, of securing to everyone a sufficient amount of property to maintain life while he snaps his fingers at the universe.'[20] The Christian ideal, according to Temple, is that no man should be compelled to work in order to sustain life, 'for so his work and service will be more nearly free, and personality will have a fuller scope'.[21] This was a remarkable change from the traditional principle, which Copec had maintained,[22] that if a man will not work neither shall he eat, but Temple makes it clear that he still accepts the moral soundness of that principle, objecting only to its use as a basis for coercive legislation.

Temple sees the establishment of the reign of law as the fulfilment of the true nature of the State in its external relations. Since war is the repudiation of law, a state which chooses to go to war is false to itself: 'It shows its true nature when it promotes that international organization which will secure the reign of law (its own true essence) in international relations.'[23] It follows from this that, in order to establish the reign of law throughout the world, a state must be prepared to 'hand over to an international assembly the determination of its own policy in matters affecting its own interest',[24] and Temple leaves no doubt that this is an expression in his own case of whole-hearted support for the League of Nations, even at the cost of some surrender of national sovereignty.

As an undergraduate at Balliol, R. H. Tawney came under the influence of Gore, and after going down from Oxford he spent three years with Canon Barnett at Toynbee Hall, developing there the almost Victorian moral earnestness which remained characteristic of all his social writing. He was a convinced Socialist, remaining a loyal member of the Labour Party despite his bitter

[20] From Temple's speech to the Anglo-Catholic Summer School, quoted in *Commonwealth*, September 1927, p. 268.
[21] *Christianity and the State*, p. 98.
[22] Copec report, *Industry and Property*, pp. 194f.
[23] *Christianity and the State*, p. 166.
[24] *Ibid.*, p. 184.

disappointment at what he considered to be its faithlessness in office, and this combination of political conviction with a profound Christian faith marked him out as an unusual figure in the academic world of the inter-war period. He made what was undoubtedly the most distinguished lay contribution to the Christian social thought of his time, and it might reasonably be claimed that his pre-eminence in this field was absolute, for, with much experience of industrial research and conciliation, and many years as lecturer (and subsequently Professor) in economic history at London University, he brought to his work a combination of practical, technical and academic qualifications which was certainly unparalleled in any of his clerical colleagues. His two most important social essays are *The Acquisitive Society* (1921), and his Halley Stewart lectures for 1929, published in 1931, *Equality*.

The Acquisitive Society begins, like so much Christian social writing, from the position outlined by the Fifth Report (which, it will be remembered, Tawney helped to produce), and in particular from its definition of the function of industry as service and its method as association. Tawney argues that the industrial order is at present built on the conviction that 'economic rights are anterior to, and independent of, economic functions. . . . The practical result of it is that economic rights remain, whether economic functions are performed or not.'[25] The criterion of function has been replaced by that of wealth, but wealth is in fact no substitute, and Tawney dismisses the theory that an all-round increase in prosperity would put an end to industrial disputes: 'For the question is one, not of amounts, but of proportions; and men will fight to be paid thirty pounds a week, instead of twenty, as readily as they will fight to be paid five pounds instead of four, as long as there is no reason why they should be paid twenty pounds instead of thirty, and as long as other men who do not work are paid anything at all.'[26] He maintains that the genuine risks of investment—frequently adduced as a reason for not paying higher wages—would be better met out of a fund maintained for the purpose than out of excessive profits which are otherwise distributed as dividends.

[25] R. H. Tawney, *The Acquisitive Society*, pp. 30f.
[26] *Ibid.*, p. 45.

As a means of achieving efficiency and security, the amalgamation of industry into large units is viewed with greater favour by Tawney than by most Christian social thinkers, although he insists that large industrial concerns must be subject to rigorous public control. On nationalization his approach is pragmatic: it is 'not an end, but a means to an end, and when the question of ownership has been settled the question of administration remains for solution',[27] an acknowledgment that nationalization does not necessarily bring any improvement in the pay or status of the employee, and a reminder that Tawney is no narrow-minded exponent of doctrinaire Socialism.[28]

His expectation that a reorganization of industry on more moral lines would lead to a great increase in efficiency and productivity is perhaps unduly optimistic.[29] Like Bull, he tends to ignore man's fallen nature, and the scope for waste, slackness and inefficiency in a Socialist economy, and he also underestimates the need to acknowledge and harness the motive of self-interest. A perceptive critic has identified the origin of this utopianism in Tawney's mistaken assumption that there is a particular Christian social order—that the Sermon on the Mount is a blueprint for social action, rather than teaching which includes a strong eschatological element.[30] But his ideal is a noble one: it calls for the abolition of 'the tyranny of functionless property', and the organization of industry as a service to the community, observing professional standards of conduct.[31] When the second Labour administration, of 1929–31, failed to pursue its own policies with boldness, Tawney reminded the Party that the objectives of Socialism must be 'to create organs through which the nation can control, in co-operation with other nations, its own economic destinies; plan its business as it deems most conducive to the

[27] R. H. Tawney, *The Acquisitive Society*, p. 149.

[28] *Cf.* 'The idea of some socialists that private property in land or capital is necessarily mischievous is a piece of scholastic pedantry as absurd as that of those conservatives who would invest all property with some kind of mysterious sanctity.' *Ibid.*, p. 99.

[29] *Ibid.*, pp. 164f.

[30] R. Preston, 'R. H. Tawney as a Christian Moralist,' in *Theology*, April, May and June 1966, pp. 157–64, 208–15, and 262–9.

[31] *The Acquisitive Society*, pp. 87–95 and 105–16. There is a hopeful reference (pp. 119–22) to the experiment of guild organization in the building industry as an alternative to collectivism.

general well-being; override, for the sake of economic efficiency, the obstruction of vested interests; and distribute the product of its labours in accordance with some generally recognized principles of justice'.[32] The political philosophy outlined in *The Acquisitive Society* was one which Tawney felt it was the duty of the Church to advocate, and although he recognized that no change of system can cure man's egotism, greed and quarrelsomeness, he did not entirely share the view that individual regeneration must precede social change. He believed that character can be changed by environment, and that the changes which he suggested would at least remove some of the factors which actively encouraged anti-social behaviour.[33]

Tawney saw that one of the greatest obstacles in the way of creating a more fully Christian social order was what Matthew Arnold described as the 'Religion of Inequality',[34] a faith carefully nurtured by an impressive number of disciples. A fine example of Tawney's powers of irony and invective is the *tour de force* of satire with which he tramples on some of the more grotesque expressions of the view that greater economic equality is undesirable or unattainable,[35] but in general his advocacy of greater equality is marked by the same critical balance as *The Acquisitive Society*, and he repudiates the idea that men are or ever can be in any sense socially equal. He does, however, subscribe to the view that 'the well-being of a society is likely to be increased if it so plans its organisation that, whether their powers are great or small, all its members may be equally enabled to make the best of such powers as they possess'.[36] He points out that this ideal is made impossible of achievement by the cumulative effect of economic privilege in a stratified social system, and that it is this cumulative process (already noticed by many writers in the case of private property) which makes such a mockery of the theoretical freedom of a *laissez-faire* economy.[37]

[32] 'The Choice before the Labour Party', in the *Political Quarterly*, Vol. 3, No. 3, July–September 1932, pp. 332f. (Also reprinted as a Socialist League pamphlet.)

[33] *The Acquisitive Society*, p. 222.

[34] *Equality*, p. 24.

[35] *Ibid.*, pp. 43–5. Dean Inge, Lord Birkenhead and Sir Ernest Benn are among his victims.

[36] *Ibid.*, p. 47.

[37] *Ibid.*, pp. 133–52.

The two methods by which Tawney would like to see economic equality more vigorously pursued are the redistribution of resources, and the development of communal organizations to prevent the domination of one group by another. Although Tawney accepts the conclusion of A. L. Bowley and Sir Josiah Stamp that there is an over-riding need for greater productivity and an increase in the national income, the main burden of Tawney's argument is to expose the confusions and misunderstandings in most discussions of the principle of redistribution. Stamp had calculated that the addition to the income of each family through the redistribution of money spent by the rich or moderately well-off on anything in the nature of luxury would not exceed five shillings a week in the first year of such redistribution, and in subsequent years would be a good deal less;[38] on the basis of this research he had sought to discount the arguments of those who were pressing for redistributive taxation. Tawney certainly echoes the Fifth Report in maintaining that the smallness of the national income makes it all the more necessary that it should be divided as fairly as possible, but he believes that Stamp, and those like him who reject the idea of redistribution, are in fact 'belabouring a phantom, in which only its critics are so ingenuous as to believe'.[39] Straightforward redistribution of income would be a wasteful and unsatisfactory course; what is wanted is 'the pooling of [the nation's] surplus resources by means of taxation, and the use of the funds thus obtained to make accessible to all, irrespective of their income, occupation, or social position, the condition of civilization which, in the absence of such measures, would be enjoyed only by the rich. . . . Collective expenditure makes possible results which would be unattainable were an identical sum distributed, without further adjustments, in fractional addition to individual incomes.'[40]

Tawney acknowledges that progress in this direction has already been made, but much greater public expenditure is, he

[38] See J. C. Stamp, *Wealth and Taxable Capacity* (1922), pp. 95–100, and the study by A. L. Bowley, *The Division of the Product of Industry* (1919), especially p. 49, on which Stamp's argument is based. Stamp's conclusions on this question are included in *The Christian Ethic as an Economic Factor*, pp. 44–8, see below.

[39] *Equality*, p. 169. [40] *Ibid.*, pp. 169f.

claims, badly needed, above all on health services and education. He denounces the argument that higher taxation would starve industry of necessary capital as 'an antiquated superstition, to which no reputable economist would lend his endorsement';[41] and he calls for an expansion of markets to absorb, in the form of increased production, the money which is at present being saved because it cannot be profitably invested. If, at some future date, excessive social expenditure should in fact begin to starve industry of capital, there would in any case be a better chance of money being invested where it was needed by a National Investment Board than at the whim of individual investors.[42] Tawney recognizes that much remains to be done, and in conclusion he reaffirms that 'though the ideal of an equal distribution of material wealth may continue to elude us, it is necessary, nevertheless, to make haste towards it, not because such wealth is the most important of man's treasures, but to prove that it is not'.[43]

Sir Josiah Stamp was born into a Baptist family, and in adult life became a Methodist, but his social thought betrays no particular sectarian bias, and was so widely respected and quoted by Anglicans that it is necessary to give some account of it here. Stamp was both a distinguished business administrator and an amateur theologian, and several of his books attempt to relate his Christian faith to the economic and industrial problems with which he was familiar. His thought on these matters is mainly to be found in *The Christian Ethic as an Economic Factor* (1926), *Motive and Method in a Christian Order* (1936) and *Christianity and Economics* (1939).[44] The first of these, the Social Service Lecture for 1926, is a good example of his down-to-earth economic realism, which made him suspicious of so much of the more woolly idealism in Christian social thought. He draws

[41] *Ibid.*, p. 218.

[42] *Ibid.*, pp. 214–26. In support of his contention that the level of taxation is not oppressive Tawney quotes the conclusion of the 1927 Colwyn Committee on the National Debt and Taxation.

[43] *Equality*, p. 291.

[44] Sir Josiah Stamp (1880–1941); Chairman of L.M.S. Railway, Director of the Bank of England, created Baron 1938. It was a mark of the conservatism of *The Christian Ethic as an Economic Factor* that it earned the approval of Dean Inge. ('Interfering Parsons', in the *Sunday Express*, 1st August, 1926.)

attention to the importance of purely physical factors in creating social problems—factors such as climate, soil fertility, communications, and to some extent the physical characteristics of man himself. These are impervious to the influence of the Christian ethic or to the lubricating effect of doses of Christian sentiment, but on the other hand there are, he acknowledges, some important social factors which can be changed by Christian influence. He particularly draws attention to the need to narrow the gap between the morality of the converted individual and that of the largely amoral organizations of which he is a member, but the emphasis in all his writing is on the attainment of higher standards of individual conduct rather than on any particular programme for the improvement of social conditions.[45]

Stamp shows how the Christian ethic can influence the physical equation of the balance of output and reward; it can create a new spirit of service, resulting in higher output, and this in turn enables a new and more favourable equation to be worked out. An important idea is that the Christian ethic can, if imaginatively embodied in financial policy, break the vicious circle of low output, low wages, low standard of living, and low efficiency. The policy which Stamp has in mind is some form of temporary deficit budgeting, by which wage increases might be granted in the expectation that increased goodwill and improved morale would lead to higher productivity, rather than as a reward for improvements already achieved.[46] He deprecates the use by Christian social enthusiasts of such phrases as 'living wage' or 'full requirements of life', which are relative in terms of both time and place, and are in any case valueless if they are unrelated to what is economically feasible. He is also unsympathetic towards the commonly held view that mass production techniques have a disastrous effect on the workers involved with them, and that it is therefore desirable to recover something of the old-fashioned concept of craftsmanship; he sees single-unit tasks as an inevitable aspect of modern industry, and suggests that 'relief is found in short hours, rest pauses, well-filled leisure and constructive

[45] *The Christian Ethic as an Economic Factor*, pp. 28–30; *Motive and Method in a Christian Order*, p. 48; *Christianity and Economics*, p. 111.

[46] *The Christian Ethic as an Economic Factor*, pp. 38f.

hobbies, rather than in a reversion to long hours to produce a very few complete articles to support the notion of craftsmanship'.[47]

Inequalities of wealth are not seen by Stamp as necessarily immoral; his objections to redistributive taxation have already been mentioned, but his case for inequality does not rest only on the arguments which Tawney found it so easy to demolish. There is a more positive aspect, in particular the truth that spending on luxuries in one generation is necessary if they are to become the common possessions of the next; writing in 1939, he refers to television as an example of such luxury spending, and in this case, at least, it is not easy to dispute the validity of his argument.[48] Moreover, Stamp is not altogether insensitive to the offence which can be caused by inequalities of wealth, and by tactless or ostentatious expenditure, and he singles out excessive payment for services as incompatible with Christian principles.[49]

Stamp sees little need or prospect of structural change in industry, and in his reliance on the wider reception by individuals of Christian ethical standards he is bound to appear conservative when compared with most Christian social thinkers, in whom the element of visionary idealism is usually present in some form. Clearly, however, it would be absurd to label him a reactionary, but that is not to say that there were no Christian social thinkers in this class. Sir Charles Marston represents the extreme right wing of Christian social concern, an approach which is admirably summed up in a publisher's note on his study of *The Christian Faith and Industry*: 'With irresistible cogency he shatters the complacency of those who affect to believe that Christianity in any way countenances the delusion that the Socialist doctrine of self-interest is any substitute for the Gospel doctrine of self-sacrifice. Fairness is one of the chief characteristics of this outstanding book. . . .' Despite these brave words, it has now sunk into the oblivion where it belongs, and it is worthwhile to resurrect it only because it evidently represented a by no means negligible point of view. P. T. R. Kirk in fact invited Marston to address an I.C.F. meeting in 1929, but Marston first demanded an assurance

[47] *Christianity and Economics*, p. 143.
[48] *Ibid.*, p. 151.
[49] *Ibid.*, pp. 153f. There is a code of ethics for expenditure which is fair and judicious.

that the I.C.F. was concerned only to convert individuals, not to change the industrial system. So blunt a challenge drove Kirk into an unwonted expression of radical commitment, and he firmly maintained the right of the I.C.F. to preach the need for change, even if it were not its business to stipulate the precise nature of that change. The correspondence between Marston and Kirk was published in the *Torch* in March, 1929, and the editor added to it a number of extracts from *The Christian Faith and Industry*, set out alongside quotations from the Fifth Report to show the gross disparity between the two.

Marston's book is in fact a passionate assault on anything which smacks of Socialism or collective responsibility, spiced with an occasional anti-intellectual sneer. He regards the trade unions as an unmitigated evil, dragging all workers down to the level of the worst and slowest, and he attacks the clergy for not bringing home to the people the value of work: 'We pride ourselves on being sportsmen, but we do not realise that the greatest sport in the world is to earn one's own living.'[50] He calls for the release of the sporting capitalist from the burdens of taxation, collectivism and red tape, and sees such a course as the only hope of restoring prosperity and thereby eliminating the social evils of bureaucracy and idleness.

This outline of various Christian approaches to the problems of society is by no means exhaustive. There were many other authors and thinkers who contributed to the debate, among them John Lee, C. E. Hudson, and A. D. Lindsay. But apart from the important group considered in the next chapter, and the work of the Oxford Conference of 1937, there was nobody who added anything distinctive to the ideas which have been surveyed in this chapter. There were basically two approaches; the theological/ethical, represented by Gore, Bull and Temple; and the political/economic, represented by Tawney and Stamp. Tawney is perhaps the most comprehensive, with a doctrine of man and society close to that of the theologians, but he attaches less importance than Stamp to economic remedies of a generally Keynesian flavour, and he lacks Stamp's firm grasp of economic realities. During the inter-war

[50] *The Christian Faith and Industry*, p. 78.

period there was in fact no writer who successfully combined theological, ethical, political and economic insights in a synthetic Christian view of society. This is perhaps an unattainable ideal, but the fact that it was achieved neither by an individual nor even by a group of writers pooling their specialized knowledge, combined with the temporary resurgence after the events of 1926 of opposition to any close Christian concern with social problems, meant that Christian social witness continued to be weak and divided.

6

The Christendom Group and the Anglo-Catholic Movement

ON MARCH 13th, 1923, a memorial signed by five hundred and ten priests of the Church of England, the Church in Wales and the Episcopal Church of Scotland was presented to Ramsay MacDonald and the one hundred and forty-three Labour members of parliament under his leadership.[1] It congratulated them on becoming, for the first time, the official opposition, expressed sympathy with the struggles of Labour to increase its political power, looked forward to the contribution which the Labour Party would be able to make to the consideration and more adequate treatment of the pressing social problems with which the clergy were familiar, and promised support for all efforts which the Labour Party might make for the 'spiritual and economic emancipation of the people'.[2] The memorial was organized privately by Lewis Donaldson, a prominent Christian Socialist and at that time Canon of Peterborough, and when its terms became known many more clergy expressed a desire to be associated with it, the number of signatories rising eventually to seven hundred.[3] This was an unprecedented gesture of political sympathy, but it did not presage a general growth in Anglican enthusiasm for the Labour Party. In fact, by a curious stroke of

[1] Ten of the original signatories later became bishops: F. R. Barry, A. W. F. Blunt, G. A. Chase, J. Darbyshire, W. H. Frere, L. S. Hunter, F. O. T. Hawkes, A. Rose, P. N. W. Strong and C. S. Woodward. Many others held high office in the Church either at the time or later. Several were cautious sympathizers who usually held aloof from political involvement, such as S. C. Carpenter, Leonard Hodgson and O. C. Quick, and one or two seem otherwise to have shown no enthusiasm for the Socialist cause. It is, for example, difficult to reconcile the signature of B. K. Cunningham, Principal of Westcott House, with an entry which he made in his diary a year later, in which he speaks of 'a deepening feeling that I am much to blame for not being able to care for those who are not by birth gentlemen'. (Quoted in J. R. H. Moorman, *B. K. Cunningham: a Memoir*, p. 105.)

[2] The details are taken from a copy of the memorial in the private possession of Dr. A. R. Vidler.

[3] *Commonwealth*, March 1924, p. 98.

irony, it was only a few weeks after the memorial was first presented that the disagreements within the Church Socialist League, hitherto the spearhead of Socialist activity in the Church of England, finally came to a head, and at a conference at Whitsun, 1923, the League in its old form was disbanded. Its place was immediately taken by the new League of the Kingdom of God,[4] which most of the former C.S.L. members joined, but the opening sentence of the L.K.G. basis shows clearly that there was a movement away from support for political Socialism:

> 'The League is a band of Churchmen and Churchwomen who believe that the Catholic Faith demands a challenge to the world by the repudiation of capitalist plutocracy and the wage system, and stands for a social order in which the means of life subserve the commonweal.'

Significant differences between this new basis and that of the old C.S.L. were the omission of any reference to public ownership, the introduction of a hostile reference to plutocracy, and the stronger emphasis on Catholic theology. A minority of C.S.L. members, whose faith in Socialism remained unshaken, disapproved of these developments, and a year later they formed a new organization, the Society of Socialist Christians, which was similar to the old C.S.L. but open to all, whether Christian or not.[5]

The way had been prepared for the transformation of the C.S.L. and the development of a new and ostensibly more theological approach to social questions by the summer schools held at Paycocke's House, Coggeshall, from 1919 to 1921, at which a group of dissatisfied C.S.L. members had worked out their sociological ideas under Widdrington's leadership. There was a growing conviction among the members of this group that the League had adopted a negative and excessively critical attitude, and had been

[4] The Chairman of the L.K.G. was T. C. Gobat, Vicar of St. James', Darlington; Reckitt was Vice-Chairman, Egerton Swann Secretary, and Widdrington National Organizer. Slesser also played a leading part in its formation.

[5] The S.S.C. of which the Chairman was Fred Hughes, was founded at a meeting held at the Food Reform Restaurant, Holborn, on February 6th, 1924, attended by representatives of the former C.S.L., of Conrad Noel's Catholic Crusade, the Crusader League, the League of Young Socialists and the Socialist Quaker Society. The *Crusader*, a left-wing pacifist periodical established in 1916, espoused the cause of the S.S.C., describing it in its editorial for May 2nd, 1924, as an amalgamation for more effective action of the remains of several sectional societies. In 1928 the *Crusader* was renamed the *Socialist Christian*, and became the official organ of the S.S.C.

wrong to remain loyal to Socialism of a Marxist flavour. It should no longer be content with social pronouncements which were 'vague untheological echoes of secular thought', but should adopt a positive and dogmatic approach to social problems, sharply distinguished both from untheological Socialism and from non-revolutionary Christianity. A collection of essays was planned to provide the outline of a Catholic sociology 'which does not require to be bolstered up by secular props, because it will be built directly upon the implications of Catholic dogma and experience'.[6]

The word sociology was intended to embrace both a theoretical Christian social philosophy, and a Christian social ethic derived directly from it—not adapted from current secular thought.[7] In a definition which found much favour with the Christendom Group, Demant later described the task of Christian social thinkers as being to move on 'from ethics to sociology',[8] from a discussion of men's motives and aspirations to a proclamation of what essentially is. The essays planned at Paycocke's were published in 1922 as *The Return of Christendom*, and they embody most of the ideas which, in a more developed form, were to become characteristic of the Christendom Group. The Group can therefore be said to have begun to develop within the C.S.L. before its transformation into the L.K.G., but it was never synonymous with either society, and the name stands for a mood and attitude rather than for a specific and definable body of individuals. W. G. Peck, one of the leading Christendom writers,[9] picked out as the distinctive mark of the Group the conviction that a reformed financial system and a guild organization for industry constitute the two pillars on which a Christian policy for society must be

[6] From L. S. Thornton's report of the 1920 C.S.L. Summer School in the *Church Socialist*, September–October 1920, p. 97. See also M. B. Reckitt, *P. E. T. Widdrington*, pp. 77–9.

[7] See an article by M. B. Reckitt on the Christendom Group in *Crucible*, October 1963, pp. 115–19, and particularly the note on the word 'sociology' on p. 116.

[8] Demant used the phrase as the title of a chapter in his *God, Man and Society* (1933).

[9] W. G. Peck (1883–1962) was a non-conformist minister before he was received into the Church of England in 1925. From 1936 to 1951 he was Director of Clergy Schools for the I.C.F., and in this capacity was chiefly responsible for the assimilation by the I.C.F. of a number of Christendom Group ideas.

built, while Egerton Swann defined the three most important ideas of a Catholic sociology as distributed property, the just price (an idea directly inherited from medieval Christendom), and a guild system for industry.[10]

In 1931 the quarterly organ of the Christendom Group, *Christendom: A Journal of Christian Sociology*, began publication, and in 1932 the Group started to hold an annual conference at St. Leonard's, but the Christendom outlook was formed well before these developments took place, and found expression in books, pamphlets, manifestoes, and the L.K.G. notes which appeared regularly in *Commonwealth*.[11] The development of Christendom thought was influenced by the alliance established in 1923 between the newly formed L.K.G. and the Anglo-Catholic movement, a factor which helped to strengthen the Catholic character of the Group. With some notable exceptions (mostly slum priests), Anglo-Catholics had tended to remain somewhat aloof from practical social issues, preoccupied with the defence of their distinctive theological position and drifting, as Widdrington put it, 'in the direction of a barren ecclesiasticism and towards a form of pietism incompatible with any strong social hope',[12] but they were sharply recalled to their social duty by the famous speech delivered by the Bishop of Zanzibar, Frank Weston, to the Anglo-Catholic Congress of 1923: 'You cannot claim to worship Jesus in the Tabernacle, if you do not pity Jesus in the slum. . . . It is folly—it is madness—to suppose that you can worship Jesus in the Sacraments and Jesus on the Throne of glory, when you are sweating him in the souls and bodies of his children.'[13] The

[10] W. G. Peck, *After Thirty Years* (1954), p. 9; N. E. Egerton Swann, *Is there a Catholic Sociology*? pp. 15–32.

[11] After the demise of the *Church Socialist* at the end of 1921, the C.S.L. notes were published in *Commonwealth*, and this arrangement was continued after the formation of the L.K.G. in 1923. But *Commonwealth* was not the official mouthpiece of the L.K.G., and its editorial opinion did not always coincide with the ideas favoured by the L.K.G. and the Christendom Group.

[12] P. E. T. Widdrington, 'The Rock whence Ye were Hewn,' in the *Church Socialist*, July–August 1920, p. 79. Widdrington was himself an Anglo-Catholic.

[13] *Report of the Anglo-Catholic Congress, London, July 1923*, pp. 185f. As an undergraduate at Oxford, Weston had been a member of the Guild of St. Matthew (H. Maynard Smith, *Frank, Bishop of Zanzibar*, p. 9). The 1923 Anglo-Catholic Congress was also notable for Studdert Kennedy's address on Salvation, which dealt particularly with social issues. See pp. 143–50 of the *Report*.

lead given by Weston inspired two clerical members of the Congress, G. D. Rosenthal and R. H. Tribe, with the enthusiastic support of Widdrington and the L.K.G., to establish the Anglo-Catholic Summer School of Sociology, which first met at Oxford in 1925. By combining the devotional tradition of the Anglo-Catholic movement with the generally Maurician theology of the L.K.G., and by welcoming members of all Christian denominations to take part in its discussions, the Summer School sometimes achieved a measure of variety and balance in its social comment which compared favourably with the utterances of smaller, sectional societies, and it was one of the most valuable activities with which the Christendom thinkers were associated.[14]

The Return of Christendom was the first attempt to express the ideas which were distinctive of the Christendom Group. It was prepared under the guidance of Gore, who contributed a cautious introduction, but he was not altogether happy with the essays. He particularly regretted the omission of any discussion of international affairs, and was sceptical about the guild organization of industry which the authors tentatively put forward. He described all the contributors as 'Socialists in a general sense',[15] but this did not imply any Fabian sympathies. As the title suggests, the authors looked for their inspiration to medieval Christendom, hoping that its principles and ideals might be recovered and applied to contemporary society. The opening essay, by Reckitt, is primarily an attack on capitalism and plutocracy, but it also includes a harsh indictment of political Socialism for its acquiescence in many capitalist illusions and fallacies. In particular, it attacks Labour's acceptance of the assumptions 'that credit must necessarily be based on securities which only capitalists can offer; that "increased production" must in itself and regardless of its nature inevitably be of economic benefit to the whole com-

[14] See R. Kenyon, *The Catholic Faith and the Social Order*, which summarizes the work of the summer schools of 1928, 1929 and 1930, and includes some penetrating comment on industrial and economic affairs. Responsibility for the summer schools was taken over in 1936 by the newly formed Church Union Association for Church Social Action, under the leadership of the Rev. Patrick McLaughlin.

[15] *The Return of Christendom*, by a Group of Churchmen, p. 9. The essays are by Reckitt (2), Slesser, Widdrington, A. J. Penty, A. J. Carlyle, Niles Carpenter, P. Bull and L. S. Thornton. There is an epilogue by G. K. Chesterton, written just before he became a Roman Catholic.

munity; that purchasing-power should only be distributed in return for work; that the multiplication of machinery is a sign, and even a condition, of economic progress; that prices must for ever serve as the "automatic register of the relation between the supply of goods and the supply of money"; that the worker must continue to receive his remuneration in the form of a wage. . . .'[16]

Essays by Thornton and Slesser emphasize the need for a dogmatic faith which, in order to envisage the redemption of society no less than of the individual, must be Catholic.[17] Widdrington, representing the most soundly Maurician point of view among the authors, calls for a recovery of the gospel of the Kingdom; Carlyle describes the medieval order of society; Penty warns against the disastrous social consequences of the mentality of industrialism—the belief that the material is more important than the spiritual.[18] Reckitt's second essay, acknowledging its debt to Tawney and to the earlier symposium *Property*, calls for the moralization of property. Once again medieval practice, with its balance between personal freedom and social function, is held up for admiration, but Reckitt goes on to claim that behind the present problem of property lies the problem of credit, the only solution of which is to be found in some form of Social Credit. Carpenter capably exposes the failure of Marxism, and Bull contributes a conventional Catholic account of the social function of the Church.

The Return of Christendom is a muddled and ill-balanced book, but it is important for its embryonic expression of the ideas of the Christendom Group. Indeed, with the exception of any reference to guilds, they may all be deduced from the quotation already given from Reckitt's first essay, which shows clearly the concern and dissatisfaction which the Group felt with the existing financial

[16] *The Return of Christendom*, p. 28. (Reckitt wanted prices to be the authentic register of the relation between the production and consumption of goods.)

[17] For a more detailed and persuasive exposition of the idea that only a Catholic theology is socially adequate, see W. G. Peck, *The Divine Society*, esp. pp. 184–7, where the author emphasizes the importance of seeing the material world as a sacrament of the spiritual.

[18] Arthur Joseph Penty, 1875–1937; by profession an architect, Penty devoted most of his time and energy from 1907 onwards to the support of guild socialism and the propagation of his own distinctive views on economics and social policy. See below.

system, and above all the orthodox view of credit. The Christendom thinkers had come to ask themselves: 'Was ownership, as we had assumed, the clue to social authority, or was there some force which could and did determine the conditions within which ownership must operate, influence the price-level, and profoundly affect the purchasing power of wages?'[19] The conclusion which they reached was that the existing financial system was even more to blame than private ownership and large-scale competitive industry for the fact that society still suffered from widespread poverty, recurrent unemployment, and a degrading system of wage labour, despite the great resources of power and machinery at man's disposal. They were influenced in this conclusion almost entirely by the plausible analysis of Britain's economic problems worked out by Major C. H. Douglas, and the remedy which he advocated under the name of Social Credit. Douglas was an engineer by profession, not a trained economist, and his system was based on a number of serious economic fallacies, but it did gain enthusiastic support from a small circle of would-be social reformers, led by A. R. Orage, editor of the *New Age*, who was converted by Douglas in 1919, and who in turn converted some of the National Guildsmen, including Reckitt.[20] It was a serious misfortune of the Christian social movement in the Church of England that many of its most active and influential leaders, including Demant and under his control the research committee of the Christian Social Council, were persuaded to advocate this fallacious panacea, rather than the economic measures which Keynes and his associates were propounding from 1923 onwards. In doing so, they were not only throwing away an opportunity of making a constructive contribution to the solution of the country's economic problems, but also bringing all Christian involvement in economics into discredit.

Writing in *The Pilgrim* in January 1922, Temple observed that the Douglas scheme was 'still in the stage of incomprehensibility to all except a few';[21] there was never in fact a time when this was not the case, and the disciples of the scheme contradicted each

[19] M. B. Reckitt, *As it Happened, an Autobiography*, p. 167.

[20] Douglas's own explanation of his scheme is set out, as clearly as anywhere, in his *Credit-Power and Democracy* (1920).

[21] *The Pilgrim*, January 1922, p. 129.

other remarkably in their idiosyncratic expositions of its working.[22] Very briefly, Douglas felt that the existing financial system was at fault because it was inherently incapable of distributing adequate purchasing power. He argued that the whole cost of production goes into the price of an article, but not into the purchasing power which is distributed in the course of its production in the form of wages, salaries and dividends. The purchasing power of the community is therefore bound to fall short of the amount needed to absorb the total product of industry at an economic price by the aggregate of bank and overhead charges and the cost of raw materials, all of which the producer must pay out in addition to the purchasing power he distributes. Douglas's solution was that goods should be sold below cost price, the difference being made up by the issue of credit to the producer. The control of credit must be in the hands of the community, rather than of private, profit-making banks, and the effective control of the producer by the consumer can be ensured only if the producer must regularly apply to a public credit-bank in order to finance his business.

In its exaltation of the consumer, the Douglas scheme was reminiscent of old-fashioned Liberalism, and although it required the public control of credit, it by no means envisaged the end of capitalism. Indeed, the flood of effective purchasing power let loose by it would have been greatly to the financial advantage of any industrialist who was meeting a need approved by a public credit-bank, and Douglas himself spoke of a 'functionally aristocratic hierarchy of producers accredited by, and serving, a democracy of consumers'.[23] He had no scruples about mass production, and was merely concerned to see that productive capacity was fully exploited, or the consumers' real demands met, whichever happened first. With this ideal in mind he rejected a system of self-governing industrial guilds on the grounds that it would be technically impractical and inefficient compared with a system which entrusted full executive power to an élite of trained experts.[24]

[22] Such confusion may be studied in three articles in *The Pilgrim*, April 1922, pp. 253–68; July 1922, pp. 388–98; July 1923, pp. 403–17. (The first of these, by Hewlett Johnson, is particularly incompetent and self-contradictory.) See also *Commonwealth*, April 1922, pp. 94–6; May 1922, pp. 124–7; August 1922, pp. 206–10; September 1922, pp. 238–43; December 1922, pp. 318–21.

[23] Douglas, *op. cit.*, p. 94.

[24] *Ibid.*, pp. 76–86.

There was much in the Douglas scheme which Christian social thinkers inspired by the ideal of medieval Christendom, deeply suspicious of large-scale industry, and inclined towards a syndicalist industrial system might have been expected to repudiate. There were in fact underlying contradictions in the Christendom Group's advocacy of Social Credit, but any misgivings they may have felt were temporarily overshadowed by their enthusiasm for two particular aspects of the Douglas plan. Most important was the fact that it attacked orthodox financial practice; the power of the banks was suspected and resented by none more strongly than the Christendom thinkers, and bankers were commonly blamed for what were in fact the inevitable results of archaic and misguided Treasury policy. Secondly, Douglas seemed to support the Christendom dislike of the wage-system in his plan to supplement wages by the payment of a national dividend—an idea bound up with his proposal to replace bank credit by the real credit of the community. He believed that the potential productive power of society should be reflected in a financial payment to each member of the community;[25] everybody would receive a dividend—'a payment, absolute and unconditional, of something due'—instead of a wage—'a dole of purchasing power revocable by authority'.[26] Eagerly seizing on these two aspects of the Douglas scheme, Christendom writers lost no time in distorting and manipulating the rest of the Social Credit theory to make it a suitable bed-fellow for industrial guilds and a relatively austere social ideal.[27]

There are two basic errors in the Douglas scheme. First, and most obviously, a fully adequate proportion of the costs of

[25] Douglas's view of credit was not as unorthodox as it may appear, however fanciful his ideas about a national dividend. The crux of the Christendom complaint was that credit, instead of being used for the most socially beneficial projects and in the interests of those whose need was greatest, was in fact commanded by those who already enjoyed financial power. The Douglas scheme was welcomed because it seemed to hold out the promise of breaking that power. (See R. Kenyon, *op. cit.*, pp. 116–44.)

[26] Douglas, *op. cit.*, p. 44. In this context Douglas seems to suggest that dividends should replace wages, but elsewhere, and more convincingly, he speaks of them as supplementing existing wages (*Social Credit*, 3rd edition, Appendix, 'Draft Social Credit Scheme for Scotland', pp. 205–12).

[27] See particularly M. B. Reckitt, 'Social Credit and the Worker', in *Commonwealth*, August 1922, pp. 206–10, in which it is claimed, with no warrant from Douglas's writings, that Social Credit provides the economic basis for a guild structure of industry.

production, other than wages paid to those responsible for the final process in the manufacture of an article, is in fact distributed at some stage as purchasing power, although not, of course, at precisely the moment at which the finished article appears on the retail market. If industry is seen as a continuous and highly complex process, instead of a series of isolated, self-contained processes—as a continuous film instead of a series of individually incomplete and meaningless stills—the folly of Douglas's argument is at once apparent. As one critic has pointed out, 'it is wages for blacksmiths, ploughmen, millers and bakers, whose final product is not yet on the market as bread, which buy the current daily output of loaves';[28] it is out of last week's pay packet that this week's output of consumer goods is bought. Secondly, Douglas was wrong to suppose that bank loans, because they are not usually fully covered by cash deposits, are imaginary creations, the repayment of which is bound to create economic disequilibrium. In fact a bank loan is always a form of saving, and to repay a loan is merely to save after the capital expenditure has been made, and out of the profits resulting from it, instead of beforehand; an advantage of the system of bank loans is, of course, that it enables those who do not already possess resources, and therefore cannot save in order to spend, to make capital expenditure and thereby add to the total product and total wealth of society.[29]

It has seemed necessary to give some outline of Social Credit and its errors, since it was an economic theory which, in one form or another, played an important part in Christian social thought of a certain school throughout the inter-war period. It is not difficult to see why this came about; there was so much economic and financial theory and practice that was utterly inept, often informed by no firmer grasp of the facts than the Douglas scheme itself, that the scope for quack nostrums was enormous, and the temptation for well-meaning but unqualified amateurs to dabble

[28] J. Lewis, *Douglas Fallacies*, p. 32.

[29] *Ibid.*, pp. 54–9. Douglas was careful to defend his scheme from the common criticism that it would lead to inflation, but neither he nor his supporters seem to have understood that the necessary control over prices and incomes would be achieved only at the cost of a bureaucratic orgy beyond the wildest Fabian dreams. The hope that the Douglas scheme could be worked by democratically controlled local credit-banks, and so eliminate bureaucratic tyranny, was perhaps the most absurd of all the aspects of its advocacy.

in economics almost irresistible.[30] But although the Christendom writers were justified in attributing the prevailing economic stagnation and the apparent paradox of poverty amidst plenty, to inflexible and unenlightened financial theory, they were guilty not only of advocating an absurd alternative, but also of grossly over-estimating both the wealth and productive capacity of the world in relation to its real needs, and the increase in efficiency which financial reform might achieve. They were actively hostile to anything which smacked of puritanism, and scornful of the traditional idea (which, despite its origin, they associated with protestantism) that if a man will not work, neither shall he eat, and yet they in fact maintained a relatively ascetic attitude towards material goods and displayed a quite extraordinary lack of imagination about possible and desirable improvements in the standard of living. The idea that the possession of a telephone, a wireless set and a refrigerator might make a real contribution to the fullness, richness and ease of life is one which seems not to have occurred to them. Even more remarkable was their failure to take account of the desperate and crushing poverty of the majority of mankind, and the immensity of the task of overcoming it.

The Christendom Group's curious and unattractive narrowness of outlook was particularly evident in the preference shown by its members for a policy of economic nationalism. As in the case of domestic financial policy, there were grounds for legitimate complaint about the existing state of affairs, and the Anglo-Catholic Summer School was right in recognizing that slavish adherence to the gold standard in the vain pursuit of international financial stability was not only failing to achieve its object abroad, but also having a disastrous effect at home.[31] Keynes had already argued in his *Tract on Monetary Reform* for a new approach to the relation of domestic to international currency control, but

[30] The form which this ineptitude most commonly took was the belief that a trade depression was likely to be cured by deflationary measures and stringent economizing. See, e.g. an article by Sir Arthur Balfour in *The Times Trade Supplement*, August 17th, 1929: 'If sufficient people go out of business and sufficient plant is broken up or dismantled, or put out of action by combinations, this might bring us a little nearer the time when we can have good trade for a reasonable period.' (Quoted inaccurately by Reckitt in *Faith and Society*, p. 330, note.)

[31] Kenyon, *op. cit.*, pp. 132–5. Britain's economic miseries were contrasted with French prosperity, the result of the devaluation of the franc.

instead of pursuing this idea, or even merely calling for closer international co-operation to achieve stability and restore confidence, the Christendom writers turned away in disgust from any form of international collaboration, repudiating policies which would lead to economic interdependence until such time as the nations had individually freed themselves from the tyranny of monetary interests.[32] Suspicion of the power of international finance was also reflected in the Christendom Group's disparagement of the League of Nations, and at a time when the League was in urgent need of the whole-hearted support of intelligent public opinion, it was denounced by Reckitt as providing an 'opportunity for secret and centralized finance to advance its own ends. There is a sense, we feel, in which suspicion in relation to the League is as much part of our duty as enthusiasm. For if the nations are controlled today by an anonymous few for the ends of avarice, so much the more is a centralized *League* of Nations liable to be so.'[33]

Another reason for the Christendom dislike of the League was that it was bound to think in terms of imposing peace, either by arbitration or by sanctions, on nations which were by nature belligerent. It was argued from the Christendom side that 'the only internationalism that can be worth very much is one which would grow naturally out of a recognisedly common culture, spontaneously felt by each nation to be one of its dearest interests', and once more the medieval ideal was praised: 'Western Europe, however much it might actually be rent by wars and fightings, at any rate knew itself to be, by rights, one, and to be so, because it held one faith. . . .'[34] The Christendom Group apparently did not

[32] For an expression of the Christendom view of international affairs, see M. B. Reckitt, *Faith and Society*, pp. 269–302. The case for economic nationalism is to be found in its least objectionable form in an article by Demant, 'Nationalism and Internationalism', in *Christendom*, March 1936, pp. 13–23.

[33] From a report by M. B. Reckitt on the work of the study circle on Economic Aspects of International Relations at the Anglo-Catholic Summer School, July 1925, in *Commonwealth*, August 1925, p. 248. For a time *Commonwealth's* editorial opinion supported this attitude towards the League of Nations, and the editorial notes for October 1926 (p. 298), although welcoming the admission of Germany, attack the League as a body of nations 'living not even on a pagan level, but definitely by the Worship of Mammon'. *Cf.* also Kenyon, *op. cit.*, p. 186, where reference is made to the fear that the League may degenerate into the 'mutual insurance society of cosmopolitan capital'.

[34] N. E. Egerton Swann, 'Christian Internationalism and Economic Realities', an article in the Lambeth Conference issue of the *New Age*, July 3rd, 1930, p. 115.

believe that, in the absence of a common culture and conscious spiritual unity, most people preferred imposed peace to wars and fightings, and although the Group's attitude was undoubtedly well-meaning, its effect was inevitably mischievous.[35]

As the international situation became more serious, the hostility of some Christendom thinkers towards the League began to falter, and at the annual conference of the movement in 1936, on the theme of Catholicism and Internationalism, there was an open split in their ranks. Demant was adamant in his view that the League did not witness to the truth and therefore should not enjoy the support of the Church, but the majority view had by this time changed. Led by Widdrington and Gabriel Gillett, most delegates felt that the League must be accepted by Christians as a real attempt to embody the truth that there is an international order; failure to support it could lead only to cynicism and disillusionment.[36]

The same pattern of impracticable idealism giving way at a late stage to a more realistic acceptance of the dangers of remaining aloof from a difficult situation may be seen in the attitude of the Christendom Group to domestic politics. Its dislike of the existing political parties is seen at its most petulant and irresponsible in two short articles which appeared in *Commonwealth* just before the 1929 general election. The first, by Widdrington, is a lament over the prevailing political apathy, the decline of the Labour Party from its original idealism, and the fact that no party affirms a spiritual criterion for society. The second, by Demant and Reckitt, maintains that it may well be a Christian duty not to vote at all, and it ends on a note of fine conceit; 'In so far as we find ourselves outside politics, as ordinarily understood, we are so because we have thrust ahead of its bewildered armies, and in no sense because we have felt it possible to skulk behind.'[37] Seven

[35] Lord Hugh Cecil had particularly provoked the Christendom Group by maintaining, in a speech to the League of Nations Union Summer School at Oxford in 1927, that the League could seek peace, but not justice; for justice could only be enforced by a sovereign power, and the League had no sovereignty over the internal affairs of member states. This remark was reported in *Commonwealth*, October 1927, p. 290, and used as evidence that the League was 'nakedly conscienceless' and therefore unworthy of Christian support.

[36] *Christendom*, June 1936, pp. 130–3.

[37] *Commonwealth*, April 1929, pp. 97–9.

years later, disillusioned at the outcome of the 1935 general election, Reckitt could still write that 'the problem for most of us is not to restrain ourselves from a too headlong immersion in secular politics, but how to retain any faith in politics at all', yet he goes on in this context to warn against the temptation to contract out of secular issues with a high-minded disdain.[38] It was a lesson which was learnt too late to be of much use.

Mention has already been made of the inherent contradictions in the espousal by the Christendom Group of the Social Credit solution to the economic malaise of the inter-war years. For a time they went unnoticed in a common enthusiasm for the attack on finance in all its sinister manifestations, both real and imaginary,[39] but the split came out into the open at the 1930 summer school, at which the theme of the discussion was 'The Redemption of Industry'. It is important to bear in mind that Social Credit, as expounded by Douglas, involved the full-scale development, exploitation and rationalization of mechanized industry, and looked forward to mass production and mass consumption on an unprecedented scale. Despite the planned increase in effective demand, the Douglas scheme was likely to lead to more and more technological unemployment, but the optimists among the Christian supporters of Social Credit believed that if this tendency were carefully controlled the result could be more leisure for everybody, rather than more unemployment for a minority. A number of Christendom thinkers, led by Widdrington, devoted a good deal of attention to the problems of the coming 'Leisure State', developing the work begun by the Copec commission on

[38] *Christendom*, June 1936, pp. 125–8.

[39] One of the more fanciful Christendom accusations against the tyranny of finance was that it was responsible for the fact 'that the dark revulsion of homosexuality stains the whole of society with perversion' (W. T. Symons, 'The Real Causes of our Present Discontents', in *Christendom*, December 1931, p. 262). This bitter hatred of finance and somewhat exaggerated estimate of its influence was not confined to the Christendom Group, and it is interesting to note a similar attitude in the Roman Catholic artist, Eric Gill. When Gill was invited to undertake a gigantic sculptural frieze in the League of Nations Council Hall at Geneva, he wished it to be of Christ turning out the money-changers, as he felt that the League should be engaged above all in ridding the world of the stranglehold of finance; in this he showed a greater faith than the Christendom Group in the integrity and ability of the League. See Eric Gill, *Autobiography*, pp. 249f.

leisure.[40] There was a certain reluctance to approve the ways in which increased leisure was likely to be spent: Widdrington attacked the entertainment industry as a dangerous social influence, and thought it a matter for regret that 80% of American families owned a car.[41] But such disapproval did not prevent many Christendom thinkers from welcoming in principle the idea of the Leisure State. The real divergence of opinion was not over how people should amuse themselves, but over the more important question of whether Widdrington and those who agreed with him were right in their belief that the Social Credit utopia of leisured affluence was compatible with Christian principles and ideals.

There was a clear division of opinion among Christendom speakers at the 1930 summer school over the Christian attitude towards industrial development and particularly the policy of rationalization, which was being canvassed in some quarters as a remedy for industrial stagnation.[42] The majority, led by Peck and Widdrington, were convinced that an industrial society and an age of plenty were compatible with Christian principles, although Widdrington was careful to distinguish between industrial society, in itself morally neutral, and what he called industrialism—an undesirable attitude fostered by industrial society, and on another occasion he recalled the warning, given originally by Figgis, that an age of leisure and affluence might well prove to be one in which the Church's task would be more difficult than ever.[43] At the summer school, strong opposition to the majority view was voiced by Slesser and Penty. Slesser maintained that the essence of Christianity lay in the transfer of interest from the material to the spiritual sphere, and he was unable to agree with

[40] See four articles by Widdrington on the Leisure State in *Christendom* for March, June, September and December 1931, pp. 42–50, 129–35, 204–12 and 289–98. The inter-relation of the questions of unemployment, leisure and Social Credit is well summed up from the Christendom point of view by W. G. Peck in 'The Church and the Future of Society', the last chapter of his book *The Social Implications of the Oxford Movement*.

[41] *Christendom*, September 1931, p. 210.

[42] See *Commonwealth*, August 1930, pp. 224–9; also Kenyon, *op. cit.*, pp. 88–93.

[43] For an elaboration of this distinction between a civilization predominantly mechanistic, and industrialism as a disease of such a civilization, see P. E. T. Widdrington, 'The Church and Industrialism', in *Stockholm*, Vol. 3, 1930, pp. 219–26. The reference to Figgis is in Widdrington's essay 'Religion and Leisure', in the symposium *Faith that Illuminates*, pp. 81f.

Peck that there must be something theologically wrong with a whole-hearted rejection of God's gift of science and invention.[44] Penty was even more radically opposed to the progressivism of the majority view; he had been invited to read a paper on the subject of industry in a revived Christendom, but found the task impossible, since the ideas of industry and a revival of Christendom were mutually exclusive: 'Industrialism is built upon the denial of everything Christianity stands for. And, if there is any truth in Christianity, the only logical deduction is that a society or system of production that denies Christian truth will be overtaken by disaster.'[45]

Penty was a prolific author, but he was also a thorough-going and very repetitive individualist, and his direct influence on Christian social thought was slight. He was always a determined opponent of Social Credit and all that it stood for, but in other ways, particularly in his admiration of medieval Christendom and his enthusiasm for the simple life, he shared the views of many in the Christendom Group. He was a regular contributor to debates and conferences on Christianity and social problems, and as early as 1915 he and Reckitt had some lively exchanges in the pages of the *Church Socialist* over the relative merits of local and national guilds. Penty was a tireless protagonist of a revival of rural life and craftsmanship, and it is possible that he was partly responsible for encouraging misgivings in the Christendom Group over some of the implications of the Douglas scheme. Although the Group continued to maintain what was basically the Douglas analysis of orthodox financial practice until after the second world war,[46] there was a gradual wavering during the thirties in its enthusiasm for the general ethos of Social Credit. Reckitt attributed this to the

[44] It is significant that Reckitt, Paul Stacy and Egerton Swann had felt it necessary to prepare a report to the C.S.L., defending their enthusiasm for Social Credit against the charge that it was a grossly materialist system and as such unworthy of Christian support. This report, 'Social Credit and Christian Values', is to be found in *Commonwealth*, March 1923, pp. 81–5. It was also published as a pamphlet.

[45] Quoted in *Commonwealth*, August 1930, p. 227.

[46] See *The Life of the Church and the Order of Society*, the report of the Malvern Conference of 1941, at which many of the speakers were members of the Christendom Group; also *Prospect for Christendom* (1945), a collection of essays edited by Reckitt. In neither of these is there any substantial change from the earlier position of the Group on financial and economic matters.

realization that its philosophy of abundance had not necessarily any sociological, let alone spiritual, significance. Penty's influence is perhaps to be seen in his conclusion that: 'To a world suffering from the accumulating devastations of mass production, mass publicity, mass creation, and mass recreation, the addition of mass consumption may seem only likely to make our spiritual confusion more confounded',[47] and one is again reminded of Penty by Reckitt's attack on those who defended Social Credit because it alone would enable modern industry to run at full blast: 'If ever there were a case of putting the cart before the horse, the inanimate before the animate, surely this is it. From a cultural, if not from a realistic standpoint, it is of precisely the same quality as the bankers' contention that men's minds and lives must be subordinated to the rules of "Sound Finance".'[48]

In some ways Penty was more realistic than many of his Christendom colleagues in his awareness of what might actually be achieved in the way of social reform. For example, he seemed to allow that the trade unions might play a part in the general evolution of the guild system,[49] and he was quite happy with private property and the wage system. But these more practical elements in his thought hardly sufficed to counterbalance his many eccentricities and the extraordinarily unrealistic quality of some of his leading ideas. He consoled himself with the belief that industrialism had reached the very limit of its possible expansion, and that its problems and difficulties were in fact the first signs of its inevitable collapse: 'Everything in modern life is congested—our politics, our trade, our professions and cities have one thing in common: they are all congested. There is no elbow-room anywhere, and, as I have said, there can be but one path of escape, and that is backwards.'[50] The use of the vague and emotive word 'congested', and the futile and impractical remedy he suggests, are typical of his most inept writing. He seems genuinely to have believed that it would be possible to destroy

[47] M. B. Reckitt, *As It Happened*, p. 176.

[48] *Ibid.*, pp. 176f.

[49] A. J. Penty, *Post-Industrialism*, Chapter 5. But Penty points out (pp. 84f). that, if his own predictions of the imminent collapse of large-scale industry prove to be well-founded, the natural industrial unit will become something much smaller than the existing trade unions.

[50] A. J. Penty, *Guilds and the Social Crisis*, pp. 25f.

existing machinery, eliminate the sub-division of labour and return to a peasant economy; the social cost of such a policy, if he ever really paused to consider it, he held to be worth the gain.[51] Among the objects of expenditure which Penty considered to be necessary chiefly because of the circumstances of urban life were the relief of the poor and the provision of police, sewerage, hospitals, asylums, baths, wash-houses, road-making and lighting: 'A community organised on an agricultural basis is for the most part free from the need of such expenditure, for when population is distributed there are few of such liabilities.'[52] It was not perhaps surprising that the implied prospect of the ill and unwashed rustic groping his way along a muddy track to his dark, insanitary cottage, unprotected from the assaults of criminals and lunatics, was not one which had a wide appeal,[53] or that Penty's unreasoning hatred of urban and industrial life, combined with his lapses into economic nonsense and his seriously mistaken assessment of the significance of the reception of Roman Law, persuaded most people to write him off as a crank.[54]

[51] There is a damaging criticism on theological grounds of those who, like Penty, advocate opting out of the problems presented by continuing social and industrial development in D. L. Munby, 'Christians and Economic Progress', Appendix A, pp. 181–90, of his *God and the Rich Society*.

[52] A. J. Penty and W. Wright, *Agriculture and the Unemployed*, p. 80.

[53] *Cf.* also an imaginary picture of the ideal distributist state of A.D. 2070, outlined by Gabriel Gillett at the Anglo-Catholic Summer School of 1927, and probably owing a good deal to Penty; this state had been set up after the revolution of 1976, when the ruling coalition of plutocrats, state socialists and scientific experts (the three *bêtes noires* of this school of thought) had been overthrown on the occasion of an attempt to introduce a bill prescribing life imprisonment for any woman giving birth to more than the statutory number of children. (Contraceptives were regarded with almost hysterical hatred by some Christendom thinkers.) Despite this repudiation of birth control, the population was remarkably and most conveniently diminished to fit in with the demands of an agricultural, distributist economy. Most social reform legislation had been repealed and free education had been abolished. In spite of the absence of health inspectors and welfare workers (hated agents of the interfering collectivist state), many children managed to survive. (*Commonwealth*, November 1927, pp. 334–7.)

[54] See A. D. Sokolow, *The Political Theory of Arthur J. Penty*, pp. 103–5 for a summary of press reviews of his books. Penty's hatred of urban and industrial life is exemplified in his fervent admiration for those Russian peasants who, he had been told, 'express their abhorrence of it by crossing themselves three times whenever they speak of the town or the factory' (*Towards a Christian Sociology*, p. 159). For his theory about Roman Law, see specially *Towards a Christian Sociology*, pp. 76–82. Nevertheless, a Pentyesque outlook on life was not uncommon: see, for example, J. B. Priestley, *English Journey*, pp. 63–5, for a disinterested description of it.

It is easy to ridicule the eccentricities of Christendom thought, and to deplore the inelegant and unnecessary jargon in which it is so frequently expounded, but in doing so one is liable to overlook its more serious shortcomings. Ronald Preston, a severe critic of the Group, has attributed its failure to think clearly and intelligently about economic issues to its wrong theology. He claims, with some justification, that the neo-Thomist philosophy of most Christendom thinkers tempted them to make a false assessment of man's ability to reach rational conclusions about a particular, technical aspect of life solely on the basis of religious conviction and common sense; in other words, there was an invalid theological reason for the reluctance of the Christendom thinkers to recognize the autonomy of the social sciences and their own need to enlist the specialized technical advice of experts.[55] Preston also claims, and this seems beyond dispute, that the Christendom estimate of the degree to which the nation could be considered Christian was absurdly optimistic; Reckitt himself describes the task of the Christendom sociologist as being 'to make plain what are the social norms to which a society striving to embody the Christian truth about man must strive to approximate',[56] but, as Preston points out, such a society is purely hypothetical. It would be more useful and realistic to 'work for the next step forward in the light of the possible alternatives open at the time'[57]—to admit, in fact, a measure of relativity in Christian social thought which the Christendom Group did not allow. The Group has also been harshly castigated by D. L. Munby for its failure to learn from expert economists,[58] and no defence of its economic thought can excuse the wretchedly bad judgment which led to the pursuit of the fantasies of Social Credit, or the Group's apparent blindness to the fact that the traditional pattern of British industry could not be maintained indefinitely—a blindness exemplified by

[55] R. Preston, 'The Malvern Conference', in the *Modern Churchman*, April 1942, pp. 15–22; and 'A Century of Anglican Social Thought', in the *Modern Churchman*, March 1943, pp. 346f. Preston has a London degree in economics.

[56] M. B. Reckitt, *Maurice to Temple*, p. 230.

[57] R. Preston, 'A Century of Anglican Social Thought', p. 347.

[58] D. L. Munby, *God and the Rich Society*, p. 158. See also 'The Disordered Economic Thinking of the National Church', a hostile review by Munby of P. Mairet, *The National Church and the Social Order* (which is a cautious apology for the Christendom point of view) in *Theology*, March 1957, pp. 92–9.

Reckitt's continuing reliance as late as 1932 on the state of the basic industries, such as textiles, mining and ship-building, as a barometer of industrial prosperity, and his assumption that any industrial recovery not reflected in these industries must be illusory.[59]

Both the Christendom Group and the Anglo-Catholic movement may also be critized on more general grounds. When C. E. Raven was invited—somewhat surprisingly, in view of his liberal and modernist leanings—to address the 1926 Anglo-Catholic Summer School, he pointed out the tendency towards pharisaism which seemed to be inherent in the Anglo-Catholic attitude towards social questions, and rebuked the Anglo-Catholics for their failure to acknowledge the realities of industrial life. It was futile, he said, to insist on exalted Christian standards in life and work when the fact was that if a workman attempted to maintain such standards he would very often run the risk of dismissal for his failure to co-operate in the petty immoralities commonly practised in so many fields of industry and commerce. Nor was it helpful, in Raven's opinion (and here he included Temple among the guilty), to speak of industry in terms of vocation and expect that the work itself would thereby become any less degrading or soul-destroying.[60] Another weakness of Anglo-Catholicism and the Christendom Group was that they were inevitably to some extent exclusive, and their repeated and explicit emphasis on the Catholic basis of their social thinking ensured that churchmen of other persuasions were deterred from co-operating with them, or providing the stimulation of a different outlook which the Catholic sociologists so badly needed.[61] There were, in fact, signs that they recognized this need, and W. G. Peck acknowledged that the feeble impact of Christian social witness was due to the fact that such witness was not unified. But he believed that, although

[59] M. B. Reckitt, *Faith and Society*, p. 69, note.

[60] *The Social Teaching of the Sacraments, being the Report of the Second Anglo-Catholic Summer School of Sociology, 1926*, edited by M. B. Reckitt, pp. 81–7.

[61] *Cf.* a letter from T. C. Gobat, one of the old guard of the C.S.L., written to G. C. Binyon *à propos* of the 1934 Summer School: 'The Widdrington–Reckitt atmosphere does not attract me much; and if I had known that breezes in other directions were blowing in (Conrad Noel), I should have come.' (quoted in Molly Gobat, *T. C. Gobat, His Life, Work and Teaching*, p. 84.)

ultimate reunion could in theory be brought nearer by means of united social action, in practice it was almost impossible to act without an agreed dogmatic basis.[62] It is true that some exchange of views was possible at the annual summer school, as was shown by Raven's presence in 1926, but the influence of outsiders is hard to discern in the writings of the Catholics. This was no doubt partly because there were not very many outside Christendom and Anglo-Catholic circles who had anything important to say about social questions, but chiefly because these circles had something of the character of a mutual admiration society; the Christendom Group certainly attracted people from all walks of life, but they tended to be people who shared its presuppositions, and the Group failed to make a serious effort to understand and assimilate the ideas of those who did not, whether churchmen, economists, industrialists or trade unionists.

This is a formidable list of criticisms, but there is also a good deal to be said on the other side, particularly in defence of the Christendom Group's reluctance to lean more heavily on the advice of economic experts. Neither Preston nor Munby makes any allowance for the Christendom thinkers on this point, but it was chiefly the manifest inadequacy of the advice of experts, as reflected in the state of the country's economy, and the apparently irreconcilable differences between, for example, Keynesian economics and the traditional Treasury view, which provoked them to look for what they called an autochthonous sociology, including (in the Douglas scheme) an economic policy which was independent of the conflicting schools of expert thought. While it was undeniably foolish of the Group to suppose that it could reject indiscriminately and with equal justification the advice of all the experts, it must be conceded that there were grounds for perplexity and frustration in the face of the economic deadlock of the twenties and thirties. One is also bound to acknowledge that the Christendom thinkers applied themselves to their task with the best of intentions, and spared no energy in their attempt to revitalize Christian social thought. Moreover, in claiming Christian support for a particular economic policy—albeit a

[62] See the L.K.G. notes which Peck contributed to *Commonwealth*, October 1928, pp. 319f.

stupid one—they were at least doing more than most Christians in the inter-war years; their insistence on the need to recover in some form the medieval principle of the just price, their desire to see property more evenly distributed and responsibility for work more fairly shared, and their concern that there should be some improvement in the status of the wage-earner, were all marks of an authentically Christian passion for social righteousness.[63] Above all, perhaps, the Christendom Group deserved credit for its understanding that social problems demanded sustained and concerted thought, and that it was a Christian duty to try to meet that demand.

The basis of the Christendom search for a relevant Christian sociology was described by Demant in the *New Age* on the occasion of the 1930 Lambeth Conference. He rejected the common preoccupation of the Church with narrowly moral issues, for 'religion is as much concerned with truth as with goodness',[64] and affirmed the duty of the Church not only to challenge the economic and financial assumptions responsible for the paradox of poverty amidst plenty, but also to point the way to truthful and valid assumptions with which to replace them: 'You cannot moralize a contradiction. But if you are ignorant that a social situation involves contradictory policies you will be looking for wrong ethical *motives* to account for the disasters—and you will mistake for these the moral perversions and poisoned relationships that spring from the strains imposed by the social dilemma.'[64] One can only regret that the rejection of one error should have been accompanied by the enthusiastic acceptance of another.

[63] A good example of the valiant efforts which were made, mostly by Christendom writers, to adapt an important principle of medieval Christendom to modern conditions was *The Just Price*, a collection of essays produced for a Christian Social Council conference in 1929 and edited by Demant. As in many other cases, the value of the work was much reduced by the fact that the essayists were arguing towards a preconceived solution—Social Credit.

[64] V. A. Demant, 'Religion and Economics', in the *New Age*, July 1930, p. 112.

7
Some Practical Issues

HOUSING

It can be claimed with some justification that the outstanding social disgrace of this century has been the country's failure to provide adequate housing for the whole population. There is perhaps no other matter in which those who do not themselves suffer contrive so successfully to remain indifferent to the plight of those who do, and the inter-war years were no exception to this dismal rule. The disastrous results of the abandonment of the Addison housing scheme in the economy campaign of 1921 were never undone, and it was only during the thirties that any substantial progress began to be made with slum clearance. Yet this was a matter in which the witness of the Church of England to the need for urgent and far-reaching reform was clear, knowledgeable and relentless; the speeches and writings above all of C. F. Garbett, as Bishop successively of Southwark and Winchester, are among the most moving and impressive signs of Anglican social concern between the wars.

It is true that house-building during the twenties was on an unprecedented scale, as Garbett himself conceded in the Lords,[1] but it always fell far short of the need, and in particular there was no sustained attempt to provide new or properly reconditioned housing at rents within the means of the poorest classes. The 1924 Housing Act, introduced by John Wheatley, Minister of Health in the first Labour administration, came nearest to meeting this need with its offer of a substantial subsidy for houses built to let, but the subsidy was reduced by the Conservative government in 1927, with a promise of further reductions in 1929, and the lack of confidence which this created prevented any long-term planning

[1] By 1932 one million nine hundred thousand new houses had been built since the war. This figure was quoted by Garbett in a debate in the Lords on November 24th, 1932. H.L. Deb., Vol. 86, Col. 50.

by local authorities. It also provided support for the building trade unions' opposition to any dilution of the existing skilled labour force, since they were understandably reluctant to open their ranks without a government guarantee that housing work would be available for a considerable time.[2]

Housing subsidies were variable and complicated, and the less conscientious local authorities were easily dissuaded from making the best use of them, but even so it was true that the provision of new houses was a more attractive proposition than slum clearance, and up to 1930 only eleven thousand slum houses had been replaced.[3] More progress was made under the Slum Clearance Act of 1930, the work of the second Labour Minister of Health, Arthur Greenwood, which increased the subsidy and linked it to the number of people rehoused, an important provision to ensure that large families and the many victims of overcrowding had a fair chance of being rehoused. This was a great step forward, as was Greenwood's encouragement of differential rents, by which the subsidy was used for the benefit of those who needed it most. But the Act was neither generous enough nor rigorously enough enforced to overcome the vested interests which opposed slum clearance, and although private enterprise quickly took advantage of the low interest rates and building costs which followed the slump in 1933, progress by local authorities continued to be very slow.[4]

Housing was frequently debated in Convocation and the Church Assembly, and in most cases the speeches were well informed and the debates of a high standard. In the House of Lords Garbett, who was acknowledged as the Church's most expert spokesman on housing, together with Lang, Winnington-Ingram and Temple, kept the Church's interest and concern in the problem constantly before the government.[5] There was little disagreement about the reforms which were necessary; the problem was always to arouse

[2] Garbett had emphasized the need for a long-term programme, to overcome the suspicions of the unions, as early as April 25th, 1923. H.L. Deb., Vol. 53, Col. 893.

[3] Marion Bowley, *Housing and the State*, p. 135.

[4] For a full account, see M. Bowley, *op. cit.*, pp. 45–54 and 135–68.

[5] See especially the *Chronicle of Convocation*, 1930, pp. 70–86; 1933, pp. 343–63. Also H.L. Deb., Vols. 53, 62, 69, 71, 75, 76, 78, 86, 87, 90, and a letter from Garbett which appeared in *The Times* on December 16th, 1933.

public opinion to the point at which the government was forced to act, and in an attempt to achieve this the Archbishops issued a joint appeal in 1933 on the occasion of the centenary of the beginning of the Oxford Movement, calling on all members of the Church of England to join in a campaign for the abolition of the slums and the provision of decent housing for everybody. In connection with the appeal Garbett was invited to write a pamphlet describing the housing problem and possible ways of dealing with it, and this probably made a greater impact than the appeal itself, written as it was with skill and restraint by a man who was known to be a master of the subject.[6] The only discordant note was struck by Hensley Henson, who was provoked by the archiepiscopal suggestion that the clergy should bring the appeal before their congregations to write to Garbett in characteristic style: 'The clergy are not likely to resent any encouragement to abandon their difficult duty of teaching religion for the far easier and pleasanter employment of declaiming against social conditions. As the most part of them have very slight knowledge of economics, and all of them are quite irresponsible, they will welcome the opportunity of "talking large", and warming themselves and their hearers with the inexpensive fervours of impracticable rhetoric.'[7]

Garbett pointed out in the pamphlet that slums and overcrowding are not necessarily found together, but both are caused by a scarcity of housing at low enough rents; moreover, any house which is seriously overcrowded tends to deteriorate quickly into a slum. When he wrote there were in England and Wales ninety-eight thousand families of five or more people living in one or two rooms, and of these 2,086 were families of six or more living in one room. Such overcrowding was usually found in houses which had some or all of the characteristics of a slum—decay, damp, lack of light and air, inadequate sanitation, vermin.[8] The

[6] C. F. Garbett, *The Challenge of the Slums*, a pamphlet published by S.P.C.K. in 1933.

[7] Quoted in C. H. E. Smyth, *Cyril Forster Garbett*, p. 221.

[8] Speaking in the Church Assembly on February 1st, 1932, Winnington-Ingram referred to an exhibition organized by the Housing Associations in London, at which were displayed (whether alive or dead is not recorded) 'the actual rats which had come out of sewers in Stepney and had been found sitting by babies' cradles' (*Report of Proceedings*, 1932, p. 8.)

results of living in such conditions were ill-health, wasted education, sexual immorality, the ruin of family life, social resentment, jealousy and violence, although Garbett also added an appreciation of the friendliness, generosity and self-sacrifice of many slum-dwellers, and emphasized the dangers and difficulties of rehousing them in new areas: apart from the problem of social readjustment, new housing estates were usually further from the place of work and rents were higher than those which the slum-dwellers had been paying; the additional cost of travel and rent was in many cases more than people could afford.[9] This question of cost, as it affected the poorest classes, was one to which Garbett made frequent reference. Speaking in Convocation in 1930 he pointed out that the lowest rent at which an unsubsidized, private enterprise, three-bedroom house could be let was eleven shillings a week; in many places, including London, the cost would be more. The average slum rent was seven shillings a week, and there was an urgent need for five hundred thousand houses to let at not more than seven shillings, with a further million at not more than eleven shillings.[10] To overcome this problem, he suggested the adoption of a system of rent differentials.[11]

Turning in his pamphlet to the question of what the Church could do, Garbett made five suggestions. First, individual Christians who owned property or shares in a property company should see that their landlords' responsibilities were scrupulously fulfilled. In this connection it was often true that the worst landlords were not large property-owners; George Orwell, in *The Road to Wigan Pier*, admitted this with some reluctance: 'Ideally, the worst type of slum landlord is a fat, wicked man, preferably a bishop, who is drawing an immense income from extortionate rents. Actually, it is a poor old woman who has invested her life's savings in three slum houses, inhabits one of them and tries to live on the rent of the other two—never, in

[9] A notorious instance of the ill-effects of rehousing slum-dwellers in new estates, which Garbett quotes (*op. cit.*, pp. 18f.), is described in the report of the Medical Officer of Health of Stockton-on-Tees for 1927: families who had moved from slums to new estates showed a higher deathrate and 50% more illness in their new surroundings, because higher expenditure on rents and travelling meant that less money was available for food.

[10] The *Chronicle of Convocation*, 1930, pp. 74f.

[11] H.L. Deb., 1930, Vol. 76, Cols. 686–8.

consequence, having any money for repairs.'[12] Fears were expressed in the *Torch* that the boom in private house-building, which was so notable a feature of the economic recovery of the 1930s, would create a large number of small landlords, and that they in turn would be likely to create new slums.[13]

Secondly, Garbett called on the Ecclesiastical Commissioners to pursue more vigorously the building of working-class flats. Contrary to frequent rumour, and to criticism which was openly voiced even in the Church Assembly, the Commissioners were in fact good landlords, and they had to their credit large numbers of working-class flats in Wandsworth, Westminster, Walworth, Vauxhall and Maida Vale, some to let at rents as low as five shillings and sixpence a week. An independent survey, which was subsequently commissioned by the Church Union and published in 1937, pointed out that the cases in which their property was not adequately maintained were the result of the property being out of their direct control on a long lease, and efforts to persuade the lessees to fulfil their responsibilities were often unsuccessful. The only valid criticism which could be levelled at the housing policy of the Ecclesiastical Commissioners was perhaps of the readiness with which they acquiesced in this legal impasse; it was only after an acrimonious debate in the Church Assembly in 1938 that the Archbishop of Canterbury was asked to appoint a committee to investigate ways in which notorious leasehold property might be dealt with.[14]

Garbett's third practical point was that Christian congregations could see that local authorities made the best use of subsidies, and of their powers to deal with defaulting landlords. He then called on Christians to support Public Utility Societies, by giving money or lending it at a low rate of interest. Garbett was not alone in urging more vigorous voluntary effort of this kind; the Social and Industrial Commission of the Church Assembly commended this course in 1925, and in 1928 sponsored the formation of the Under-Forty Club to further this work. The Copec movement gave birth to the

[12] *Op. cit.*, p. 57. The same point was recognized by Charles Jenkinson, a great Christian housing reformer whose work is described below. See H. J. Hammerton, *This Turbulent Priest*, p. 60.

[13] The *Torch*, January 1934, p. 5.

[14] *Report of Proceedings*, 1938, pp. 164–90.

Birmingham Copec House Improvement Society, and in 1924 Church Army Housing was formed to work on the same lines. The most famous example of Christian involvement in voluntary housing work, that of Basil Jellicoe at St. Pancras, is described below.[15]

Finally, Garbett urged support for a National Housing Corporation, to plan and co-ordinate house-building on a large scale and provide capital, backed by a government guarantee, at a specially low rate of interest.

Much was said and written about housing, but this was a sphere in which practical action was also possible. The housing problem was one with which the clergy were face to face in their parochial work, whether urban or rural, but it was the priests in slum areas of cities who were most vividly aware of the need to tackle it. G. C. Ommanney, Vicar of the slum parish of St. Matthew's, Sheffield, from 1882 until 1936, was typical of these, fighting a largely unsuccessful battle with the city authorities, who were in Sheffield even more complacent than usual. On one occasion he made representations to them about the state of the drains: 'It was the way in which things were done in Sheffield and therefore it was all right, was the argument with which I was met.'[16] An unexpected difficulty which Ommanney and many others met with was the sullen acquiescence of the slum-dwellers in their living conditions: 'The people are too contented, and if we could get a little more "divine discontent" into them there would be changes.'[17]

When Basil Jellicoe was appointed missioner at the Magdalen College Mission in Somers Town, St. Pancras, he found housing conditions at least as bad as those described by Ommanney, and the same inertia on the part both of the local authority and of the slum-dwellers. In December 1921, he decided to devote himself

[15] The structure and functioning of Public Utility Societies, as the voluntary associations were called, is described in T. Speake, *The Housing of the Poor*, 1928, to which the Bishop of Lichfield (Kempthorne) contributed an introduction.

[16] *Ommanney of Sheffield, Memoirs of G. C. Ommanney*, edited by F. G. Belton, p. 57.

[17] *Ibid.*, p. 56. *Cf.* part of a statement by a deputation of Leeds clergy to the city council in 1931: 'It is sometimes said that slum conditions create revolution; but to many of us the more terrible fact is that people learn to acquiesce in these sad conditions.' (Quoted in H. J. Hammerton, *op. cit.*, p. 74.)

to an effort to clear away the worst of the slums and replace them by decent housing at a rent which the existing tenants could afford to pay. His biographer emphasizes that he was not moved solely by a desire for social reform, but also by his conviction that the housing in Somers Town was 'essentially a blasphemy against God, a fearful mockery, a recrucifixion of Christ'.[18] He always saw his housing work as first and foremost that of a priest, and emphasized the Christian inspiration behind it. The St. Pancras House Improvement Society was founded in 1924, and a national publicity campaign was launched; Lord Robert Cecil and Neville Chamberlain wrote to *The Times* and John Galsworthy to the *Observer*, urging public support for the Society, and by the end of 1926 its original capital of two hundred and fifty pounds had grown to forty-two thousand. The Society's work was to recondition, or more often replace, the worst houses in Somers Town. Most of these were fairly substantial, originally built for middle-class owners, but by 1920 badly deteriorated and seriously overcrowded. It was a strict and creditable principle of the Society that everybody should be rehoused in the same area, maintaining valuable social continuity, and this meant that flats rather than houses had to be provided. Jellicoe claimed that the work was conducted strictly as a business undertaking, and until 1953 all the building was in fact done with invested capital, albeit loan stock paying only 3%.[19]

The advantages of a voluntary housing scheme, as opposed to one undertaken by the local authority, were considerable. Not only were the tenants rehoused in the same area, which involved the provision—very unusual in municipal housing of the twenties and thirties—of accommodation specially designed for large families and old people, but the whole scheme was managed on the lines pioneered by Octavia Hill, with housing managers in personal contact with the tenants, and ready to provide help and advice whenever necessary. This system greatly reduced the

[18] Kenneth Ingram, *Basil Jellicoe*, p. 35. Most of the information about Jellicoe's work is taken from this source.

[19] John Gowing, *Forever Building; A Short History of the St. Pancras Housing Society, 1924–54*, p. 11. The interest rate was reduced after the last war to 2½%. Gifts of money were used for propaganda or for the provision of supplementary social services.

difficulty of what was known as 'decanting'—the temporary removal of slum tenants to other property while their own was being reconditioned or replaced. The reluctance of tenants to move, misled and disillusioned as they had often been by unscrupulous landlords, was a considerable hindrance to the work of many local authorities. The St. Pancras Society was able to set high standards in both accommodation and management, in the hope that local authorities might be encouraged to follow suit. But under Jellicoe's direction it did even more than that; it provided many other services for its tenants—a nursery school, a savings club, a furniture shop and, most controversial, a public house, for Jellicoe was convinced that the right kind of pub, designed consciously as a social centre, was a vital part of the life of any community.

Despite these advantages, however, and despite the fact that the work of the Society not only continued to expand in St. Pancras but also inspired the formation of similar societies in many other towns and cities, it remained true that voluntary effort could only scratch the surface of the housing problem.[20] It seems likely that voluntary schemes made a considerable impact on public opinion, and thus indirectly on the work of local authorities, but it was only in this accidental way that Jellicoe himself made any contribution to the long-term political solution of the national housing problem. A very different approach was that of Charles Jenkinson, who was appointed Vicar of St. John's, Holbeck, Leeds, in 1927, and who was well aware of the fact that the housing problem could be solved only by quick and vigorous municipal action.[21] Leeds contained seventy-two thousand back-to-back houses, of which thirty-three thousand, in continuous rows of seventy or more to the acre, were much too bad to be worth reconditioning, and Jenkinson saw that the only way in which he could contribute to the solution of a problem of such magnitude was by entering the political life of the city. He was

[20] Garbett paid frequent tribute to the voluntary societies, but was careful to put their work in perspective. Speaking in Convocation in 1933, he pointed out that, of the one million nine hundred thousand new houses built between 1919 and 1932, only thirty thousand were the work of public utility societies. (The *Chronicle of Convocation*, 1933, p. 349.)

[21] The account of Jenkinson's work is taken from his biography, H. J. Hammerton, *op. cit.*

elected to the city council in 1930, and when his housing proposals were rejected as too ambitious by the Conservative majority, he printed twenty thousand copies of the speech he had made; the resulting pressure of public opinion in his favour secured a partial reversal of the council's decision. In 1933 control of the council passed to Labour, and Jenkinson became chairman of the housing committee. He was convinced of the need for a really imaginative housing programme, and replaced the original proposal, prepared on the basis of the 1930 Greenwood Act, to replace two thousand houses in five years, with a plan to replace thirty thousand houses in six years, rehousing a hundred and ten thousand people at a cost to the city of twelve million pounds and to the government, making full use of available subsidies, of ten million. Such a scheme would not only provide urgently needed housing, but also make possible proper overall planning, employ a large labour force, and greatly reduce expenditure on the welfare services which had to be provided as a direct result of bad housing conditions. Jenkinson was in some ways ruthless, riding roughshod over opposition and even over the genuine hardships of those who would suffer as a result of his plans, but it was vital to complete the scheme before the withdrawal of the Greenwood subsidy, and to have it so far advanced that possible defeat at the next election could not prevent its completion. This great rehousing scheme in Leeds, completed in 1939, was one of the most remarkable results of Christian social concern between the wars. If it seemed to some that Jenkinson's neglect of his parish work in favour of the housing project was curious behaviour for a priest of the Church of England, the fact that his parishioners asked the bishop not to accept his resignation of the living of St. John's—tendered because he realized that his pastoral work was suffering—was a vindication of Jenkinson's conviction that he could best fulfil his calling by carrying through his plan to rehouse the slum-dwellers of Leeds.

A vital part of Jenkinson's scheme was the introduction of differential rents, so that the subsidy was used strictly according to the needs of each family. The amount which a family needed to spend on food, calculated on the basis of information provided by the B.M.A., was deducted from its total income, and the rent assessed in the light of what remained. In some cases the full economic rent would be payable, in others none at all. By this system, decent housing could be brought within reach of all wage-earners—an arrangement which seemed to Jenkinson logical and necessary, but one which nevertheless raised what was in effect a moral issue. Any system of rent differentials involved a means test, and although it was generally accepted that this was the only way of sharing limited resources among people whose needs varied widely, it was a method which met with some opposition on allegedly Christian grounds. There was also similar opposition, for the same reasons, to the principle of family allowances, which seemed to many to be not only a fair one, but the only possible way of providing an adequate standard of living for the members of large families out of the existing national income.[22] The Christian opposition came from a small group of Christendom thinkers, who regarded any form of means test as an intolerable invasion of the individual's privacy, an unworthy abandonment of the principle of the living wage for all in favour of what was found to be expedient, and yet another move in the unwelcome direction of the enslaving mechanism of state doles, patronage and dependence, of alleviation by subsidy rather than emancipation by property.[23]

The wholesale condemnation of means tests was, however, unusual, and it was only a few Christians who found the principle morally objectionable. But differential rents and the methods used by voluntary housing societies also raised a not unrelated economic question: was it in the long run desirable or prudent to provide subsidized housing, either by means of artificially low costs made possible by charitable investment at a low rate of interest, or by means of allowances against the normal rent? Might it not have been better for Christian social reformers to

[22] See Eleanor Rathbone, *The Disinherited Family* (1924). She argued that there was no chance at that time of providing for all workers a minimum wage which would be high enough to constitute a living wage even for the largest families. It is perhaps significant that in France, Germany, Belgium and Holland, where family allowance systems were in force, it was the Christian trade unions which supported the principle, while the Socialist unions opposed it. (See J. H. Richardson, 'The Family Allowance System', in the *Economic Journal*, September 1924, p. 384.)

[23] See, e.g. M. B. Reckitt, 'Family Endowment or Family Enslavement', in *Commonwealth*, June 1927, pp. 172–4.

concentrate on a campaign for higher wages, out of which the economic rent could be paid? This was not the same issue as family allowances, since it might still have been necessary to provide for the feeding and clothing of children, but was more concerned with the economic health of the building industry. A speaker at the 1930 C.S.C. conference on the Ethics of Interest and Investment, J. H. Higginson, attacked philanthropic investment at 2% or 3% in charitable housing projects, on the ground that the long-term results of such investment would be the permanent diversion of private-enterprise building away from the provision of working-class housing, and an end to the hope that the building industry would ever be able to cater economically for the majority of the working population.[24] The respective advantages of high wages and subsidized services were not fully worked out on this occasion, but a more thorough treatment of the problem is alluded to in *Commonwealth* for January–February 1931. This was an article by Keynes in the *Political Quarterly*,[25] which argued that although many of the traditional economic objections to high wages were discredited, in particular the wages fund theory, there was still some justification in the circumstances of 1930 for restraint in wage claims. The campaign for high wages as the means of achieving a decent standard of living put up production costs and thus tended to drive money out of the country; the Treasury's reaction to this was to increase the bank rate, partly to attract short-term investment in Britain, but partly also because 'the bank rate, in its internal aspect, is essentially a means of ensuring that there shall be enough unemployment to put effective pressure on wages so as to cause them to fall to a level which is in equilibrium with external conditions'[26]—a slow, wasteful and painful process, and one which had been partly responsible for the chronic industrial stagnation of the twenties. Keynes therefore considered it inexpedient to attempt to improve the working-man's lot by campaigning for higher wages, since this would inevitably reduce the reward of capital below what was obtainable in other countries. To squeeze the capitalist in the act of earning

[24] *Commonwealth*, April 1930, pp. 111f.
[25] The *Political Quarterly*, Vol. I, 1930, pp. 110–24.
[26] *Ibid.*, p. 116.

Housing conditions—a slum family in Bethnal Green, 1923

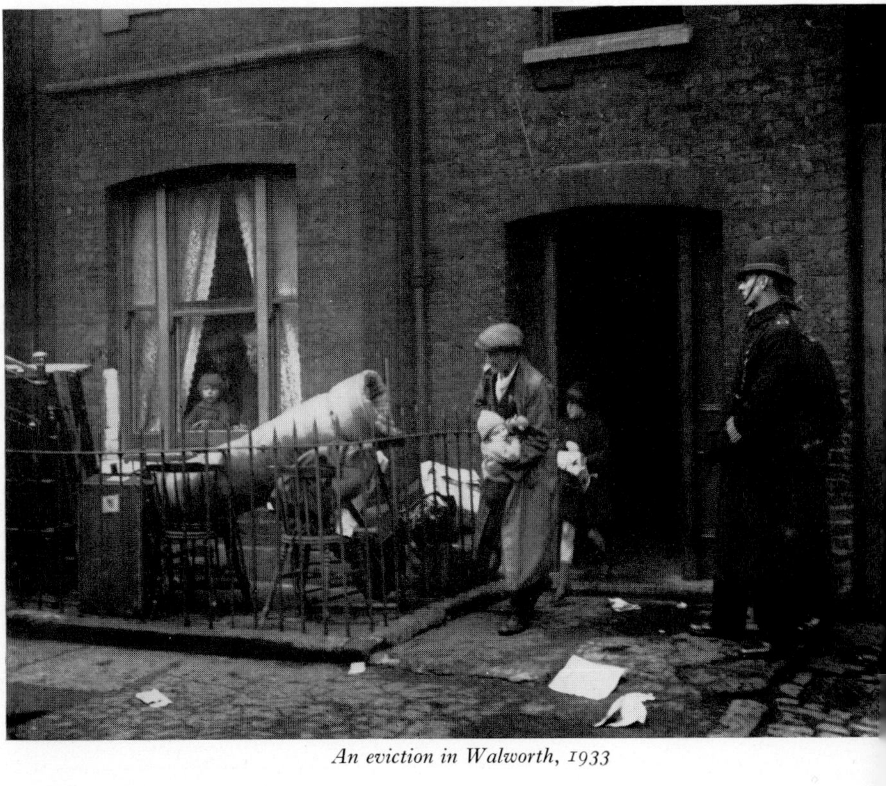

An eviction in Walworth, 1933

his profits was to squeeze him in the wrong place. But that did not mean that he could not be squeezed at all: 'We must not starve the goose that lays the golden eggs before we have discovered how to replace her. We must tax her eggs instead.'[27] Keynes went on to deal with the ways in which higher taxation should be used for the benefit of society as a whole, and these significantly included family allowances and subsidized housing—a convincing economic vindication of the efforts of Christian social reformers in these two directions. It was to the credit of the editor of *Commonwealth*, G. W. Wardman, that he singled out Keynes's point of view for commendation, particularly since it was at variance with the long-standing opposition of the Christendom Group and the L.K.G.—so often expressed in the pages of *Commonwealth*—to any state provision of welfare services.[28]

UNEMPLOYMENT

The most dangerous and demoralizing result of the economic policies of successive governments in the twenties and thirties was the chronic unemployment problem.[29] The plight of the unemployed provoked much Christian sympathy and a good deal of practical action, but Christian social thinkers cannot be said to have contributed much to the long-term solution of the problem. In 1931 Demant's research committee submitted to the Christian Social Council *This Unemployment, Disaster or Opportunity? An Argument in Economic Philosophy*. This conscientious and ingenious piece of work reviews the history of the events leading up to the prevailing economic crisis and the various measures suggested to deal with it, but, based as it is on the usual economic fallacies underlying Christendom Group expositions of the

[27] *Ibid.*, p. 120.

[28] For hostility to state welfare services, see, e.g., *Commonwealth* for April 1930, pp. 113–16. With the inauguration of *Christendom* in 1931, there was no longer any pressure on *Commonwealth* to provide a platform for the views of the Christendom Group, and its comment on social and economic issues became notably more open-minded.

[29] There were never less than a million unemployed during the twenties, and the depression which began in 1929 caused the figure to rise sharply to a maximum of 2·95 m. in January, 1933. Recovery from this point was slow, and the January unemployment figures for successive years were: 1934, 2·4 m.; 1935, 2·29; 1936, 2·13; 1937, 1·67. (*Board of Trade Statistical Abstract for the United Kingdom*, 1939, p. 132.)

supposed shortcomings of the existing financial and industrial system, and relying on the principles of Social Credit, it is of little intrinsic value. Unemployment was an urgent and desperate problem, moral and spiritual no less than material, and the fact that the ostensible Christian experts could do no better than this as their contribution to its solution was one of the saddest results of their misguided economic theories.

The unemployment problem could be solved only, if at all, by political action, and it was the failure of the second Labour government to find a solution, coupled with the financial implications of its continued reliance on the heavily overdrawn unemployment insurance fund, which was largely responsible for its ignominious fall in the summer of 1931.[30] It is interesting to note that even in this wretched affair, the one Cabinet minister who made any creditable effort to persuade his colleagues to pursue an intelligent policy to deal with unemployment was George Lansbury, an avowed churchman who made no secret of the Christian inspiration behind his political work.[31] A letter from Lansbury, published in *The Times* on October 11th, 1932, just over a year after the National government had taken office, also reflected the good sense of his views on economics; as well as calling for Christian leadership in a campaign of prayer and action to overcome the poverty and demoralization of the unemployed, Lansbury put his finger on the need for stimulation of the economy, for more consumption rather than more thrift. Lansbury's call for a reversal of the government's continued policy of economic restraint was supported on October 17th by a letter from six distinguished economists, including Keynes and Stamp, but his observations on the Christian duty to the unemployed produced a mixed response. On October 14th, there was a letter from W. J. A. Price, Vicar of Holy Trinity, Birkenhead, which denied Lansbury's

[30] Writing in the *Socialist Christian* (the journal of the Society of Socialist Christians) in September 1931, R. W. Sorensen described the Labour government's fall as 'a revelation of the callous blackmail that can be exercised by the priests of the Golden Calf', and ridiculed a statement by the Bishop of Peterborough (C. M. Blagden), who had expressed the hope that the new economy measures, including reduced unemployment allowances, could, if accepted 'without squealing', act as 'a wholesome discipline and medicine of the soul' (Quoted, *op. cit.*, p. 57.)

[31] Raymond Postgate, *The Life of George Lansbury*, pp. 252–9.

allegations of poverty and hunger: 'The facts are that no one is starving and no one is destitute. . . . I must protest against the sacred name of Our Lord being dragged into Mr. Lansbury's travesty of the facts.' Hensley Henson, in what Reckitt described as 'the familiar spectacle of the Bishop of Durham wringing his hands in a paroxysm of spiritual impotence',[32] pointed out the confusion behind Lansbury's letter: 'The world needs, not sentimental rhetoric, albeit expressed in religious language, but sound knowledge, courageous statesmanship, honest and patient administration, and above all, a generous public spirit which will accept large sacrifices of private interest in the cause of the community.'[33] The relatively conciliatory, and even socialistic, tone of this is unmistakable, and it accords with the significant change in Henson's attitude towards the problem of unemployment which is reflected in his *Retrospect*; in 1930 he had been urged by many of the clergy in his diocese to launch an appeal on behalf of the unemployed, in particular to provide shoes and clothing for the children, but he had declined to do so, believing that his better judgment was here in conflict with his natural sympathies. But two years later he had changed his mind, and a letter from him appeared in *The Times* on December 13th, 1932, describing the most pressing needs of the unemployed and their families.[34]

Taking the country as a whole, there was undoubtedly a good deal of hardship among the unemployed. In the euphemistically styled 'special areas'[35] the trouble was that poverty was so widespread and persistent that the morale of the people was gradually worn down; it was impossible to replace clothing or household equipment out of unemployment benefit, or to pay for the entertainments and excursions which might have helped to make the boredom and monotony of idleness more bearable. In other areas,

[32] *Christendom*, December 1932, p. 244.

[33] *The Times*, October 13th, 1932.

[34] H. Hensley Henson, *Retrospect of an Unimportant Life*, Vol. II, pp. 398f. Nearly five thousand pounds was contributed in response to his appeal.

[35] The 'special areas', where unemployment was highest, were those where most of the heavy industries—traditionally the backbone of the British economy—and industries depending largely on the export market were to be found, i.e. South Wales, Lancashire, north-east England and south-west Scotland. Maximum unemployment figures in the worst-hit industries were: coal 41% (1932); cotton 44% (1930); ship-building 63% (1932). (Quoted in E. Lipson, *The Growth of English Society*, p. 426.)

the chief difficulty was often the humiliation experienced by those who were unemployed among a population still largely at work; the one advantage of being unemployed in a 'special area' was that there were so many obviously able-bodied, capable and conscientious men out of work that no special stigma attached to the fact.[36] A good deal was done by voluntary effort to soften the hardships of unemployment, and the lead in such work was in many cases taken locally by church congregations. Occupational centres, clubs and social activities were provided, and special help was also given to supplement the exiguous unemployment benefit.[37] Hardship was particularly severe after economy cuts in the benefit rates were imposed by the National government in 1931, and the uncovenanted benefit—the notorious dole—which had since 1921 been payable to all those whose entitlement to unemployment insurance benefit had run out, was made dependent on a searching means test, which often resulted in the humiliating experience of parents having to be supported by the earnings of their children. Responsibility for conducting the much-resented inquisition into the family circumstances of each applicant was placed on the local Public Assistance Committees, which administered the vestiges of the old Poor Law—a fact not calculated to endear them to the unemployed. However fair and reasonable it was in principle, the system of means tests was bitterly resented in practice, partly because it was harshly and unsympathetically conducted in some places, and partly because the rates payable by P.A.C.s varied widely, some making no allowance for rent and others paying what was, over a considerable period, just too little to make ends meet.[38]

Conservative, Labour and National governments all seemed to be more interested in finding the most economical way of main-

[36] See George Orwell, *op. cit.*, pp. 85–90. Walter Greenwood's novel *Love on the Dole* is also a penetrating account of the demoralizing effect of long-term unemployment.

[37] For details of some of the clubs and centres provided for the unemployed see the annual reports of the I.C.F., the *Torch*, March, June, July, 1932; *Men Without Work* (a report to the Pilgrim Trust), pp. 298–377. H. Jennings, *Brynmawr*, describes a more ambitious project financed by the Society of Friends.

[38] See especially *Memoirs of the Unemployed*, edited by H. L. Beales and R. S. Lambert; Fenner Brockway, *Hungry England*; John Newsom, *Out of the Pit*.

taining the unemployed than in providing them with work, and the longer unemployment lasted, the more serious were the results of this policy. The long-term effects of unemployment were particularly damaging for young people who had never had a job, and consequently had never become used to regular work. The dangers of protracted unemployment and the particular difficulties of juveniles were themes to which Garbett repeatedly came back in his speeches in the Lords and in Convocation: 'Unemployment is the factory of the unemployable. Most of that class who are the despair of social reformers—the men who cannot work—come from those periods of unemployment between the ages of fourteen and eighteen. They have lost the discipline of school. They have not the help of their home. They have not the discipline of work.'[39] To reduce the evil effects of juvenile unemployment, he called for the registration of all between the ages of fourteen and sixteen (when they were not covered by any form of compulsory insurance), and obligatory attendance at unemployment centres, which should come under the Minister of Education rather than the Minister of Labour, and should take the place of the continuation schools envisaged by the Fisher Education Act of 1918, but never in fact established.[40]

Not all churchmen shared Garbett's wise and well-informed approach to the unemployment problem, as was shown by A. C. Headlam, Bishop of Gloucester, in a speech in Convocation on January 19th, 1930. He denounced the campaign to maintain wages at what he regarded as an artificially high level, and attributed much of the blame for its popularity to the work of the I.C.F., an organization whose utterances he seldom read 'without thinking of the enormous amount of harm it was capable of doing'.[41] He then expounded the wages fund theory in its crudest

[39] H.L. Deb., Vol. 60, Col. 574.

[40] *Ibid.*, cols 571–8. See also H.L. Deb., Vols. 66, 69 and 86, and the *Chronicle of Convocation*, 1933, pp. 122–6. Garbett had long been interested in the problem of unemployment, and had been elected to the library committee of the Oxford Union—the first step towards the presidential chair on which he had set his heart—on the strength of his speech on November 26th, 1896, opposing the motion: 'That, in the opinion of this House, the problem of the unemployed is really the problem of the Unemployable.' (Quoted in C. H. E. Smyth, *Cyril Forster Garbett*, pp. 46f.)

[41] The *Chronicle of Convocation*, 1933, p. 129.

form, and called for the abolition of unemployment insurance and the halving of taxation. This was an exceptional display of economic ignorance, for which Headlam was immediately rebuked by Lang, but it was nevertheless true that there was a good deal of genuine perplexity and misunderstanding about the facts of unemployment, as was clearly shown by the Interim Report on Unemployment of the Church Assembly Social and Industrial Commission, C.A. 484, commissioned in 1932, published in 1935, and debated in the Assembly on February 6th and 7th, 1935. The contention of the report that the unemployment problem indicates 'some fundamental defect or disorder in the present social and economic system'[42] is in line with the Fifth Report, and its recommendations for short-term action, including an increase in Public Assistance benefits, raising of the school-leaving age to fifteen, and the provision of more occupational centres and allotments, are unremarkable. It was the final section, consisting of three different theories of the best long-term solution, which proved controversial, particularly since a good deal more space is devoted to the third possibility, that of Social Credit, than to the other two, the Conservative and Socialist solutions.

The proponents of the third view (Widdrington and Reckitt were members of the Commission) point out that the advocates of the first two theories 'confessedly desire no fundamental change in the financial system', although the Socialist solution would involve 'drastic and far-reaching changes in its control'.[43] Neither the name Social Credit, nor that of Major Douglas, appears in the Report, but there can be no doubt that this is the inspiration behind the conclusion of the third view that 'a true economic objective cannot be pursued by means of the present money economy and its present methods of administration by the banking system'.[43] In conclusion, the report calls for a government commission to study this third theory, with the important qualification that none of its members should be 'persons who have a controlling interest in the present financial system',[44] a reflection of the widespread suspicion of the advocates of Social Credit that their ideas had never been seriously and sympathetically examined, and that the universal condemnation of Social Credit by orthodox

[42] C.A. 484, p. 3. [43] *Ibid.*, p. 10. [44] *Ibid.*, p. 11.

economists was a sinister example of vested interests seeking to stifle new and creative thinking.

One member of the Commission, J. H. Higginson, issued a memorandum of dissent, in which he rejected this call for a further examination of Social Credit, pointing out that Major Douglas had been heard at great length and with exemplary patience by the Macmillan Committee of 1931. Higginson also ridiculed the idea of an amateur inquiry into a highly technical subject, and singled out the need to restore business confidence and stimulate the investment of idle capital as the key to a solution of the unemployment problem.[45]

The debate on this Report showed how the level of the Church Assembly's treatment of social issues was slowly rising. Against a background of bewilderment and confusion, there were clear signs of a new thoughtfulness and compassion, and even Lord Hugh Cecil, who criticized the Report at some length, spoke in gentler and more measured terms than might have been expected. The most discordant note was struck by the Bishop of Jarrow, J. G. Gordon, who expressed the view that the clergy were 'not to be concerned with making society fit for men, but with making man fit for society', a particularly unhappy opinion in view of the desperate plight of Jarrow itself, and one which was not unexpectedly seized upon with some relish by a contributor to *Christendom*.[46] The wording of the resolution finally passed by the Church Assembly was significantly watered down; in its original form it urged Christians to demand that 'financial, industrial and economic policy be so reconstructed as to express more adequately the moral and religious principles which are the only sure foundations of social order', but this was amended to avoid the clear implication that such reconstruction was in fact required.[47]

The Church Assembly frequently returned to social issues during the thirties, usually in connection with the underlying problem of unemployment, and speeches were often of a high standard. In 1934, in a debate on the destitute poor, Prebendary W. F. H. Randolph struck a modern note in his claim that the

[45] *Ibid.*, pp. 18–23.
[46] *Report of Proceedings*, 1935, p. 71; *Christendom*, March 1935, p. 11.
[47] *Ibid.*, 1935, pp. 63–111.

work of dealing with poverty must be done by the State, but that it was the duty of the Church to see that the work was well done. A resolution was passed maintaining that 'individual attempts to deal with the homeless poor are inadvisable, and that no relief should normally be given except through the medium of some corporate agency of a public or charitable nature',[48] a point which had been urged on the Assembly by the Church Army in view of the difficulties created by indiscriminate charity. This was a sensible policy, but by no means new; it was no more than had been taught more than thirty years previously by Canon Barnett.

Another important Church Assembly debate was initiated by P. T. R. Kirk in November 1936, on the effect of long-term unemployment in the distressed areas—'islands of depression and hopelessness amid the rising tide of prosperity'. Kirk asked that the government should be urged to give more power to the Commissioners for the Special Areas, referring to local unemployment figures still as high as 80% in some areas of Durham, Cumberland and South Wales, and to the recent resignation of Sir Malcolm Stewart, the Commissioner for England and Wales, who had despaired of being able to achieve any real improvement while working within the limitations imposed by the Treasury. The Assembly passed Kirk's resolution with only minor changes, after a debate which was notable for a far-sighted speech by H. Shaw, a Tyneside delegate, who called for a regional planning scheme for the whole North East, and a system of Board of Trade licences for all new factories which would make possible some measure of direction of industry to the Special Areas.[49] This debate and resolution may have added weight to the resignation of Sir Malcolm Stewart, and to the march of two hundred men from Jarrow to London with which it coincided. At all events, the Special Areas (Amendment) Act was passed in 1937, offering remission of rates, rent and income tax for up to five years for any firm which was established in the Special Areas.[50]

One of the most serious effects of long-term unemployment was

[48] *Report of Proceedings*, 1934, pp. 330 and 337.
[49] *Ibid.*, 1936, pp. 570–94.
[50] C. L. Mowat, *op. cit.*, p. 466. The government's refusal to meet an all-party deputation of the Jarrow marchers was bitterly attacked in *Christendom*, December 1936, p. 250.

the slow but unmistakable spread of malnutrition, especially among mothers and children, and the I.C.F. in particular was active in collecting evidence of this problem and bringing it before the public. In 1934 it produced a memorandum, *Unemployment and the Subsistence Level*, on the basis of research carried out in London, Manchester and Sheffield, showing that unemployment assistance for large families in particular fell well below the B.M.A. minimum-needs standards.[51] The 1931 cuts in benefit were in fact restored in the 1934 budget, but the problem remained and became more serious as unemployment dragged on in the Special Areas, and its victims were increasingly tempted to spend some of their meagre resources on anything which would relieve the soul-destroying boredom of idleness, rather than on dull but wholesome food. As soon as recovery began in earnest, with the re-armament drive of the mid-thirties, the cost of living began to rise, in 1937 by as much as 9%, and this aggravated the problem for those on a fixed rate of benefit. This particular development was noticed by a number of Christian writers,[52] and lay behind an I.C.F. pamphlet published in 1938, *The Fact of Malnutrition*. Commenting on this pamphlet, a writer in *Christendom* showed how it raised again the problem which had lingered on ever since the principle of 'less eligibility'—now known as the wage-stop—had been enunciated by the Poor Law of 1834, that of the very low wage-level of some manual workers, above which the U.A.B. scale of benefit was not allowed to rise. It was pointed out that some system of family allowances was the only way at present open for overcoming this problem of low wages.[53]

The Church Assembly debated the problem of the malnutrition of mothers and children in 1938, and Kirk moved a resolution couched in provocatively precise and political terms, calling for increased Unemployment Assistance and Insurance allowances for children, free milk and school dinners, and cheap milk for nursing and expectant mothers. This debate revealed the Assembly in unsympathetic and reactionary mood, and despite some sensible speeches in favour of family allowances rather than relief in kind,

[51] The *Torch*, March 1934, pp. 40f.
[52] *Ibid.*, January 1938, pp. 1–3; The *Socialist Christian*, December 1937, p. 88.
[53] *Christendom*, September 1938, pp. 170f.

a feeble, generalized and complacent amendment was carried in place of Kirk's resolution.[54]

In all attempts at dealing with unemployment and its attendant evils, the lack of reliable and authoritative facts was a constant hindrance to action, and could be used as an excuse by those who were disinclined to contemplate drastic measures. It was much to the credit of the Church, and particularly of Temple, who took the initiative, that this lack was largely met by a very thorough survey of unemployment which was carried out for the Pilgrim Trust, at the expense of the trustees.[55] The research began in 1933, when unemployment was at its worst, and although the results of the survey were not published until 1938, by which time it was too late to make much use of its conclusions and recommendations, it still constitutes an invaluable study of long-term unemployment in all its aspects. The report ended by expressing the hope that the work done by voluntary agencies for the unemployed might become the foundation for a new system in which men could find opportunities to develop new interests and new friendships, and despite social changes since the last war, which have reduced the need and scope for such a system, the ideals sketched out in the report have to some extent been realized in new forms of adult education and leisure activities.

EDUCATION

The foundation in 1811 of the National Society for the Education of the Poor in the Principles of the Established Church was one of the most important events in the history of popular education in Britain, and it marked the beginning of a period during which the Church of England established something approaching a monopoly of educational work among all but the wealthiest classes. Even after the establishment by the State of School Boards from 1870 onwards, the Church continued to play an important part in education under what was known as the Dual System, an arrangement by which the Church Schools maintained their independent status as 'non-provided' schools alongside those run

[54] *Report of Proceedings*, 1938, pp. 547–52.

[55] *Men without Work: A Report made to the Pilgrim Trust*, with an introduction by the Archbishop of York (Temple) and a Preface by Lord Macmillan.

by the State. From 1902 onwards the non-provided schools began to receive financial assistance from the local authorities, and the educational concern of the Church of England during the inter-war years was largely focused upon the delicate and continually evolving relationship between Church, State and local authority in the sphere of education. There was of course a constant interest among many Christians in all aspects of educational theory and practice, as was shown by the Copec report on education, and by the writings in particular of R. H. Tawney, but the debates of Convocation and Church Assembly, although often devoted to educational matters, were primarily concerned with the narrower question of the Church–State relationship, and with the provision of religious instruction in State schools.

The Education Act of 1918, the work of H. A. L. Fisher as President of the Board of Education, was among the most ambitious of the government's essays in post-war development. Many of its best proposals in fact came to nothing, smothered by the same wave of economy measures as saw the abandonment of the Addison housing scheme, and the part-time continuation schools proposed under the Act for all children between fourteen and sixteen were in most cases never established. The Fisher Act opened up important new possibilities in the sphere of religious instruction, and offered new terms to the Church of England for a revision of the existing Dual System. Fisher's proposals in fact amounted to a virtual abolition of the System, but on terms which were not unfavourable to the interests represented by the Church. They envisaged unity of administration, with Church schools transferred to the Local Education Authorities, but the retention of diversity of type—the diversity consisting partly in the fact that children in the former Church schools would still enjoy the right of denominational instruction on two days a week. The concessions on the part of the State were that there should be proper theological training for all student teachers in State colleges who did not wish to contract out on grounds of conscience and, most important of all, that there should be universal religious instruction in all State schools on the basis of an agreed syllabus. This was a significant development, and one which might have been expected to win over even the most zealous defenders of the

Church's stake in education, particularly as the concession of universal religious instruction was certain to become more and more valuable with the extension of secondary education, a development in which the Church, for financial reasons, could not hope to play more than a very small part.

In a debate in the Lower House of Canterbury Convocation in May 1919,[56] it was clear that Church opinion was open to the possibility of abandoning the Dual System on the terms offered by Fisher, and a number of speakers gave the impression that they did not believe the system could survive the far-reaching plans for reorganization which were at that time expected to be implemented without delay. The commonest fear was that children who had been enjoying denominational instruction might be denied it under the reorganization scheme, and the so-called Cowper-Temple clause,[57] by which no denominational instruction was allowed in a State school, came under attack. When the Upper House debated the same subject, Gore, in one of his last Convocation speeches as Bishop of Oxford, exposed the vagueness of the hopes expressed in the Lower House that children might not in fact lose their right to denominational teaching when they were transferred at the age of eleven to central, provided schools, and he emphasized the enormous expense which would be involved if the Church were to attempt to set up its own non-provided secondary schools.[58]

The crux of the matter throughout the inter-war years was the disagreement within the Church about the acceptability of agreed syllabuses, which carried on the Cowper-Temple principle of non-denominational instruction. The particular difficulty over secondary education was not pressing, as no significant steps were taken to reorganize the schools until further impetus was given to the movement by the work of C. P. Trevelyan, Minister of Education in the first Labour government of 1924. At his instigation a consultative committee was set up under Sir Henry Hadow, and produced a report which recommended that the school-leaving age should be raised from fourteen to fifteen, that

[56] The *Chronicle of Convocation*, 1919, pp. 279–98.

[57] Section 14 of the Education Act of 1870. W. F. Cowper-Temple was a leading Broad Churchman.

[58] The *Chronicle of Convocation*, 1919, pp. 377–85.

the break between primary and secondary education should be established for all children at the age of eleven, and that new types of secondary school—the technical and the modern—should be created for those children for whom the grammar school curriculum would not be suitable.

In the early post-war years it looked as though the case for the abolition of the Dual System would win the day. The first report of the Education Committee of the newly established Church Assembly (N.A. 52) welcomed the proposals of the Fisher Act, and recommended the handing-over of Church schools on certain conditions, which were held to have been met in Fisher's own exposition of the Act. These conditions included provision for the withdrawal of children from State schools to receive denominational instruction if this was desired by the parents.[59] In an important debate in the Assembly in February 1922, most speakers favoured acceptance of this Report, although some expressed misgivings about losing the distinctive atmosphere of a Church school, and the right of entry enjoyed by parish clergy.[60] Davidson, in an influential speech, referred to significant changes in the climate of opinion on the question of religious instruction; he claimed that there was a greater recognition of the need to provide religious instruction and to see that it was given by fully qualified teachers, that there was a more sympathetic understanding of what the Church of England had been trying to achieve—an education that was religious through and through—and that there was a greater readiness on all sides to hammer out a new, efficient, unified educational system.[61] There was some sense of urgency in the debate, and Hensley Henson spoke of national goodwill towards the Church as a wasting asset; it was important to accept the favourable terms offered by the Fisher proposals while they were still open, since money could not be found to maintain independent Church schools at all levels under the reorganized system.[62]

It is both curious and regrettable that this sense of urgency,

[59] The right of withdrawal for denominational instruction was provided by the Anson by-law, but acceptance of this was not obligatory for all local authorities until it was made so by the 1936 Education Act.

[60] *Report of Proceedings*, 1922, pp. 45–78.

[61] *Ibid.*, pp. 72f.

[62] *Ibid.*, pp. 76–8.

and the impetus for change which was so clearly present in the early twenties, should have given way to an increasingly narrow preoccupation with the retention of a diminishing number of Church schools under the Dual System. The failure to carry through large-scale reorganization was of course the government's fault, prompted by the worsening economic situation, and Christian comment on the economies in educational expenditure under the Geddes axe has been mentioned in an earlier chapter, but it is nevertheless true that enthusiasm for change quickly evaporated in Church circles; the case for maintaining the Dual System became increasingly popular in subsequent discussion of the education question. A speaker in Canterbury Convocation in 1928, for example, referred to the inadequacy of any form of non-denominational religious instruction, proudly pointed to the fact that the Church of England had raised one million pounds in three years for its own schools, called for this level of giving to be maintained, and complained that co-operation with L.E.A.s might be interpreted as acquiescence in anything that the State was prepared to offer.[63]

There was a fairly clear division of opinion on this matter according to churchmanship. The *Socialist Christian*, representing the left wing of Christian social concern, complained in July 1929 that Catholics, both Roman and Anglican, were too much concerned with 'definite religious teaching' in schools,[64] and a memorandum published in the same periodical ten years later, outlining a policy for Education in the Socialist Christian State, came down unhesitatingly against denominational instruction. All education would be 'religious' in its respect for the individual, for the growth and development of the children in a co-operative society, and in its emphasis on their training in social behaviour. The Bible would be studied as literature and history, but denominational teaching must remain the private concern of parents or Church organizations.[65]

The proposals of the Hadow Report of 1926, which involved greater reorganization than that envisaged by the Fisher Act,

[63] The *Chronicle of Convocation*, 1928, pp. 216f.
[64] The *Socialist Christian*, July 1929, p. 152.
[65] *Ibid.*, January 1939, pp. 85f.

re-opened the vexed question of Church participation in secondary education. The abandonment of the Dual System was by this time no longer a serious possibility, and the Church was faced with a difficult choice, between abandoning its stake in secondary education altogether, or raising a great deal of money to establish its own secondary schools. Most dioceses in fact tried to maintain a foothold in the secondary sphere, although this was inevitably a very much smaller share than that which the Church still enjoyed in primary education. The aspect of the reorganization scheme which excited most Christian interest, however, was the proposal to raise the school-leaving age to fifteen, particularly as it was felt that an extra year at school would help to reduce the level of juvenile unemployment. There was repeated and widespread criticism of the government's failure to implement this proposal, and a motion calling for action was passed in the Church Assembly in 1934, with the support of Lang and Temple. The speeches were not all on one side, in fact, and there was strong feeling against the raising of the school-leaving age, with Lord Hugh Cecil not unexpectedly leading the opposition.[66]

The following year, 1935, saw the publication of *The Next Five Years, an Essay in Political Agreement*, signed by 152 public figures (including, from the Church of England, Temple, Raven, Lewis Donaldson and F. R. Barry), and this repeated the criticism of the government's slowness in putting the Hadow proposals into effect. By March, 1934, only 53% of pupils over eleven were in reorganized schools, and even these were not enjoying the full benefit of reorganization, which could be felt only when the school-leaving age was raised.[67]

The increasingly unfavourable effect on the Church of the reorganization schemes prompted a reconsideration in 1934 of the original Fisher terms for abolishing the Dual System. Canon J. J. Davies, speaking in the Church Assembly, asked that these proposals should be commended to the newly reconstituted National Society, now known as the Central Church Council for Religious Education. It is by no means certain that the Ministry of Education would still have been prepared to offer the same

[66] *Report of Proceedings*, 1934, pp. 399–409 and 467–80.
[67] *The Next Five Years*, pp. 192–7.

terms for a concordat, and although the motion was passed, nothing came of it. There was notably more opposition to the idea than when it had first been discussed in the Assembly, and the Bishop of Pontefract in particular (C. R. Hone) urged the Church to maintain and strengthen its position by investing in more of its own secondary schools.[68] The Dual System received further support from the Education Bill of 1936, by which the government offered grants to assist in the provision of Church secondary schools, and it is significant that when this new offer was debated in the Church Assembly in February 1936, nobody raised any objection on the grounds that the Dual System would thereby gain a further lease of life. There was one further attempt to move towards its abolition, instigated by Hensley Henson in November 1936; he took his usual gloomy view of the future of Church schools, and again spoke in favour of making the best possible terms with the State, but although Lang supported his long-term ideal of a unified State system with adequate provision for religious instruction, the feeling of the debate was that this was a utopian ideal.[69]

Thus it was that when war broke out in 1939 there was still a measure of uncertainty and confusion over the future of Church schools, and the provision of religious instruction in State schools. It was unsatisfactory that, after the failure of the Fisher proposals, the way was not prepared in the inter-war years for a better solution to these problems than that offered by the Education Act of 1944.

BIRTH CONTROL

Charles Gore's dislike and disapproval of artificial contraceptives has already been noticed, and it was typical of many of the older generation of Christians between the wars. This attitude was often largely intuitive, based on aesthetic rather than on logical or ethical grounds, but there was one factor of great importance in the debate on birth control, whose significance and influence is not easy to comprehend in a world overshadowed by the problem of the population explosion. This was the declining

[68] *Report of Proceedings*, 1934, pp. 536–41.
[69] *Ibid.*, 1936, pp. 463–90.

Unemployment: the Jarrow marchers near Bedford, October 26th, 1936

Unemployment: a poor relief soup kitchen

birthrate in Britain and most of the developed countries of the world; the decay of Western civilization, even to the point of its extinction by the rapidly growing numbers of black, brown and yellow men, was widely foretold. There were many who saw more enthusiastic procreation as a Christian duty, and many more for whom the declining birthrate was a good argument against the use of contraceptives, which were in any case most popular among the better educated and more talented sections of the community, those whose offspring were most urgently needed to uphold the fabric of civilization. An example of the seriousness with which this decline in the population was treated was provided by a debate in the Lower House of York Convocation in June 1938; the Reverend W. E. Kemp, moving a resolution welcoming a parliamentary private member's bill, the Contraceptives (Regulation) Bill, made much of the declining birthrate, and showed that if fertility and mortality remained constant the population of Britain would be no more than thirty-seven million in 1970, and twenty-eight million in the year 2000. If the decline in fertility continued, the results would be even more disastrous.[70]

Opposition to the use of contraceptives was not, however, based solely, or even primarily, on considerations of national well-being; this was a factor which provided added impetus for a campaign which found its inspiration elsewhere. The issues were clearly defined and expressed, and the debate about birth control is more than usually easy to follow. It is possible to trace a clear movement of opinion during the inter-war years, with the anti-contraception lobby steadily losing ground; this trend can be seen most obviously in the differences between the pronouncements of the 1920 and 1930 Lambeth Conferences on this matter.

In 1920 the committee appointed to consider problems of marriage and sexual morality observed that there was 'sad evidence at the present time of a widespread lowering of moral conditions', namely an increase in the number of illegitimate births, despite a lower total birthrate; more divorces; and the widespread incidence of venereal disease.[71] In discussing the question of contraception the committee acknowledges its incompetence to deal with medical

[70] *York Journal of Convocation*, 1938, pp. 131–6.
[71] *The Lambeth Conferences, 1867–1948*, p. 100.

considerations, and recognizes that 'the physical union of husband and wife has a sacramental value by which is expressed and strengthened the love that the one ought to have for the other', but goes on to urge 'the paramount importance of deliberate and thoughtful self-control', and ends with an 'earnest warning against the use of any unnatural means by which conception is frustrated'. This advice is clear and unambiguous, but the report does admit the existence of a considerable weight of responsible opinion on the other side; the reasons put forward in favour of the rigorist position are that the moral and religious issues should be given more importance than medical, financial and social factors (it is assumed, although without explicit theological support, that morals and religion tend towards the repudiation of contraceptives) and that, despite the need to control the problem of venereal disease, 'the distribution, or use before exposure to infection, of so-called prophylactics . . . cannot but be regarded as an invitation to vice'.[72]

The report of the committee appointed by the 1930 Lambeth Conference to discuss the life and witness of the Christian community includes an important and sensitive discussion of the matter of birth control. It describes the declining birthrate in the civilized world as one of the most urgent and perplexing problems of the day, and attributes this decline largely to the use of contraceptives. There is a passing reference to the strong tradition in the 'Catholic Church' (this may be a deliberately ambiguous usage) that all preventive methods are unlawful for a Christian; this is in any event a misleading over-simplification, but although the weight of the traditional testimony is acknowledged, the committee is unable to accept that it is necessarily final.[73] There are, it claims, circumstances in which it is necessary to limit the size of a family; in particular, 'it can never be right for intercourse to take place which might lead to conception, where a birth would involve grave danger to the health, even to the life, of the mother, or would inflict upon the child to be born a life of suffering; or where the mother would be prematurely exhausted, and additional children would render her incapable of carrying out her duties to the existing family'.[74] It is allowed that circumstances of income,

[72] *The Lambeth Conferences*, 1867–1948, pp. 102f.
[73] *Ibid.*, p. 199. [74] *Ibid.*, p. 200.

housing and education may also be relevant, but these need careful scrutiny, and pleasure or self-indulgence should not be the motive for determining to limit or refuse parenthood.

The 1930 Lambeth Report shows important changes, both in letter and spirit, from that of 1920, and the new wording was flexible enough to allow of a good variety of interpretation, particularly as the birthrate and population figures increased rapidly after the second world war. But the Lambeth Reports, although representing clearly the movement of opinion which took place in the Church of England between the wars, leave a good deal to be desired, both in terms of theological and philosophical justification for the conclusions reached, and in so far as they do not expound, side by side, the opposing points of view. This latter task is at least attempted in the Copec report of 1924, *The Relation of the Sexes*. Here there are three distinct attitudes towards contraception, clearly summarized and juxtaposed. The first is the rigorist position, held by those who believe that the question is closed. The use of contraceptives means, on this view, that the spiritual side of sex is overshadowed by the material, and 'the whole relation suffers degradation'. Analogies with the use of anaesthetics or spectacles, as a rightful part of man's encroaching control over nature, are rejected as invalid. 'Better the strain and effort of abstinence and the sublimation of the instinct to high purposes . . . than any debasing of the supreme expression of married love.'[75]

The second point of view regards contraceptives in much the same way as drugs: there may be exceptional cases in which their use is justified, but habitual resort to them is bound to have undesirable results. 'The moral fibre of the nation must be lowered by the elimination of self-control from the most intimate mutual experience of human life', quite apart from the temptation offered by contraceptives to indulge in sexual intercourse outside marriage.[76]

The third approach to the question of contraception starts from the conviction that physical acts cannot be judged apart from their motive, and maintains that the 'splendour of parenthood', which is acknowledged to be the primary end of marriage,

[75] *The Relation of the Sexes*, p. 156. [76] *Ibid.*, pp. 157f.

'can best be secured if parenthood is made a responsible act, instead of a casual and often undesired consequence of union'.[77] In a reference to the reputedly evil effects of repression or enforced abstinence from sexual activity, those who hold this third point of view are in complete disagreement with the rigorists, and are happy to accept the use of contraceptives as part of man's progress in the subjugation to his will of the processes of nature.

The Copec report thus provides an unusual opportunity to compare the differing Christian points of view on the use of contraceptives. The one matter in which all the committee members seem to have been agreed was the undesirability of advertising contraceptives and making them too readily available: 'The Christian rule of chastity makes it impossible for us to acquiesce in the doctrine that personal behaviour, even if it has no directly anti-social effects and runs no risk of detection, lies outside the scope of society's powers of interference.'[78]

There were, of course, other shades of Christian opinion on this matter besides the three expounded in the Copec report. Not unexpectedly there was a distinctive Christendom Group point of view, explained by Reginald Tribe in *The Christian Social Tradition.* This reveals a characteristic and admirable grasp of the living conditions of the poorer classes, and sees that large families are an important cause of abject poverty, but Tribe is not thereby tempted to recommend the use of contraceptives; the answer is to be found not in limiting the size of families, but in some form of family wage, deducted from the earnings of all workers, but distributed according to need, and also—more important in the long run—in a 'solution of our financial impasse'.[79] The precise nature of the impasse is not spelt out, but it is clear that we are here on familiar Christendom Group ground; Tribe makes a typically extravagant claim that there is enough potential wealth to support families of six or eight children, even at middle-class levels of comfort, if only the stranglehold of orthodox finance could be broken. With such an optimistic assessment of the world's productive capacity, there remains no need for contraceptives, and their use is condemned on 'pragmatic and social grounds'.

[77] *The Relation of the Sexes*, p. 158. [78] *Ibid.*, p. 162.
[79] R. Tribe, *The Christian Social Tradition*, p. 243.

Contraconception (*sic*) 'implies the exploitation of the emotional life without the complementary demand that comes to parents from the duties entailed upon them by children. It may thus easily lead to the oversexing of those who employ such means.'[80] A further objection to contraceptives is alleged to be that their long-continued use may lead to sterility on the part of the woman, although no evidence is adduced in support of this belief.

It may be that Tribe, with his fear of oversexing, was the type of Christian thinker whom Kenneth Ingram had in mind in his book *The Modern Attitude to the Sex Problem.* Ingram, who favours the judicious use of contraceptives, criticizes much Christian opposition to birth control as springing from an unhealthy sexual outlook: 'The conventional religious approach to sexual problems is itself much too sexual.'[81] He is, however, acutely aware of the possible dangers inherent in the use of contraceptives, in particular the fact that the relative certainty of avoiding conception may provide an excuse for a husband to make excessive sexual demands on his wife, and encourage sexual exploitation which is at present inhibited by fear of the consequences. Ingram also concedes that contraceptives may foster promiscuity, and minister to the selfishness of those who frivolously reject the responsibilities of parenthood, but these dangers do not in his opinion justify the rigorist point of view.

RACE RELATIONS

The question of race relations is another sphere in which it is important not to overlook the great changes which have taken place within the last thirty years. References to racial matters in the speeches and writings of influential Christian leaders between the wars were often astonishingly different in tone from what would be taken for granted in the sixties as an enlightened and moral point of view. Indeed, the occasional, unguarded references to racial matters which are to be found in the Christian social literature of the inter-war years are of particular importance for a proper understanding of the climate of Christian opinion, since they go far to counterbalance the impression given by the definitive

[80] *Ibid.*, p. 241.
[81] K. Ingram, *The Modern Attitude to the Sex Problem*, p. 89.

study of the subject, J. H. Oldham's *Christianity and the Race Problem.*[82] This is a sensitive and compassionate book, and ranks alongside the most distinguished work of Tawney, Garbett and Temple as an example of enlightened and expert Christian social thought, but it is clear from many other sources that Oldham's ideas were by no means the common equipment of all his Christian contemporaries.

There was a widespread sense of the need for much research and more facts on which to base a Christian racial policy, and a feeling that there was plenty of time before the racial problem was likely to become an urgent one. Sir Josiah Stamp and Charles Raven were in somewhat improbable agreement at least on this point, and there is a noticeably theoretical and unrealistic air about their remarks. Stamp claimed in *Christianity and Economics*, written in 1939, that Christian doctrine could give 'no lead upon general immigration and racial problems', and had 'no clear message upon problems of population, or even self-determination of racial groups'. He attacked Christian utopianism on such matters—'the vision of a world state and pure internationalism, but little guidance in an interim ethic, pending that distant or millennial day',[83] and a few years earlier he had made the unquestioning assumption that mixed marriages were regarded with a repugnance which had a sound biological basis, and was 'not due to a low standard of Christian tolerance or brotherhood'.[84] Raven's plea was for biological research to discover whether mixed marriages in fact have a eugenic or dysgenic effect, and whether there is 'any biological justification for the widespread psychic revulsion against members of other races which produces the colour bar'.[85]

If either Stamp or Raven had consulted Oldham's book, he would have found a great deal of the material for which he was hopefully looking. Written in 1924, when Oldham was Secretary of the International Missionary Council, *Christianity and the*

[82] Joseph Houldsworth Oldham (b. 1874); Secretary of the International Missionary Council, 1921–38; Chairman of the Research Commission of the Universal Christian Council for Life and Work, 1934–8.

[83] J. Stamp, *Christianity and Economics*, p. 190.

[84] J. Stamp, *Motive and Method in a Christian Order*, p. 44.

[85] C. E. Raven, *Is War Obsolete?*, 1934, p. 174.

Race Problem examines every aspect of the matter with commendable thoroughness and impartiality, although even Oldham is willing to accept uncritically the attitude that one would not wish one's daughter to marry a black man.[86] He begins his study with a survey of some of the sources of racial antagonism, and admits the need for more knowledge of the facts behind racial problems. But he points out the limitations of the scientific method in this sphere, since concepts of morality, generosity and sympathy have an important part to play, and social and psychological factors may easily invalidate apparently impartial attempts to compare white and coloured races in terms of natural endowment. Intelligence tests which show American negroes to be less able than whites, and reveal an arrest in negro development at adolescence, take no account of the social and educational factors which are involved.[87] Oldham, like Tawney in another context, acknowledges that absolute equality is an altogether unrealistic ideal to pursue; there are great differences between the races in experience and attainment, and the only practicable working principle is that all men 'are entitled to have their point of view taken into consideration and their claims fairly judged in relation to the common good.'[88] This is perhaps surprisingly cautious, but Oldham is a thoroughgoing realist. He refuses to abandon the belief that colonial rule may be necessary in order to protect backward peoples, despite the hypocrisy with which this argument is frequently used to cover exploitation. Similarly, the right of a nation to restrict immigration in order to protect its own living standards must be observed, and migratory pressures controlled by reciprocal arrangements for immigration quotas.[89]

Oldham sees that social equality among the races, within a framework of complete integration, is the Christian ideal, but he accepts the difficulty of achieving this in countries where white and coloured races are both present in large numbers, or where one racial group feels threatened in some way by another. There is cautious approval of racial segregation as a short-term means of maintaining harmony, but if two races share in a common economic or political life, integration must eventually come, and

[86] J. H. Oldham, *Christianity and the Race Problem*, pp. 159f.
[87] *Ibid.*, pp. 73f. [88] *Ibid.*, p. 92. [89] *Ibid.*, pp. 126–44.

it is a distinctively Christian duty to further this process.[90] Oldham sees political equality between the races as another fertile ground for hypocrisy, and subjects South Africa to some harsh criticism in this respect. One of Oldham's particular concerns, both in this book and elsewhere, was to discredit the arguments used at various times by General Smuts to defend white supremacy.[91]

In a long and unusually far-sighted chapter on population, Oldham sees that Malthus's devil, thought to have been laid to rest in the nineteenth century, now stalks the world again, despite the low birthrate in European countries. Although this problem is not directly relevant to the racial issue, and Oldham claims rather surprisingly that the white races are—taking the world as a whole—multiplying at least as fast as any other, he mentions it as one which cannot be solved without a disciplined and compassionate sharing of the world's resources which transcends racial barriers. This is in fact the way in which Christianity can most usefully help to resolve all racial problems; it 'gives a way out of the circle in which we are confined by our prejudices and dislikes. It widens, and so transforms, the issue by bringing in God.' Christian insights, concludes Oldham, need to be reinforced by more research, developed by more discussion on the lines of Copec, and implemented in a new sense of missionary responsibility.[92]

In May 1935, an anonymous article in the now obviously ailing periodical *Commonwealth* suggested emigration as a solution to the problem of unemployment, but in terms which made it relevant to the racial issue. Describing the colonies as Britain's safety valve, the writer urges the population of these areas with Anglo-Saxons, if only to prevent their occupation by a preponderance of aliens, for that 'would be the first unmistakable indication of our decay as a nation. Furthermore, we must provide that our colonies become populated by an overwhelming proportion of Anglo-Saxons in order to ensure the continuance of a clean and virile race.'[93]

[90] J. H. Oldham, *Christianity and the Race Problem*, pp. 170–5.
[91] *Ibid.*, p. 188. See also Oldham's *White and Black in Africa: a Critical Examination of the Rhodes Lectures of General Smuts* (1930).
[92] *Christianity and the Race Problem*, pp. 223f.
[93] *Commonwealth*, May 1935, p. 181.

This was an unusually candid expression of a point of view which the Bishops had singled out at the 1930 Lambeth Conference as 'the greatest single obstacle to racial understanding and co-operation . . . the so-called "superiority complex" of the dominant races, and especially of the Anglo-Saxon'.[94] The report of the Lambeth sub-committee on racial matters affirms the Christian doctrine of the spiritual unity of all men, and although the difficulties caused by economic pressures are acknowledged, they cannot obscure the Christian duty to build on this spiritual unity, in an attitude of respect and reverence for the individuality of men of all races, and with a proper understanding of the principle of interdependence.[95] This report provided a basis for Conference resolutions condemning racial discrimination and affirming that the colonial principle of trusteeship must lead on to partnership.[96]

It can thus be claimed that Christian standards in the matter of race relations were upheld in both individual and official pronouncements, although with a significant number of dissentient voices. The potentially explosive nature of the racial problem was understood by very few, and its significance on the international scene was overshadowed by the many political problems of the inter-war years, particularly those which affected the League of Nations.

FOREIGN AFFAIRS AND THE LEAGUE

The unhappy beginnings of the League of Nations have already been mentioned in an earlier chapter, and in general the record of its achievements continued to be disappointing. Throughout the twenties international relations were bedevilled by three major problems—reparations, disarmament and security. The economic and political consequences of the reparations clauses of the Treaty of Versailles continued to prevent the restoration of normal diplomatic and trade relations between the Allies and Germany; the failure of the Allies, and especially of France, to disarm was a breach of the promise made to the German delegation at Versailles; and no agreement was reached on the question of how security could be guaranteed, whether by a League police force or other-

[94] *The Lambeth Conferences, 1867–1948*, p. 204.
[95] *Ibid.*, pp. 204f. [96] *Ibid.*, p. 167.

wise, in such a way that there could be no danger in large-scale allied disarmament. Prejudices were at times in damaging conflict, with simultaneous opposition from old-fashioned nationalists to disarmament, and from pacifist idealists to the idea of an international security force. But there was a brief period when the League seemed to be on the brink of real success, and this moment of optimism coincided with the 1930 Lambeth Conference.

While the Bishops failed, to the disappointment of many Christian social thinkers, to add to what they had said in 1920 about social and industrial matters, they did devote a good deal of attention to international affairs, appointing sub-committees on Race and on Peace and War. The report of the latter shows very clearly the optimism which was widely felt about the League of Nations at the time, gratefully welcoming the Kellogg Pact of 1928, by which fifty-eight signatories had renounced war as an instrument of national policy and undertaken never to settle differences with other powers except by pacific means. Moreover, fifty-two of the signatories had also signed the so-called Optional Clause, by which they agreed to submit any dispute likely to lead to a rupture of international relations to the Court of International Justice.[97] The report speaks of nationalism, the grievances of minority groups, mutual suspicion and economic competition as the principal causes of war, but sees ground for hope in the many factors making for peace: the League itself, whose principles the Archbishop of Canterbury had himself claimed to be in accord with the Spirit of Christ;[98] the League of Nations Union; the World Alliance, which by 1930 had national councils in thirty-one countries; and the Continuation Committee of the Stockholm Conference, which furthered international co-operation in its discussion of social welfare. The report calls for Christian support for disarmament, which it sees as the acid test of the sincerity of a nation's allegiance to the Kellogg Pact. On the question of the

[97] *The Lambeth Conferences, 1867–1948*, p. 206. The report does not mention the fatal weakness of the Kellogg Pact—the lack of any provision for its enforcement. The fact that so many nations signed the Pact but at the same time continued their massive expenditure on armaments explains *Commonwealth*'s complaint that the Pact was 'dangerously near to being a piece of deliberate hypocrisy'. (September 1928, p. 258.)

[98] *Ibid.*, p. 208. Lang had appealed to all members of the Church of England to support the League.

international effects of trade and industry, the report acknowledges that selfishness and greed create the war spirit, and claims that world peace can best be built on the industrial and social peace of each nation, but the Lambeth committee, unlike some members of the Christendom Group, also recognizes the interdependence of nations, emphasizing the need to tackle problems of unemployment and finance by international action.[99]

During 1930 the international outlook remained quite bright. Britain, the U.S.A. and Japan reached agreement at the London Naval Conference, and the problems of security and disarmament came a little nearer to solution when thirty members of the League agreed to a convention promising financial help to any country threatened with aggression. But the operation of this plan was made conditional on the completion of a disarmament treaty, and despite this new incentive such a treaty never materialized. French fear of Germany was the most powerful reason for the failure of the Allies to disarm, but the British government must bear a heavy responsibility for its failure of will; at the crucial moment it made no serious attempt to resolve the deadlock between France and Germany by insisting on international inspection to prevent secret rearmament, coupled with a system of collective security which would enable France to disarm in accordance with her treaty obligations.[100] There was still considerable hostility among British supporters of the League to the idea of an international police force—hostility which, understandable as it may have been in the first flush of post-war idealism, could scarcely be justified after ten years of the plainest proof that a toothless Covenant and protestations of mutual goodwill could not suffice to maintain the peace. Apart from the spurious objections raised by the Christendom Group, there was a good deal of well-meaning Christian opposition to anything which involved the use of force; in 1933 the editor of *Crockford's* made much of the difficulties of maintaining an international security force, and dismissed the idea as belonging to 'the worlds in which Alice moved rather than to the one in which we have to live'.[101] Even Arthur Henderson,

[99] *Ibid.*, pp. 208–11 and a series of resolutions, see pp. 168f.
[100] See Lord Robert Cecil, *A Great Experiment*, pp. 212f.
[101] *Crockford's*, 1933, Preface, p. vi.

who was Foreign Secretary in the second Labour government and chairman of the unsuccessful Geneva Disarmament Conference which sat from 1932 to 1934, betrayed a naïve confidence in the power of international morality. Speaking of the Kellogg Pact he said: 'The obligation is absolute and if the Governments which accepted are acting in good faith, it follows that wars of conquest or aggression to gain national ends are things of the past, and force is eliminated as a means of settling international disputes.[102] The possibility that a government might act in bad faith, or go back on its word, was not one which he considered. On the other hand, there was much intelligent Christian comment on the question of disarmament. Kempthorne, Temple and Lang spoke vigorously in favour of disarmament in a Church Assembly debate, and Temple looked forward to the creation of an international police force.[103] At the beginning of 1932 the Council of Christian Ministers on Social Questions issued an appeal for the remission of reparation payments and war debts, and the Convocations showed an awareness of the need for disarmament, if not of the consequences of failing to achieve it.[104]

Many people were pinning their hopes on the Disarmament Conference, which opened in Geneva on February 2nd, 1932. Temple preached in Geneva before the Conference began, making a notable attack on the clause in the Treaty of Versailles which laid the whole blame for the 1914–18 war on Germany and her associates—a clause which Temple described as an offence against the Christian conscience.[105] This was a brave and not altogether popular attempt to pave the way for the removal of what was a justifiable source of grievance to Germany, but the Conference as a whole failed to reconcile the conflicting aims of Germany and France, the fault, according to Lord Robert Cecil, of Britain.[106] The German Chancellor, Brüning, was unable to show any success, and resigned in the summer of 1932; six months later Hitler came to power. In 1930 Theodore Woods, Bishop

[102] A. Henderson *Consolidating World Peace* (The Burge Memorial Lecture for 1931), p. 19.

[103] *Report of Proceedings*, 1932, pp. 118–34.

[104] The *Chronicle of Convocation*, 1932, pp. 54–8 and 60–6. *York Journal of Convocation*, June 1932, pp. 27–35.

[105] F. A. Iremonger, *William Temple*, pp. 375–7.

[106] Lord Robert Cecil, *A Great Experiment*, pp. 240f.

of Winchester, had written: 'By the documents they sign, the nations look towards peace. By the military preparations they make they look towards war. They face both ways, an attitude neither dignified nor definite.'[107]

At that time, as Woods implied, it was urgently necessary that the nations should bring their actions into line with their professed intentions, and be ready if necessary to take risks in the interests of peace. But by the summer of 1933 the opportunity for such risks had slipped away; there was little doubt about the direction in which Germany was determined to go, and it was a mark of his failure to grasp the significance of the changes which had taken place that Lang could comment as he did, in introducing the summer session of Canterbury Convocation, on the first manifestations of National Socialism in Germany: 'I am sure we all sympathize with the remarkable outburst of national feeling, the resurrection of national self-confidence and self-respect, which we are witnessing in Germany. But we venture to plead with that great people that they will not express their strong national sentiment in words and deeds provocative to other nations, or in any way check the growth of that general spirit of peace and goodwill among nations which is essential alike to the security and recovery of the world.'[108] The gentle remonstrance which he added over the persecution of the Jews served only to make it more obvious that the politicians had no monopoly of the language of appeasement.

Confusion continued to prevail in Christian circles about a right attitude towards international problems, and the long-drawn-out debate on the League, collective security, disarmament, rearmament and pacificism failed to produce anything approaching an agreed Christian point of view. Conflicting movements continued to grow in strength and influence. On the one hand there was the Peace Ballot of 1934–5, which showed overwhelming public support for collective security and the imposition, if necessary, of military sanctions against an aggressor, and which prompted Baldwin to appoint Anthony Eden as Minister for League Affairs in 1935. This policy of trusting and strengthening

[107] F. T. Woods, 'Is it Peace?', in *Stockholm*, 1930, Vol. 3, p. 210.
[108] The *Chronicle of Convocation*, 1933, p. 220.

the League was enthusiastically supported by many Christian writers and speakers, notably in the perceptive bulletins on international affairs which began to appear in the rejuvenated I.C.F. magazine, the *Torch*, in June 1933.[109] On the other hand there was the pacifist movement, led by George Lansbury and H. R. L. Sheppard, and distinctively Christian in inspiration. Both these movements enjoyed increased support when it became apparent in 1934 that the diplomatic negotiations at the protracted Geneva Disarmament Conference had failed to achieve any success, and both found many enthusiastic advocates among churchmen. There was even a measure of relief in Christian circles that rearmament and old-fashioned alliances came back into favour in default of any more satisfactory means of securing world peace.[110]

Enthusiasts for the League, although growing in number and influence during the early thirties, found it increasingly difficult to defend their cause, as the League repeatedly failed to deal satisfactorily with the crises with which it was faced from 1931 onwards. The Japanese invasion of Manchuria in 1931, the Italian invasion of Abyssinia in 1935, the German reoccupation of the Rhineland in March 1936, and the outbreak of the Spanish Civil War four months later, were all occasions on which the weight of world opinion and the machinery of collective action might have been mobilized and brought to bear with salutary effect, but in each case the League proved powerless to prevent aggression or even to agree on effective economic sanctions, although in the Abyssinian crisis there was a moment when the League seemed to be about to play a decisive role. This is not the place to record the details of successive international problems, but merely to indicate some Christian reactions to the pattern of events. In general the weight of Christian opinion was in favour of a stronger and more effective League and of the principle of collective security, although some commentators were unable to resist the temptation to reflect sarcastically on the practical

[109] From January 1935 the *Torch* was renamed the *I.C.F. Journal*, to distinguish it from the parish magazine inset which was widely circulated as the *Torch*.

[110] See e.g. the *Torch*, July 1934, pp. 105f., and a Church Assembly debate on November 19th, 1936 (*Report of Proceedings*, 1936, pp. 523–5).

impotence of the League, and some even considered a temporary abandonment of the ideals for which it stood. An article in the *Socialist Christian* in 1936 described the League as looking like a short cut to peace, and therefore something to which people were naturally attracted. But, it went on, 'it should now be clear that no real League of Nations exists or has existed. . . . The great powers, on whom alone collective security depends, have never been prepared to take action except in support of their purely selfish interests.'[111] The confusion of principle with expediency in the actions of the Baldwin government provoked the *I.C.F. Journal* to ask 'For what are we prepared to fight? . . . The present Government seem likely to make the worst of all worlds. They will get rearmament with its burdensome cost . . . with its fatal contribution to world politics and ultimately to world events. But it seems that they will not use it to defend any principle or to vindicate any ideal in the progress and struggle of the human race.'[112]

Support for the policy of appeasement, in order to create a breathing space in which the mood of the member nations could catch up with the idealistic requirements of the League Covenant, came both from the Royal Institute of International Affairs and from the Archbishop of Canterbury. The former, meeting at Chatham House during the summer of 1936, considered such suggestions as the limitation of the League's sphere of influence to Europe, and the authorization of territorial changes by a two-thirds majority in the League Council and Assembly; such obvious readiness to make concessions under pressure was seized upon with glee by *Christendom*, as further proof that the League and its advocates were unworthy of support by true idealists.[113] The Archbishop's proposals came during the course of a presidential address to Convocation in 1936; he observed that the League's record in the Abyssinian crisis was not such as to reflect or inspire confidence, and he called for an interval which might be used 'to secure such a general appeasement of the situation, at least in Europe, as may make the revival of the League . . .

[111] Charles Record 'The Way to Peace', in the *Socialist Christian*, February 1936, p. 110.

[112] *I.C.F. Journal*, July 1936, pp. 108–10.

[113] *Christendom*, December 1936, pp. 300–3.

possible and hopeful'. Eighteen months later, Lang could still speak of the desirability of appeasement, and call for a fuller and more generous recognition of Hitler's professed desire to do all in his power to maintain the peace of Europe.[114]

The perplexity of Christians faced by the menacing international situation of the late thirties was clearly revealed by the debate on Peace and National Defence which took place in the Church Assembly in February 1937. An uncontroversial motion, largely in the terms of the 1930 Lambeth Report, rejected war as a means of settling disputes and deplored the programme of large-scale rearmament, but clearly recognized the need for Britain to maintain enough armaments to enable her to fulfil her obligations under the Covenant. The Dean of Winchester (E. G. Selwyn) condemned the growing wave of pacifist feeling in the Church, speaking of a widespread and vigorous propaganda campaign to claim pacificism as the only true interpretation of the teaching of Christ, and went on to justify the use, in certain circumstances, of military force to maintain a stable moral order. Opposition to this speech came from the Bishop of Birmingham (Barnes) and from H. R. L. Sheppard, who spoke passionately in defence of the pacifist cause. He described any form of war as 'mass murder, a betrayal of God, and a blasphemy against the future of man', and pleaded for an acceptance of pacificism as the vocation of the Church.[115] Temple, speaking at the end of the debate, distinguished absolute moral principles from the need to judge each situation in relative terms, and criticized the humane arguments of the pacifists which seemed, from a Christian point of view, too much concerned to avoid physical death. He quoted the dominical injunction not to fear those whose power is limited to the killing of the body, and this theological point seems to have found favour with the members of the Assembly.[116]

In terms of votes the pacifists were on this occasion in a minority, but the Christian attitude remained uncertain. The Church spoke on international affairs with a variety of voices, and certainly did not accept any single vocation. The pacifist

[114] The *Chronicle of Convocation*, 1936, pp. 50f; 1938, p. 2.

[115] *Report of Proceedings*, 1937, p. 182.

[116] *Ibid.*, pp. 194–7. *Cf.* Temple's *Christianity in Thought and Practice*, p. 92, where he again affirms that justice is more sacred than life.

William Temple on his way to his enthronement as Bishop of Manchester, February 1921

Lord Robert Cecil speaking at the Women's International League on January 20th, 1932, before leaving for the Geneva Disarmament Conference

point of view continued to be popularly expounded by Lansbury and Sheppard, and also, more intellectually, by C. E. Raven and by D. M. MacKinnon in the pages of *Christendom*,[117] but despite this persuasive advocacy it failed to win over the majority of British churchmen. The publication of MacKinnon's articles was a notable gesture by Reckitt, as editor of *Christendom*, for he himself came to an increasingly firm conviction that the Fascist leaders must be matched by strength, and this unresolved divergence of opinion within the pages of *Christendom* was symptomatic of the uncertainty with which the Church was to meet the crisis which was soon to engulf the whole of Europe.

[117] *Christendom*, June 1938, pp. 149–51; June 1939, pp. 139–43.

8

An End and a New Beginning: Oxford 1937 and the Onset of War

IT MIGHT have been expected that the economic and financial crisis of 1930–3 would provoke some very hard and concerted thinking among churchmen, even among those who had previously felt that it was no business of the Church to comment or pronounce upon secular affairs, and *Christianity and the Crisis*, edited by Percy Dearmer and published in 1933, appears at first sight to be the fruit of such thought. A book of over six hundred pages, its thirty-two contributors include the Archbishops of Canterbury and York, five other bishops and two deans of the Church of England, and a number of Anglican laymen. It ranges over all aspects of the prevailing crisis in its discussion of the intellectual, moral, social, economic, international and even cultural confusion. There is a weighty exposition of Christianity, a survey of the history of the Church in its social aspect, and a comprehensive account of what was held to be the Christian solution. Some of the essays are judicious and well-informed, such as the treatment of problems of marriage and divorce by the Bishop of Liverpool (A. A. David) and an outstanding essay on Christian unity by the Bishop of Croydon (E. S. Woods), but it is in general a lamentable book, unco-ordinated, contradictory, inadequate and yet repetitive—a fair reflection, it would not be too harsh to say, of the state of Christian social thought in 1933. The distinguished nature of so many of the contributors does not seem to have earned for their work much influence or popularity, and there are few references to it either in contemporary literature or in surveys of the Christian thought of this period. Despite the fact that it includes an essay by Reckitt and an exposition of the Douglas Social Credit scheme, it was not even welcomed in Christendom circles, and Ruth Kenyon, reviewing it in the *Torch*, complained of its preponderantly liberal protestant flavour, relieved only by the valiant efforts of the Christendom contributors to unmask the bogey of finance.[1]

The essays in *Christianity and the Crisis* seem to have been assembled hastily and without consultation among the contributors, which accounts for their lack of harmony; moreover, they constitute an unhappy juxtaposition of the eccentric views of the Christendom Group and a numerically stronger representation of the somewhat discredited optimism of Copec. These faults are partly due to editorial slackness, but the book is nevertheless sadly typical of the general disarray in the field of Christian social thought in the early thirties. Die-hard opposition to the principle of Christian involvement in the problems of society had certainly declined since the war, but indifference among Christians to the social implications of their faith, and uncertainty about what social action they might take, were still widespread. It is true that in 1933 the Christendom Group was at the height of its popularity and influence, and its outlook was to dominate the Malvern conference of 1941,[2] but it never succeeded in permeating the Church of England as a whole. In 1933 Demant published *God, Man and Society*, an exposition in moderate terms of the Christendom Group's understanding of Christian sociology at that time. It is devoted partly to a relatively uncontroversial survey of the nature and scope of Christian social duty, and is less vitiated than much Christendom writing by the economic beliefs of this school of thought, but it adds nothing to the ideas previously worked out by Christendom writers, and the fact that it is in many ways disappointingly derivative hints at the staleness and exhaustion which were soon to bring about the decline of the Christendom movement.

The year 1933 marked in many ways the lowest point between the wars in the economic position of Britain, and correspondingly the moment of greatest social misery—at least for the great mass of the unemployed and their dependants. The impetus and enthusiasm for social change which had been so strong at the end of the war finally foundered under the stress of the economic, financial and international crises of the years 1929–33, and the

[1] The *Torch*, June 1933, pp. 85f.

[2] See the report of the Conference, *Malvern, 1941: The Life of the Church and the Order of Society*.

optimism of the Fifth Report and Copec was seen to have been misplaced. In so far as it is possible to determine with any precision the course of large movements of thought, it may be claimed that 1933 saw the end of an era of Christian social concern, and created new conditions which had to be met in new ways. *Christianity and the Crisis* was a disappointing and unsuccessful attempt by Christian thinkers to rise to the occasion, but there were other more promising portents.

The generally higher level of the Church Assembly and Convocation debates has already been referred to; there was not only a greater Christian interest and competence in social matters, but also a widening of the concern felt by Christians, in the sense both of the subjects which it embraced and the number of people who were involved in the movement of thought. A sign of this—in itself of no great importance, but a significant indication of the new tendency—was a lively and well-informed debate in the Church Assembly in February 1935, on the problem of road accidents. Concern was expressed at the fact that more than seven thousand people were being killed on the roads each year, and Christians were urged to set an example of courtesy and care. The frequent attribution of accidents to bad roads and traffic conditions was rejected as being at variance with the facts; far more important were recklessness and the influence of alcohol.[3]

More important as a sign of the wider Christian interest in social problems was a great public meeting held at the Albert Hall in London on November 5th, 1935, under the chairmanship of Temple, to discuss Christian Action in Social Problems. Its object was to display the concern of the Church about social issues, and to deepen and mobilize that concern for more effective corporate action. Those who were present at the meeting were invited solemnly to affirm their conviction that the state of society, in particular the continuance of enforced and destitute idleness, malnutrition and overcrowded slum housing, was a defiance of God, and to pledge themselves to action as individuals and through their parishes.[4]

[3] *Report of Proceedings*, 1935, pp. 132–42.

[4] Advance notice of the meeting, and the wording of its resolutions, was given in *Christendom*, September 1935, p. 172.

A further sign of a steady growth in the Church of an enlightened and sensitive social conscience was provided by the obvious warmth and unanimity of the welcome given to the Criminal Justice Bill introduced by the Home Secretary, Sir Samuel Hoare, in November 1938, and outlining far-reaching changes in the treatment of offenders. The proposals for dealing with young people were particularly praised, including as they did a system of remand homes and compulsory attendance centres as opposed to imprisonment or the harsh regime of a Borstal institution. The Bill also proposed, against the advice of the judiciary, the abolition of corporal punishment, except for violent attacks on prison officers, and the extension of psychological treatment for certain prisoners. The *Church Times* of November 25th described the Bill as 'a courageous attempt at Christian statesmanship', and the *Guardian* of the same date, complimenting Hoare on his record at the Home Office, described these latest proposals as 'a fine testimony to his humanity and Christian purpose'. The 1938 Bill was the culmination of a gradual humanizing of prison conditions and the treatment of criminals which had proceeded during the inter-war years, and although it had not been passed at the outbreak of war, and was abandoned in November 1939, Temple was still able to point to penal reform as one of the three areas in which Christian social concern had been most fruitful between 1918 and 1939.[5]

One of the factors which helped to cultivate a new sense of realism in the field of Christian social thought was the increasing impact on Christianity in England of thinkers belonging to other Christian traditions. This had the effect in some cases of exposing the fallacies in hitherto widely accepted ideas, and also of enlarging the horizon of Christian concern, showing more clearly the need for relativism in approaching social problems. One of the most influential figures during the latter half of the thirties was the American, Reinhold Niebuhr, whose powerful writing convicted both those pietists who had ignored the insistent demands made on Christians by the society in which they live, and the optimists who had supposed that Christian ethics could virtually be identified

[5] *Malvern, 1941*, p. 217. The others were the extension of secondary education and the large-scale provision of new houses.

with human benevolence, or the will of God with specific programmes of social reform. An extended review in *Christendom* of Niebuhr's *An Interpretation of Christian Ethics* showed how the Christendom Group in particular could benefit from Niebuhr's insistence on the relative nature of Christian social ethics,[6] and it is perhaps not fanciful to trace his influence in the consistently realistic *Christendom* comment on the international crises of 1938 and 1939—a striking but short-lived change from the dogmatism and unreality of so much earlier Christendom thought.

Niebuhr was, however, only one of the Christian thinkers to bring new insight to the Christian social movement within the Church of England. An article by E. L. Mascall in *Christendom* for June 1938, traced the influence on the Christendom Group of Berdyaev and Maritain, and the 1937 Church Union Summer School heard an address by l'Abbé Köthen on the work of Catholic Action in Europe, including the movement known as 'Jocisme', from the initial letters of Jeunesse Ouvrière Chrétienne, started in Belgium by Cardinal Cardijn to bridge the gap between the Church and young workers.[7] The influence of Maritain, together with that of such diverse figures as Tawney and Demant, confessedly lies behind T. S. Eliot's Boutwood Lectures for 1939, *The Idea of a Christian Society*. This outline of a possible Christian social pattern, which is similar in spirit to a good deal of Christendom Group writing, is interesting mainly for its revival in a new guise of Coleridge's 'clerisy'—the idea that society, at present in Eliot's view neither Christian nor pagan, could be guided in a Christian direction by the influence of a nucleus of spiritually and intellectually developed Christians. But it was not only the Catholic wing in England which received stimulus from abroad; the Socialist Christian League, which had been formed in 1932 by an amalgamation of the Society of Socialist Christians and a smaller propaganda body called the Christian Socialist Crusade, was in touch with a number of Socialist Christian organizations abroad, notably in France, Germany, Austria, the United States of America and Scandinavia. The S.C.L. periodical, the *Socialist Christian*,

[6] *Christendom*, June 1937, pp. 143–8. See also the *Socialist Christian*, January 1940, pp. 7–9, and C. E. Hudson, *Preface to a Christian Sociology*, p. 22.

[7] *Christendom*, June 1938, pp. 129–40; June 1937, pp. 105–7.

contained frequent references to the activities of these groups, the suffering and persecution of those in Germany and Austria under the Nazis, and to the meetings and conferences at which Socialist Christians shared their ideas and discussed their problems. Interest was also shown by the S.C.L. in the theory and practice of brotherhood economics in Japan, a system of Christian co-operatives organized by the Japanese Christian Socialist, Kagawa.[8]

Christian social thinkers were inevitably caught up in the revival of interest in Marxism in the mid-thirties, a movement which was stimulated by Victor Gollancz's Left Book Club, founded in 1936, and also by the plight of the Republicans in the Spanish Civil War. *Christianity and the Social Revolution*, a symposium published in 1935, included contributions from Christians, Communists, and those who claimed to be both, and set out 'to give emphasis to the revolutionary character of the Christian faith, and to demonstrate that it has always contained strongly Communistic elements; to set out the grounds of Communist opposition to religion and the Church; and to advance considerations which suggest that it is in the better mutual understanding of the two movements, and even, perhaps, in their synthesis, that the hope of the future lies.'[9] This account of the book's purpose is from the introduction by C. E. Raven; other Anglican contributors were Conrad Noel and G. C. Binyon, and Niebuhr provided a concluding essay. This was an attempt to close the gap between Christianity and Communism, to emphasize the common ground between the two, and especially to claim the strongest possible Christian authority for an active and revolutionary sociology.

By 1935, however, it was by no means clear that Communism would not be swallowed up by Fascism, and some Christians felt that the choice was between one and the other; Christianity must throw in its lot with either the Right or the Left. This view of the Christian dilemma inspired Kenneth Ingram's impassioned question—*Christianity—Right or Left?* The choice, he maintained, must be made. 'Now the ranks are closing. Those who believe that Christianity is dependent on the maintenance of the old

[8] *The Socialist Christian*, September 1937, p. 59.

[9] *Christianity and the Social Revolution*, edited by J. Lewis, K. Polanyi and D. Kitchin, p. 28.

order, on the traditional outlook and mode of thought, on the preservation of society as it now exists, must take their place on the side of the Right. Those who are conscious that Christianity is greater than any of its forms, who do not seek to limit the work of the Holy Spirit to the confines of their own traditional conceptions, are natural allies of the Left.'[10] Roger Lloyd, in *Revolutionary Religion*, one of the first volumes written for the S.C.M.'s Religious Book Club, challenged Ingram's conclusion that Christians should align themselves on the Left, although he acknowledged that most Christians would probably be temperamentally more inclined towards Communism than Fascism, and that Communism in Britain would be less harsh and brutal in its working than in Russia. He pointed instead to a better course, a Christian *via media*, avoiding the excesses which are bound to accompany any purely political programme, and resulting in an altogether better social pattern, a society 'peopled by free citizens living in fellowship, and not by automatically conditioned human machines who have no voice or will but that which authority dictates'.[11] He went on to show that Ingram's presentation of the issue as a choice for Christians was itself a misunderstanding of the nature of the gospel: it was precisely the conflict between Right and Left which was making life unbearable for countless men and women, and making war even more likely. To side with Communism or Fascism would be 'to make terms with, and thus guarantee the increase of one or other of the forms of the very Anti-Christ which Christians are in the world to overcome'.[12]

All these developments were signs of a new realism in Christian social thought, a more sensitive awareness of the difficulty of being a Christian in society, and a more resolute determination that the Church should bear its witness in the world as it was, rather than remain in the realm of utopian idealism. Denominational and national barriers were breaking down, and it was becoming increasingly difficult to isolate the Christian social thought of any particular branch of the universal Church. This was above all true of the most important and impressive sign of

[10] K. Ingram. *op. cit.*, p. 196. [11] R. Lloyd, *op. cit.*, p. 99.
[12] *Ibid.*, p. 180.

the new Christian social concern in the late thirties, the conference of the Universal Christian Council for Life and Work which was held at Oxford from July 12th–26th, 1937, under the title Church, Community, and State. This meeting, the culmination of five years' preparatory work, was the sequel to the Stockholm conference of 1925 to which, it will be recalled, Great Britain contributed the Copec reports.

But the scope and membership of the Oxford conference were very different from those of its predecessor; there came to Oxford four hundred and twenty-five delegates (of whom only eighteen were members of the Church of England), together with four hundred associate members and visitors, representing forty different nations, and every branch of the Christian Church throughout the world apart from the Roman Catholic Church, which declined to play any official part in the proceedings, and the German Evangelical Church, whose delegates were prevented by the Nazi government from attending. Various preliminary meetings and discussions had shown that most contemporary social problems were bound up with the nature and claims of the modern state, and it was decided in 1934 that a Research Commission should be set up under the chairmanship of J. H. Oldham to prepare for a world conference. The theme was to be the relation of the Church to the all-embracing claims of the communal life, the problem—to use the words of a Roman Catholic writer—'how religion is to survive in a single community, which is neither Church nor State, which recognizes no formal limits, but which covers the whole of life and claims to be the source and goal of every human activity'.[13] Oldham had elsewhere, in a preparatory pamphlet, identified the real threat to Christianity as the 'Secular Mind', that attitude which sought 'to use the supreme authority of the State and all the agencies at its command to impose on the whole community a philosophy of life and a pattern of living which are wholly, or in important respects, contrary to the Christian understanding of the meaning and ends of human existence',[14] a threat which made it essential for the Church to witness in and

[13] Christopher Dawson in the *Tablet*, 26th June, 1937; quoted in *The Churches Survey their Task*, edited by J. H. Oldham, (The Report of the Oxford Conference), p. 9.

[14] J. H. Oldham, *Church, Community and State: a World Issue*, p. 14.

against society, and not merely through the lives of individuals.

The task of the conference itself was to co-ordinate and amplify the work of the preparatory commissions. The papers contributed by the members of these commissions were published separately in six volumes at the end of 1937, while preliminary reports were prepared by five sections of the Research Commission and circulated to delegates before the conference met. These reports, entitled *Church and Community*; *Church and State*; *Church, Community, and State in relation to the Economic Order*; *Church, Community, and State in relation to Education*; and *The Universal Church and the World of Nations*, were then revised during the conference debates and finally published in the conference report, *The Churches Survey their Task*. As well as the section debates, there were plenary sessions of the conference at which addresses were given by representatives of the main Christian traditions. A recurring theme in these addresses was the universality of the Church, and the need to release the power which would come from an awareness among Christians that they were members of a world-wide community. Examples were quoted from the mission field of a realization of the truth of Christian community in a form unknown in the older Churches of the west, and speakers urged that Christians should abandon the narrow concept of the worshipping community in favour of creating an all-embracing Christian community life. Oldham himself criticized the narrow, clericalized view of the Church which encouraged people to think of Christian action in the social sphere in terms only of what might be achieved by the Church in a corporate capacity, and he showed how individual Christians, with the support, inspiration, prayers and fellowship of the organized Church behind them, could be a powerful influence in society, bringing Christian insights into the world of business and politics in a way which was impossible for the Church as a corporate institution. The hope was expressed that as well as a growth in ecumenical fellowship, the future would also see an intensification of the Christian life of individuals, through their participation in cells for study, prayer and discussion. Finally, one of the most important achievements of the plenary sessions of the conference was its approval, with only two dissentients, of proposals to combine the Life and Work movement with that of Faith and Order in a new World Council of Churches.[15]

A message to the Churches was issued by the conference, condemning the idolatrous deification of nation, race or class, or of political or cultural ideals, calling for the removal of the injustices which are the root cause of war, and making particular mention of the persecution of Christians by totalitarian regimes: 'Our hearts are filled with anguish as we remember the suffering of the Church in Russia. Our sympathy and gratitude go out to our Christian brethren in Germany; we are moved to a more living trust by their steadfast witness to Christ and we pray that we may be given grace to bear the same clear witness to the Lord.'[16]

The report of the section which considered *Church and Community*, under the chairmanship of Sir Walter Moberly, identifies society's attempt to be self-sufficient as the cause of its sickness and disintegration; Christians are themselves to some extent infected with the ills of society, and feel themselves in perpetual tension and conflict, often uncertain whether they are called to work together with movements which only partially approach the will of Christ, or whether they are called to repudiate the structures of secular society. The report identifies three particular problems, namely those which concern the Church and the national community, or *Volk*—so pressing in view of the happenings in Germany—the Church and the various racial groups of mankind, and the Church and the Common Life. Although the report cannot be said to have any particularly remarkable advice to offer on these problems, the preparatory work for it included a masterly essay by Temple on the course which Christians must in practice steer between idealism and expediency.[17]

The report on *Church and State* is useful for its definition of the distinctive character of the Church's activity as 'the free operation of grace and love', while that of the State's activity, whatever its constructive function in the cultural and social

[15] The proceedings of the plenary sessions are summarized in *The Churches Survey their Task*, pp. 28–50.

[16] *Ibid.*, p. 63.

[17] *Ibid.*, pp. 67–76. Temple's essay is to be found in Volume IV of the Church, Community and State series, *The Christian Faith and the Common Life*, pp. 45–65.

spheres may be, is 'the power of constraint, legal and physical'.[18]

Church, Community, and State in relation to the Economic Order is by far the longest report, and includes an analysis of the features of life in a capitalist society which tend to subordinate God's purpose for human life to the demands of the economic process; these are held to be the enhancement of acquisitiveness; the maintenance of indefensible inequalities; the creation of centres of economic power which are not responsible to any organ of the community and therefore may be tyrannical over sections of it (this oblique reference to the malign influence of high finance was the only point in the whole conference at which the views of the Christendom Group may perhaps be detected); and the prevention of a sense of Christian vocation in daily life through unemployment or unworthy employment. Christian teaching in relation to the economic order should be governed by three main considerations: it should deal with ends, standards and principles, in the light of which each particular problem or remedy must be tested; it should uncover the true facts of each case, and especially the human consequences of economic policies; and it should clearly point out the human obstacles and objections which stand in the way of economic justice.[19] The report also includes outstandingly sensitive and judicious analyses of the relation of theoretical Christian concern with social issues to Christian approval or disapproval of specific social systems or measures, and of the relative merits of private enterprise and socialist theories of society. It emphasizes the need for the most careful and critical avoidance both of implied acquiescence in an unsatisfactory status quo, and of the mistaken identification of some particular nostrum with the will of God.[20]

The report on *Church, Community, and State in relation to Education* is interesting mainly for its summary of the ideal of Christian education (a) in a state which is favourable to Christian opinion, and (b) in a non-Christian or anti-Christian setting. In the former case, which is relevant for the Church of England, there are many instances of Church schools and colleges struggling to hold their own alongside increasingly superior secular provision,

[18] *The Churches Survey their Task*, p. 82. [19] *Ibid.*, pp. 104–9 and 114–25.
[20] *Ibid.*, pp. 94–7 and 109–14.

and here the report calls on the Church to 'concentrate her efforts upon creating and maintaining a smaller number of schools of differing types, which by their distinctive quality serve as a demonstration of educational standards that are fully Christian'.[21] There must be complete freedom of conscience about religious instruction—not merely freedom to opt out altogether, but freedom also, for those who want it, to receive a fully Christian education, which may mean providing Church Schools as well as Bible teaching in State Schools, but the report is by no means unenthusiastic about agreed syllabuses. In the second case, the report distinguishes between Christian education in a neutral and in a hostile environment. There are many developing countries which are not Christian in any corporate sense, but in which the government welcomes the pioneering educational work of the Church. In such cases it is most important that the Church should not wrongly exploit its opportunity, but should respect the liberty of conscience of non-Christians who come to Church schools or colleges. The Church must also be ready to hand over educational responsibility as the State itself achieves higher standards—'she must not accept a tinge of added piety as an excuse for inefficiency', and must again concentrate her resources in the provision of a small number of centres of excellence.[22]

In places where no Christian teaching is permitted, personal witness and voluntary work among students may be valuable and important. Even in anti-Christian states the Church must render to Caesar his due, and recognize the importance, especially for developing countries, of building up loyalty and patriotism among the people. 'The point where patriotic reverence becomes idolatry is not easy to define. It is the point where an absolute loyalty is given to an external human authority rather than to the voice of God made known in Christ and in the inward voice of conscience and truth. If and where this point is reached Christian teachers and students must and will still be ready to suffer persecution.'[23]

The report on *The Universal Church and the World of Nations* speaks of the change which has come over men's view of the international situation within ten years, from an optimistic faith in the possibility of creating a true international order, to the present

[21] *Ibid.*, p. 157. [22] *Ibid.*, pp. 161–3. [23] *Ibid.*, p. 165.

bewilderment and dejection. Some, at least, of this disillusionment is attributed to the excessively high hopes, of an almost religious quality, which were pinned on specific human schemes, ignoring the universal taint of sin and imperfection in any human endeavour. But this is not to belittle the part which Christians can play in international politics—it is merely another call to realism. The League of Nations has been able to achieve only what the governments of member states have wished, and despite much valuable work by the technical agencies and the I.L.O., no substantial progress will be made until the mentality of national power politics is abandoned.

War of any kind is condemned as a particular demonstration of the power of sin in the world and a defiance of the righteousness of God, but the report accepts that individual Christians differ widely in their attitude to the practical problems posed by war. Some are thoroughgoing pacifists, some reluctantly accept that war may be justified by international law or by the dictates of conscience, while others believe that one of the duties of a citizen is to obey the call of the State to fight in all causes which are not obviously evil. Special considerations and opportunities for the Church in the international sphere are mentioned; these include the need to remove all racial barriers within the Christian community, the importance of maintaining full religious freedom for all, and the value of generous mutual Church aid, including the offer of money, advice and leadership to small or weak branches of the Church.[24]

As Oldham points out in *The Churches Survey their Task*, the significance of the Oxford conference lay not so much in any remarkable and detailed contribution to Christian social thought on individual problems, as in the fact that so great and so representative a gathering of Christians could say so much with a united voice, and find such fellowship and community of feeling despite the difficult nature of the problems they were discussing. Oxford 1937 undoubtedly marked a new step forward in the realization of the ecumenical, as opposed to merely international,

[24] *The Churches Survey their Task*, pp. 167–87. The Christian pacifist position is well set out in a paper contributed by C. E. Raven to Volume VII of the Church, Community, and State series, 'The Religious Basis of Pacifism', pp. 285–315.

character of the Church, and it spoke with sober realism and considerable spiritual wisdom to a bewildered world. In a sense it gives the impression of already looking forward to the end of the war which was beginning to seem inevitable, and many of the ideas worked out at the conference—Christian cells, lay participation, mutual Church aid, and the need for a new sense of Christian community—are still part of the contemporary theological scene, more than thirty years later.

The delegates who made their way home from Oxford were not, however, plunged at once into the horrors of war. There followed for most of them more than two years of uneasy peace, and a succession of critical moments which presented Christians with the opportunity of witnessing in a world which was aware to an unusual degree of international issues, and ready as seldom before to grasp at any source of hope or insight which seemed to offer guidance in the gathering gloom. There was much concern in Anglican circles during this period with the fate of Christians and Jews in Nazi Germany, and that of the refugees and victims of war in Abyssinia, Spain and China, and there were frequent references to their sufferings in Convocation and the Church Assembly. In January 1938, the Bishop of Chichester (Bell) moved a resolution expressing the sympathy of the Bishops with their fellow Christians in Germany, and rejoicing at the steadfastness of the priests, pastors and lay people who had chosen to suffer rather than fail in their witness to the freedom of the gospel. A solitary voice of protest at this motion, on the grounds that it was political, was that of the Bishop of Gloucester (Headlam), but he found no supporters for his point of view. The *Church Times*, observing that Headlam was in a minority of one in the Upper House of Convocation, later called for his resignation from the post, which he somewhat incongruously held, of Chairman of the Church of England Council on Foreign Relations.[25]

Headlam tried hard to spread his own account of the situation in Germany, and contributed a long article to the *Guardian* of September 2nd, 1938. In this he claimed to be revealing the truth, and attacked what he described as the ill-informed and tactless

[25] The *Church Times*, August 12th, 1938. The Convocation Debate is recorded in the *Chronicle of Convocation*, January 1938, pp. 110–12.

support which the Church of England was giving to the Confessional Church in Germany: 'It is quite untrue to say that National Socialism is incompatible with Christianity . . . and it is a foolish and dangerous thing to say so . . . If (Hitler) is irritated by the continued opposition of the Confessional Church and the activities of the English bishops . . . he might use his power against the Church: that is why a moderate and intelligent policy is so essential.' Apart from one or two expressions of gratitude for the 'weighty knowledge' of the Bishop's observations, the correspondence columns of the *Guardian* subsequently carried some angry attacks on his misrepresentation of the facts, and it is certainly hard to see how Headlam can possibly have been unaware of the fate of Dr. Martin Niemöller, who had been imprisoned without trial for seven months and had finally chosen to go to a concentration camp rather than remain silent in his Christian witness. This case had recently received wide publicity, and was only one of many instances of Nazi persecution which had already taken place.

The most important test of Christian opinion in 1938 came with the Czech crisis of September. Hitler had been steadily increasing the pressure of his demands for the dismemberment of Czechoslovakia and the return of the Sudetenland to Germany, and Britain and France were nearly involved in war in May 1938. In the face of what seemed to be Anglo-French determination, Hitler was content to bide his time, fixing October 1st as the deadline for a settlement of the Sudetenland question. Chamberlain was determined not to risk British involvement again and resolutely pursued his policy of appeasement, which culminated in the unprecedented flight to Berchtesgaden to meet Hitler on September 15th, followed by meetings at Godesberg and Munich on the 22nd and 29th, so completing the ruin of Czechoslovakia and the humiliation of Britain and France.

Europe had lain for weeks under the shadow of almost certain war, and it would have been extraordinary if Chamberlain's success in postponing open conflict had not been ecstatically welcomed by many unthinking people, despite the appalling price demanded of Czechoslovakia—a price which on any reckoning constituted betrayal by Britain and France, who did not even

Unemployment: a miner at Wigan still out of work in 1939

consult the victim.[26] But the warmth of the praise bestowed on Chamberlain—the journalist Godfrey Winn wrote 'Praise be to God and to Mr. Chamberlain. I find no sacrilege, no bathos, in coupling those two names'[27]—was astonishing evidence of the almost universal suspension of moral sensitivity, and there were few exceptions to this state of mind even among leading churchmen. Lang, in a broadcast on the evening of September 28th, before Chamberlain had even flown to Munich, spoke of Hitler's final invitation as 'an answer to the great volume of prayer which has been rising to God. More than one member of Parliament said to me today as we all trooped out into the lobby: "This is the hand of God". I feel sure that many of you, when you heard the news could not help saying "Thank God". Yes, in your prayers tonight thank God. . . .'[28] A letter from Temple appeared in *The Times* of October 4th, in which he joined in the chorus of gratitude to Chamberlain, qualifying this only by the suggestion that, as a sign of British gratitude, the government should calculate what it would have cost to wage for one week the war which had been avoided, and give that sum to Czechoslovakia to help with the resettlement of refugees from the Sudetenland.

The *Church Times* on September 23rd, before the final settlement, indulged in a long and somewhat uneasy justification of Anglo-French conduct, opining that any postponement of war was welcome in so far as it offered further time for the innate sanity of the German people to assert itself against the madness of their rulers. A week later it, too, was thanking God for Neville Chamberlain—'No man in history has fought so strenuously to prevent war.' The *Guardian's* leading article on October 7th was also a tortuous and uncomfortable apologia for the Munich settlement, ending with an acknowledgment that the terms imposed on Czechoslovakia were humiliating and cruel: 'The sorrowful and bitter words of the Czech government to Great Britain and France must leave us sad and uneasy while our memory lasts.' The hope that it would quickly fade was not actually expressed.

[26] For a concise account of the Czechoslovak crisis see Mowat, *op. cit.*, pp. 604–19.
[27] Quoted by Mowat, *op. cit.*, p. 619.
[28] Reported in *The Times*, September 29th, 1938.

The Munich settlement was not, however, immune to Christian attack, and some churchmen rose to the occasion with considerable vigour. One of the most notable was the Reverend St John Groser, whose ministry at Christ Church, Watney Street, in the East End of London, was in the finest tradition of Anglo-Catholic involvement in the problems of society, a mixture of unbounded pastoral compassion and fiery Socialist zeal. In a letter to the *Guardian* of October 7th, Groser expressed his burning indignation: 'Blackmail has succeeded. The threat of force has triumphed. . . . That Mr. Chamberlain should talk of "peace with honour" when he has surrendered to this blackmail, torn up Article 10 of the League Covenant without reference to Geneva, and sacrificed the Czechoslovaks in order, as he says, to prevent a world war, is bad enough; but that the Archbishop of Canterbury should say that this is the answer to our prayers . . . is beyond endurance.' Groser was not unsupported, and for several weeks the correspondence columns were full of a rare savagery and sarcasm. The more specialized Christian social publications also added their criticisms, and Reckitt's editorial in the December issue of *Christendom* showed cynical contempt for the Archbishop's readiness to identify the hand of God in the activities of the Prime Minister, pointing to the price of appeasement: 'In proportion as a nation dreads and shrinks from war are those who oppose it strengthened in the pursuit of their purposes. Perhaps already our hatred of war has so armed the forces of ruthlessness that they have become irresistible.'[29] The *Socialist Christian* was even more outspoken in its denunciation of 'the combination of blasphemy and superstition that has characterized the attitude of many of our Christian churches in the hour of need and in the subsequent relief. . . . The day Mr. Chamberlain came home hundreds of churches that had been open for prayer until that time, were closed. The crisis was over. The trick had been done. There was nothing more to pray about'; not even the fact that 'injustice, foul and cruel, was being forced on Czechoslovakia'.[30]

There were second thoughts about Munich in the popular mind, and imperceptibly the mood of the country changed.

[29] *Christendom*, December 1938, pp. 243–5.
[30] The *Socialist Christian*, November 1938, pp. 65f.

Perhaps the one unmistakable gain from the postponement of war for eleven months was that by the time it finally came there was a resolution, a unity of purpose, and a determination to see it through which had certainly been lacking in September 1938. The declaration of war on September 3rd, 1939, met with almost the same measure of approval as had greeted its avoidance in the previous year, and the dominant Christian attitude was well summed up by Reckitt: 'If resistance to Nazism does not call for war, what does it call for? What other means are still open to us to secure that a minimum basis of civilized life, if no more, is restored to Europe?'[31] There was a general sense of relief that the uncertainty and moral equivocation were finally at an end, and just before the outbreak of war Kenneth Ingram, writing in the *Socialist Christian*, captured this mood: 'I do not believe that if the Government attempted to do a second Munich, they could now get away with it.'[32] But this sense of relief and determination did not blind Christians to the horrors which war would entail; D. M. MacKinnon expressed his approval of an attitude of 'Christian materialism which cannot condemn as irrelevant the physical agony of millions that such a conflict as the next war would seem likely to involve', and Reckitt, looking round at the brutality which was already rampant in so many parts of the world, sombrely reminded his readers of 'the weight of human anguish which a European war would so vastly extend'.[33]

The impression given by this study of the Anglican contribution to Christian social thought between the wars is inevitably that it was weaker and less effective than it should have been, and for this there were perhaps four main reasons. Most important was the profound ignorance of many of those who wrote and spoke about social issues—an ignorance which was evident above all in the field of economic theory. Even Tawney, whose passion and sincerity were unsurpassed, was an economic historian rather than an economist, and his writing on social questions is distinguished more by its moral fervour and political conviction than by its

[31] *Christendom*, December 1939, p. 245.
[32] The *Socialist Christian*, July–August 1939, p. 3.
[33] *Christendom*, June 1939, pp. 143 and 86.

economic insight. His convictions often led intuitively to sound economic conclusions, but intuition was no substitute for a complete mastery of the subject as a weapon with which to do battle against the established orthodoxies of the Treasury and the vested interests of the City. The only important writer who combined a thorough understanding of contemporary economic theory with a lively Christian conviction was Sir Josiah Stamp, but his own relatively unadventurous economic views, combined with his narrow conception of the Christian faith, were not such as to inspire a new Christian initiative.[34] The charge of ignorance applies also in other spheres besides that of economics, and a glance at the really well-informed writings and speeches of, for example, Garbett on housing or Temple on education serves to show how the contribution of experts such as these towers above the generality of Christian comment on such matters.

Secondly, the continuance of partisan differences had a damaging effect on Christian social witness. These differences were chiefly of two kinds, between modernists and Catholics on the one hand, and between Socialists and anti-Socialists on the other, although the various points of view overlapped and these labels fail to do justice to the complexity of the situation. The annual Summer Schools of Sociology provided an opportunity for the Anglo-Catholics to share their discussion of social issues with Christians of other traditions, but they remained jealous enough of their own point of view to make real co-operation difficult and unusual, and even among their own ranks there was a good deal of bewilderment and confusion, particularly on the part of those who had been most radical in their social views. W. E. Moll, who had been Stewart Headlam's curate and a leading figure in the C.S.L., wrote to Widdrington of his despair at the result of the 1931 general election: 'Here I am humanly speaking in sight of the grave after years of fighting, and I am sad beyond power of words at what has come in these latter days.'[35] Widdrington himself, in a

[34] See e.g. Stamp's *Christianity and Economics* (1939), p. 177, where he claims that the Christian faith can validly express itself only by 'informing and vitalizing the individual man with particular ideals and morals'. This was a point on which the Christendom Group's theology was more satisfactory.

[35] From Widdrington's obituary of Moll in *Christendom*, September 1932, p. 221.

letter to Reckitt in 1936, expressed doubts about the wisdom of continuing to pursue the social policies originally worked out in *The Return of Christendom*, and confessed his own perplexity in view of 'the strength of the forces opposed to us and their ruthlessness, and also of the inertness, the passivity of the Church'.[36] There were certainly grounds for Widdrington's complaint, for the other parties in the Church of England were, with the exception of isolated individuals, almost uniformly indifferent to social issues; theological debate, prayer book revision and the controversy over religious education combined to distract attention away from the problems of society. A few of those whose work has been described in earlier chapters were members of the Modern Churchmen's Union—notably J. G. Adderley, C. E. Raven and Charles Jenkinson—but it could still be said that most Modern Churchmen were 'less in touch with the youth and religious problems of the day than were the Catholics they despised. They were academic, pedantic, scholastic men. . . .'[37]

The division between those Christians who sympathized with political Socialism and those who opposed it was less clear than the distinction of churchmanship, but it was a significant factor in preventing co-operation between some of the most active leaders of Christian social thought. Tawney, for example, was a lifelong member of the Labour Party, and felt it his duty, if he disapproved of its principles or conduct, to apply himself to their correction. The Christendom thinkers, on the other hand, were in principle bitterly opposed to any extension of State responsibilities and functions, and it is hardly surprising that the achievements of the Labour governments of 1924 and 1929–31 failed to convert them to the Socialist cause. They feared in particular that social welfare schemes might prejudice the development of their Catholic sociology: 'The tacit acceptance of Social Service . . . as a permanent and healthy thing is one that unless closely watched may easily outflank any demand for a change in social structure which a Christian Sociology might make. Many of the things now done as Social Service can never be regarded by Christians as anything

[36] Quoted by M. B. Reckitt in *P. E. T. Widdrington*, p. 122.

[37] From R. E. Roberts, *H. R. L. Sheppard, Life and Letters*, p. 270. Sheppard, whose opinion Roberts is quoting, was at one time a Vice-President of the Modern Churchmen's Union.

but *ad hoc* temporary necessities, doing for men what in a Christian society they would be able to do for themselves.'[38] Demant was referring in this context to voluntary social service in America, but the objection applied even more forcibly to the assumption by the government of responsibility for social welfare.

A third reason for the weakness of Christian social witness was that it continued to meet with opposition in principle from a number of influential churchmen. An extreme example of old-fashioned hostility towards the involvement of the Church in political and economic matters, in this case coupled with remarkable economic ignorance, was provided by Inge's 1930 Social Service Lecture, summed up by his claim that 'The Gospel is a message of moral and spiritual regeneration, not of social reform. As Christians, our business is with the inside, not the outside, of the cup, with the building up of character, not with the improvement of external conditions.'[39] There was always a possibility that exponents of the social gospel might get their priorities wrong and see the improvement of external conditions as the principal end of Christian effort, but in practice this was seldom the case in Britain, and it became less of a danger as time went on; Inge's presentation of the problem as a choice between alternatives shows his failure to understand the arguments, deriving from Maurice and Westcott, for bringing social questions within the sphere of Christian judgment and concern. But this is not to say that ninety years of propaganda had been altogether without effect; hostility of this kind was becoming quite rare, and its decline was probably more rapid between the wars than at any time since the days of Maurice, Kingsley and Ludlow. Even such a redoubtable conservative as Hensley Henson was not above giving credit where it was due, and, despite his staunch opposition to Socialism, he paid tribute in his diary to the achievements of the Labour-controlled local authorities in the provision of social welfare services in County Durham.[40]

Finally, from about 1930 the theological climate became increasingly unfavourable towards the predominantly liberal

[38] V. A. Demant, 'The Prospects of Christian Sociology in America', in *Christendom*, March 1931, p. 39.

[39] W. R. Inge, *The Social Teaching of the Church*, pp. 91f.

[40] H. Hensley Henson, *Retrospect of an Unimportant Life*, Vol. II, pp. 406f.

protestant outlook of the Fifth Report and Copec, and it was not until the late thirties that the development of a more satisfactory theological basis for Christian social thought was begun. By the time the new insights were commonly available, largely through international and ecumenical exchange, the world was on the brink of war, and the opportunity for applying and embodying them in the life of the Church and the community was temporarily lost.

In what he described as his Meditation on an Historical Theme, *The Church of England, 1900–65*, Roger Lloyd bestows high praise on the Christian Social movement between the wars, claiming that it not only kept pace with secular events, but that 'its prophetic thinking went deeper with every year, continually extending the area of its competence until it was dealing in every utterance with nothing less than the entire range of human social life and the whole nature of the human beings who lived it'.[41] This is clearly an extravagant estimate of the achievements of Christian social thinkers, and one which does not attempt to do justice to the complex and chequered development of this area of Christian concern, but its underlying optimism is not altogether unjustified. It is not easy to trace the course of Anglican social thought in the inter-war years, but a certain broad pattern does emerge; from the time of the General Strike, if not before, weaknesses became increasingly apparent in the courageous but inadequate approach to social issues which was represented by the Fifth Report and Copec, preached by the I.C.F., and reflected in Lambeth conference reports and the debates of Convocation and the Church Assembly, but this Christian attitude towards society was nevertheless largely responsible for the continued growth of awareness among both clergy and laity of the existence of social problems, and for the fine achievements of many individual members of the Church of England in various fields of social thought and action. The more eccentric and imaginative nostrums of the Christendom thinkers are mostly now forgotten, but much that was said and written by churchmen about the Christian ideal for society has its memorial in subsequent social legislation, and in improvements which have come about in the structure and life of society. Furthermore, apart from any measurable achievements or results,

[41] Roger Lloyd, *op. cit.*, p. 308.

the social thought of the Church of England in the years between the wars remains of permanent value as an indication of the need to take disciplined and realistic account of the facts of each social problem and the possibilities of solving it, and as a warning against the folly of presuming to dispense with the services of the expert, whether economist or theologian.

WOLVERHAMPTON TEACHERS
COLLEGE LIBRARY

BIBLIOGRAPHY

The place of publication is London unless otherwise stated

1. OFFICIAL AND SEMI-OFFICIAL PUBLICATIONS

The *Chronicle of Convocation* SPCK.
Crockford's Clerical Directory, Prefaces.
Hansard, Parliamentary debates.
The National Assembly of the Church of England, Report of Proceedings SPCK.
York Journal of Convocation York, W. H. Smith.

2. PERIODICALS AND NEWSPAPERS

Commonwealth edited by Henry Scott Holland until his death in 1918, subsequently by Christopher Cheshire and G. W. Wardman.
Christendom edited by M. B. Reckitt; the organ of the Christendom Group; from 1931.
The *Church Socialist* the organ of the Church Socialist League; until 1921.
The *Crusader* from 1924 the unofficial organ of the Society of Socialist Christians; became the official publication of the S.S.C. in 1928, renamed the *Socialist Christian.*
The *Green Quarterly, an Anglo-Catholic Magazine*; from 1924.
The *Pilgrim* edited by William Temple; 1920–27.
Stockholm: International Review for the Social Activities of the Churches; 1928–31.
The *Torch* the organ of the Industrial Christian Fellowship. Consulted from 1924; earlier volumes not available. Renamed the *I.C.F. Journal* in 1935.
The *British Gazette* and the *British Worker*, newspapers published only during the general strike of 1926; see Chapter 4.
The Times, the *Church Times* and the *Guardian* have also been frequently consulted, together with occasional issues of other periodicals and newspapers as indicated in the text.
Periodicals and newspapers were published throughout the period under review—1918–39—unless otherwise stated.

3. PAMPHLETS AND MANIFESTOS

Various, particularly those published by the Church Socialist League, the Industrial Christian Fellowship, the League of the Kingdom of God, and the Anglo-Catholic Congress.

4. CONFERENCE AND COMMITTEE REPORTS

Christianity and Industrial Problems, the Report of the Archbishops' Fifth Committee of Enquiry SPCK, 1918; page references in the text are to the edition of 1926.

The Church and Social Service, the Report of a Committee appointed by the Archbishop of Canterbury SPCK, 1920.

The Churches Survey their Task, the Report of the Conference of the Life and Work Movement at Oxford, July 1937, on Church, Community and State, introduced by J. H. Oldham Allen & Unwin, 1937. This is Volume VIII of the Church, Community and State series; other titles, published in connection with the Oxford Conference, are:

I. *The Church and its Function in Society*, by W. A. Visser't Hooft and J. H. Oldham
II. *The Christian Understanding of Man*
III. *The Kingdom of God and History*
IV. *The Christian Faith and the Common Life*
V. *Church and Community*
VI. *Church Community and State in Relation to Education*
VII. *The Universal Church and the World of Nations*

Volumes II–VII consist of collections of papers written as part of the preparation for the Conference. All volumes were published by Allen & Unwin in 1937.

Copec: *The Proceedings of C.O.P.E.C.*, a report of the meetings of the Conference on Christian Politics, Economics and Citizenship at Birmingham, April 1924, edited by Will Reason Longmans, Green, 1924.

Reports of Copec Commissions Longmans, Green, 1924:

1. *The Nature of God and his Purpose for the World*
2. *Education*
3. *The Home*
4. *The Relation of the Sexes*
5. *Leisure*
6. *The Treatment of Crime*
7. *International Relations*
8. *Christianity and War*
9. *Industry and Property*
10. *Politics and Citizenship*

11. *The Social Function of the Church*
12. *Historical Illustrations of the Social Effects of Christianity*
The Report of the Commission on Rural Life appointed by the Copec Continuation Committee Longmans, Green, 1927.
The Fourfold Challenge of Today, a record of the proceedings of the Sheffield Regional Copec Conference, edited by Henry Cecil Longmans, Green, 1925.

Malvern, 1941: The Life of the Church and the Order of Society Longmans, Green, 1941.

Lambeth Conferences:
The Five Lambeth Conferences (1867–1908) SPCK, 1920.
The Lambeth Conferences, 1867–1948 SPCK, 1948.

The Report of the First Anglo-Catholic Congress, London, 1920 SPCK, 1920
The Report of the Anglo-Catholic Congress, London, July 1923 Society of SS. Peter and Paul, 1923

The Stockholm Conference, 1925, edited by G. K. A. Bell OUP, 1926

5. BOOKS: PRIMARY SOURCES (other than the publications mentioned above, which are of great importance in this category.)

Barker, Edwin (with Ronald Preston)	*Christians in Society* SCM, 1939
Barnett, S. A.	*The Perils of Wealth and Poverty* Allen and Unwin, 1920; published posthumously
Bull, Paul	*The Economics of the Kingdom of God* Allen & Unwin, 1927
Bussell, F. W.	*The National Church and the Social Crisis* Robert Scott, 1918
Cecil, Lord Hugh (Lord Quickswood)	*Nationalism and Catholicism* Macmillan, 1919
Cecil, Lord Robert (Viscount Cecil of Chelwood)	*All the Way* Hodder & Stoughton, 1949
	A Great Experiment Jonathan Cape, 1941
	International Arbitration Burge Memorial Lecture for 1928 published in the collected lectures for 1927–33, OUP, 1933
	The Moral Basis of the League of Nations Lindsey Press, 1923
Competition, A Study in Human Motive	Written for the Collegium by John Harvey, J. St. G. C. Heath, Malcolm

Spencer, William Temple and H. G. Wood Macmillan, 1917

Cunningham, W. — *Personal Ideals and Social Principles* SPCK, 1919

Dearmer, P. (Ed.) — *Christianity and the Crisis* Gollancz, 1933

Demant, V. A. — *Faith that Illuminates* (edited by Demant) Centenary Press, 1935
God, Man and Society SCM, 1933
The Just Price (edited by Demant; essays prepared for a conference in 1929 of the research department of the Christian Social Council) SCM, 1930;
Religion and the Decline of Capitalism, the Scott Holland Lectures for 1949 Faber & Faber, 1952
This Unemployment: Disaster or Opportunity? SCM, 1931

Eliot, T. S. — *The Idea of a Christian Society* Faber & Faber, 1939;
Selected Essays, 1917–32 Faber & Faber, 1932

Figgis, J. N. — *The Fellowship of the Mystery* Longmans, Green, 1914
Hopes for English Religion Longmans, Green, 1919

Fox, R. M. — *The Triumphant Machine* Hogarth, 1928

Garbett, C. F. — *The Challenge of the Slums* SPCK, 1933
In an Age of Revolution Hodder & Stoughton, 1952

Gore, Charles — *Christ and Society*, the Halley Stewart Lectures for 1927 Allen & Unwin, 1928
Christianity Applied to the Life of Men and of Nations, the Essex Hall Lecture for 1920, reprinted, with an introduction by R. H. Tawney John Murray, 1940
The League of Nations, the Opportunity of the Church Hodder & Stoughton, 1918

Green, Peter — *Betting and Gambling* SCM, 1924

Greenslade, S. L. — *The Church and Social Order* SCM, 1948

Groser, St J. B. — *Politics and Persons* SCM, 1949

Headlam, A. C. — *The Church and Industrial Questions* SPCK, 1919

Henson, H. Hensley — *Letters of Herbert Hensley Henson*, edited and introduced by E. F. Braley SPCK, 1950

Quo Tendimus? The Primary Charge delivered at his Visitation to the Clergy of his Diocese in November, 1924 Hodder & Stoughton, 1924

Retrospect of an Unimportant Life, 3 volumes OUP, 1942, 1943 and 1950

Hudson, C. E. — *Preface to a Christian Sociology* Allen & Unwin, 1935

Inge, W. R. — *Diary of a Dean* Hutchinson, 1949

Outspoken Essays 2 series, Longmans, Green, 1921 and 1922

The Social Teaching of the Church, the Social Service Lecture for 1930 Epworth, 1930

Ingram, K. — *The Modern Attitude to the Sex Problem* Allen & Unwin, 1930

Christianity—Right or Left? Allen & Unwin, 1937

Jones, Stanley — *Christ and Communism* Hodder & Stoughton, 1935

Kennedy, G. A. Studdert — *The Best of Studdert Kennedy*, selected from his writings by a friend Hodder & Stoughton, 1947

Democracy and the Dog Collar Hodder & Stoughton, 1921

Lies! Hodder & Stoughton, 1919

The Wicket-Gate Hodder & Stoughton 1924

G. A. Studdert Kennedy, by His Friends — Preface by J. K. Mozley Hodder & Stoughton, 1929

Kenyon, Ruth — *The Catholic Faith and the Industrial Order*, Based on the proceedings of the Anglo-Catholic Summer School of Sociology, 1928–30 Philip Allan, 1931

The Social Aspect of the Catholic Revival, in *Northern Catholicism*, edited by N. P. Williams and C. Harris SPCK, 1933

Lee, John — *The Social Implications of Christianity* SCM, 1922

Lewis, J. (Ed., with K. Polanyi and D. K. Kitchin) *Christianity and the Social Revolution* Gollancz, 1935

Lindsay, A. D. (Lord Lindsay) *Christianity and Economics* Macmillan, 1933

Pacifism as a Principle and Pacifism as a Dogma SCM, 1939

(Ed.) *Christianity and the Present Moral Unrest* Allen & Unwin, 1926

Lloyd, R. B. *Revolutionary Religion* SCM, 1938

Mairet, Philip *The National Church and the Social Order*; an enquiry conducted by the Social and Industrial Council of the Church Assembly, written by Mairet with the authority of the Council and in order to express the Council's views Church Information Board, 1956

Marchant, J. (Ed.) *The Future of the Church of England* Longmans, Green, 1926

Marston, C. *The Christian Faith and Industry* SPCK, 1927

Men without Work A report made to the Pilgrim Trust, introduced by W. Temple CUP, 1938

Mess, H. A. *Casual Labour at the Docks* G. Bell,1916

Factory Legislation and its Administration P. S. King, 1926

The Facts of Poverty SCM, 1920

Industrial Tyneside Ernest Benn, 1928

Studies in the Christian Gospel for Society SCM, 1923

Munby, D. L. *Christianity and Economic Problems* Macmillan, 1956

God and the Rich Society OUP, 1961

The Next Five Years: an Essay in Political Agreement Macmillan, 1935

Niebuhr, Reinhold *An Interpretation of Christian Ethics* SCM, 1936

Moral Man and Immoral Society Scribner's, 1933

Reflections on the End of an Era Scribner's, 1934

Noel, Conrad *An Autobiography* edited by Sidney Dark Dent, 1945

Socialism in Church History Frank Palmer, 1910

Oldham, J. H. — *Church, Community and State: a World Issue* SCM, 1935
Christianity and the Race Problem SCM, 1924
White and Black in Africa: a Critical Examination of the Rhodes Lectures of General Smuts Longmans, Green, 1930

Osborne, C. E. — *Christian Ideas in Political History* John Murray, 1929

Peck, W. G. — *After Thirty Years* SPCK, 1954
The Divine Society SCM, 1925
The Church and the Future of Society, in *The Social Implications of the Oxford Movement* New York, Scribner's, 1933
The Salvation of Modern Man Centenary Press, 1938

Penty, A. J. — *Guilds and the Social Crisis* Allen & Unwin, 1919
Post-Industrialism Allen & Unwin, 1922
Protection and the Social Problem Methuen, 1926
Towards a Christian Sociology Allen & Unwin, 1923

(with William Wright) — *Agriculture and the Unemployed* Labour Publishing Company, 1925

Phillips, Mary — *The Responsibility of the Christian Investor* Christian Social Council, 1933

Porter, Alan (Ed.) — *Coal: a Challenge to the National Conscience* Hogarth, 1927

Property, its Duties and Rights — Essays introduced by C. Gore Macmillan, 1913

Raven, C. E. — *Is War Obsolete?* Halley Stewart Lectures for 1934 Allen & Unwin, 1935

Reckitt, M. B. — *As it Happened* an autobiography Dent, 1941
Faith and Society Longmans, Green, 1932
Religion in Social Action Unicorn Press, 1938
The World and the Faith Faith Press, 1954

(with C. E. Bechhofer) — *The Meaning of National Guilds* Cecil Palmer, revised edition 1920 (with C. E. Hudson) *The Church and the World*, Vol. 3 Allen & Unwin, 1940

(Ed.) *Prospect for Christendom* Faber & Faber, 1945

(Ed.) *The Social Teaching of the Sacraments* the report of the 2nd Anglo-Catholic Summer School of Sociology, 1926 Society of SS. Peter and Paul, 1927

Relton, H. M. *Religion and the State* Unicorn Press, 1937

The Return of Christendom by a Group of Churchmen, introduced by C. Gore Allen & Unwin, 1922

Slesser, H. H. *Judgment Reserved* Hutchinson, 1941

Religio Laici Mowbray, 1927

Spencer, Malcolm (Ed.) *The Kingdom of God in Industry*, a collection of essays issued by a Joint Social Council of the Churches associated with Copec Independent Press, 1927

(Ed.) *Social Discipline in the Christian Community* Longmans, Green, 1926

Stamp, J. (Lord Stamp) *The Christian Ethic as an Economic Factor* Epworth, 1926

Christianity and Economics Macmillan, 1939

Motive and Method in a Christian Order Epworth, 1936

Swann, N. E. E. *Is there a Catholic Sociology?* SPCK, 1922

Tawney, R. H. *The Acquisitive Society* G. Bell, 1921 (expanded version of *The Sickness of an Acquisitive Society* Fabian Society, 1920)

Equality, the Halley Stewart Lectures for 1929 Allen & Unwin, 1931

Temple, W. *Christianity and the Social Order* Penguin, 1942

Christianity and the State, the Scott Holland Lectures for 1928 Macmillan, 1928

Christianity in Thought and Practice SCM, 1936

Essays in Christian Politics and Kindred Subjects Longmans, Green, 1927

Introduction to *The Industrial Unrest*

	and The Living Wage The Collegium and P. S. King, 1913
	Thoughts on some Problems of the Day Macmillan, 1931
Tribe, R.	*The Christian Social Tradition* SPCK, 1935
Westcott, B. F.	*Christian Social Union Addresses* Macmillan, 1903
	The Incarnation—a Revelation of Human Duties SPCK, 1892
	Address on Socialism in *The Report of the Church Congress, Hull, 1890*

6. BOOKS: SECONDARY SOURCES: histories and commentaries on Christian social thought; biographies of individuals directly involved in the Christian social movement.

In this section there are two books which deserve particular mention, and which have been found most valuable:

D. O. Wagner's *The Church of England and Social Reform since 1854*, published in 1930, New York, Columbia University Press, is an excellent and thoroughly judicious account of the long period with which it deals, but it is inevitably lacking in detail, and finishes at 1926.

M. B. Reckitt's Scott Holland Lectures for 1946, *Maurice to Temple*, Faber & Faber, 1947, are also extremely useful, but again cover a long period, and are the work of one who was himself deeply committed to a particular school of Christian social thought between the wars. Other relevant books are:

Anson, Peter	*The Call of the Cloister* SPCK, 1955
Canon Barnett, his Life, Work and Friends	by his wife; 2 volumes John Murray, 1918
Bell, G. K. A.	*Randall Davidson, Archbishop of Canterbury*; 2 volumes OUP, 1935
Belton, F. G.	*Ommanney of Sheffield*, memoirs of G. C. Ommanney, Vicar of St. Matthew's, Sheffield, 1882–1936 Centenary Press, 1936
Bettany, F. G.	*Stewart Headlam* John Murray, 1926
Binyon, G. C.	*The Christian Socialist Movement in England* SPCK, 1931
Brown, C. K. F.	*The Church's Part in Education, 1833–1941* The National Society and SPCK, 1942
Carpenter, James	*Gore, a Study in Liberal Catholic Thought* Faith Press, 1961

Christensen, T. *The Origins and History of Christian Socialism, 1848-54* Aarhus, University Press, 1962.

Craig, Robert *Social Concern in the Thought of William Temple* Gollancz, 1963

Gobat, Molly *T. C. Gobat: His Life, Work and Teaching* Letchworth, G. W. Wardman, 1938

Gowing, John *Forever Building: a Short History of the St. Pancras Housing Society, 1924–54* St. Pancras Housing Society, 1954

Hammerton, H. J. *This Turbulent Priest* biography of Charles Jenkinson Lutterworth, 1952

Hunter, L. S. *Years of Change and Revolt, 1904–57* paper read to the London Society for the Study of Religion, winter 1957–8. (Privately communicated)

Ingram, K. *Basil Jellicoe* Centenary Press, 1936

Iremonger, F. A. *Men and Movements in the Church* Longmans, Green, 1928

William Temple, Archbishop of Canterbury, His Life and Letters OUP, 1948

Jasper, Ronald *Arthur Cayley Headlam, Life and Letters of a Bishop* Faith Press, 1960

Lansbury, George *My Life* Constable, 1928

Laun, J. F. *Social Christianity in England* SCM, 1929

Lloyd, R. B. *The Church of England, 1900–65* SCM, 1966

Lockhart, J. G. *Cosmo Gordon Lang* Hodder & Stoughton, 1949

Mansbridge, Albert *Edward Stuart Talbot and Charles Gore* Dent, 1935

Paget, Stephen *Henry Scott Holland, Memoir and Letters* John Murray, 1921

Peck, W. G. *William Temple as a Social Thinker*, in the symposium (no editor named) *William Temple, an Estimate and an Appreciation* J. Clarke, 1946

Prestige, G. L. *The Life of Charles Gore* Heinemann, 1935

Purcell, William *Woodbine Willie*, biography of Studdert Kennedy Hodder & Stoughton, 1962

Reckitt, M. B. *P. E. T. Widdrington, a Study in Vocation and Versatility* SPCK, 1961

Roberts, R. E. — *H. R. L. Sheppard, Life and Letters* John Murray, 1942

Smith, H. Maynard — *Frank, Bishop of Zanzibar*, biography of Bishop Weston SPCK, 1926

Smyth, C. H. E. — *Cyril Forster Garbett* Hodder & Stoughton, 1959

Sokolow, A. D. — *The Political Theory of Arthur J. Penty* Yale, 1940

Spinks, G. L. (with E. L. Allen and J. Parkes) — *Religion in Britain since 1900* Dakers, 1952

Stephenson, Gwendolen — *Edward Stuart Talbot, 1844–1934* SPCK, 1936

Stevens, T. P. — *Father Adderley* Werner Laurie, 1943

Tatlow, Tissington — *The Story of the S.C.M. of Great Britain and Ireland* SCM, 1933

Tawney, R. H. — *Religion and the Rise of Capitalism*, the Scott Holland Lectures for 1922 John Murray, 1926

Troeltsch, Ernst — *The Social Teaching of the Christian Churches*; 2 volumes Allen & Unwin, English translation by Olive Wyon, 1931

Tuckwell, Gertrude — *Constance Smith, a Short Memoir* Duckworth, 1931

Woods, E. S. (with F. B. MacNutt) — *Theodore, Bishop of Winchester*, biography of Bishop F. T. Woods SPCK, 1933

7. BOOKS: THE BACKGROUND: historical, political, social and economic.

In this section there are again two books which require special mention: the first is C. L. Mowat, *Britain Between the Wars*, Methuen, 1955, which is the outstanding history of the period—thorough, balanced and most readable; it is an essential for understanding the background of the Christian social movement. Much less thorough and less reliable, but typically stimulating, is A. J. P. Taylor, *English History, 1914–45*, OUP, 1965.

Fiction is also a useful source of information about life in Britain between the wars; Walter Greenwood's novel, *Love on the Dole*, Jonathan Cape, 1933, written with first-hand experience of conditions in the depressed areas, is the best known and one of the most important of the spate of novels inspired by the events of the early 1930s. Other examples are:

Brierley, Walter — *Means Test Man* Methuen, 1935

Cronin, A. J. — *The Stars Look Down* Gollancz, 1935

Greenwood, Walter	*His Worship the Mayor* Jonathan Cape, 1934
Hodson, J. L.	*God's in his Heaven . . .* Gollancz, 1935
Mitchison, Naomi	*We have been warned* Constable, 1935

Other non-fiction books which have been found helpful include:

Abrams, M.	*The Condition of the British People, 1911–45* Gollancz, 1945
Beales, H. L. (with R. S. Lambert)	*Memoirs of the Unemployed* Gollancz, 1934
Birkenhead, the Earl of	*Frederick Edwin, Earl of Birkenhead, the Last Phase* Butterworth, 1935
Blythe, Ronald	*The Age of Illusion* Hamish Hamilton, 1963
Bolitho, Hector	*Alfred Mond, First Lord Melchett* Martin Secker, 1933
Bowley, A. L.	*The Division of the Product of Industry* Oxford, Clarendon, 1919
(with A. R. Burnett-Hurst)	*Livelihood and Poverty* G. Bell, 1915
Bowley, Marion	*Housing and the State* Allen & Unwin, 1945
Brockway, A. Fenner	*Hungry England* Gollancz, 1932
Bullock, Alan	*The Life and Times of Ernest Bevin*, vol. I Heinemann, 1960
Cameron, A. M.	*Civilization and the Unemployed* SCM, 1934
Carr-Saunders, A. M. (with D. Caradog Jones and C. A. Moser)	*A Survey of Social Conditions in England and Wales* OUP, 1958
Cole, G. D. H.	*British Trade Unionism Today* Gollancz, 1939
(with Raymond Postgate)	*The Common People, 1746–1946* Methuen, 4th edition, 1949
Cooke, Colin	*The Life of Richard Stafford Cripps* Hodder & Stoughton, 1957
Douglas, C. H.	*Credit-Power and Democracy* Cecil Palmer, 1920
	Social Credit Eyre and Spottiswoode, 3rd edition, 1933
Evans, Trevor	*Bevin* Allen & Unwin, 1946
Gill, Eric	*Autobiography* Jonathan Cape, 1940
Glass, S. T.	*The Responsible Society* Longmans, Green, 1966

Graves, Robert (with Alan Hodge) — *The Long Weekend, a Social History of Great Britain, 1918–39* Faber & Faber, 1940

Hammond, J. L. and B. — *The Rise of Modern Industry* Methuen, 5th edition, 1937

Harrod, R. F. — *The Life of John Maynard Keynes* Macmillan, 1951

Henderson, Arthur — *Consolidating World Peace*, Burge Memorial Lecture for 1931, published in the collected lectures for 1927–33 OUP, 1933

Hilton, John — *Rich Man, Poor Man*, the Halley Stewart Lectures for 1938 Allen & Unwin, 1944

Hodson, H. V. — *Slump and Recovery, 1927–37* OUP, 1938

Hutt, Allen — *The Post-War History of the British Working Class* Gollancz, 1937

Jennings, Hilda — *Brynmawr: a Study of a Depressed Area* Allenson, 1934

Jones, J. H. — *Josiah Stamp: Public Servant* Pitman, 1964

Keynes, J. M. — *Can Lloyd George do it?* The Nation, 1929
The Economic Consequences of Mr. Churchill Hogarth, 1925
The Economic Consequences of the Peace Macmillan, 1919
The End of Laissez-Faire Hogarth, 1926
A Revision of the Treaty Macmillan, 1922

Laver, James — *Between the Wars* Vista, 1961

Lewis, J. — *Douglas Fallacies: a Critique of Social Credit* Chapman & Hall, 1935

Lipson, E. — *The Growth of English Society* A. & C. Black, 1949

Lloyd, E. M. H. — *Stabilization* Allen & Unwin, 1923

Lyman, R. W. — *The First Labour Government, 1924* Chapman & Hall, 1958

Masterman, C. F. G. — *England After War* Hodder & Stoughton, 1922

McElwee, William — *Britain's Locust Years 1918–1940* Faber & Faber, 1962

Montgomery, John — *The Twenties* Allen & Unwin, 1957

Muggeridge, Malcolm — *The Thirties* Hamish Hamilton, 1940

Newsom, John	*Out of the Pit* Oxford, Blackwell, 1936
Nichols, Beverley	*The Sweet and Twenties* Weidenfeld & Nicolson, 1958
Nicolson, Harold	*King George V, his Life and Reign* Constable, 1952
Orwell, George	*The Road to Wigan Pier* Gollancz, 1937
Percy, Lord Eustace	*Democracy on Trial* The Bodley Head, 1931
Postgate, Raymond	*The Life of George Lansbury* Longmans, Green, 1951
Priestley, J. B.	*English Journey* Heinemann, 1934
Rathbone, Eleanor	*The Disinherited Family* Edward Arnold, 1924
Raymond, John (Ed.)	*The Baldwin Age* Eyre & Spottiswoode, 1960
Rowntree, B. S.	*The Human Needs of Labour* Nelson, 1918
Speake, T.	*The Housing of the Poor* Garden Cities and Town Planning Association, 4th edition, 1928
Stamp, J. (Lord Stamp)	*Wealth and Taxable Capacity* P. S. King, 1922
Symons, Julian	*The General Strike* Cresset, 1957
Tawney, R. H.	*The Choice before the Labour Party* Socialist League Pamphlet
	Education, the Socialist Policy ILP, 1924
Webb, Beatrice	*My Apprenticeship* Longmans, Green, 1926
Youngson, A. J.	*The British Economy 1920–57* Allen & Unwin, 1960

Acknowledgements

The thanks of the author and publishers are due to the following for permission to quote extracts:

George Allen & Unwin Ltd., *Christ and Society* by Charles Gore, *Christianity, Right or Left?* by K. Ingram, *The Churches Survey their Task*, edited by J. H. Oldham, *The Return of Christendom* by a Group of Churchmen and *Equality* by R. H. Tawney; G. Bell & Sons, Ltd., *The Acquisitive Society* by R. H. Tawney; Jonathan Cape Ltd., and the Executors of the Estate of the late Viscount Cecil of Chelwood, *A Great Experiment* by Lord Robert Cecil; J. M. Dent & Sons Ltd., *As It Happened* by M. B. Reckitt; Victor Gollancz Ltd., *Christianity and the Social Revolution* edited by J. Lewis; Hodder & Stoughton Ltd., *England After War* by C.F. Masterman; Longmans, Green & Co. Ltd., *The Future of the Church of England* edited by J. Marchant; the Public Trustee and the Society of Authors, *Heartbreak House* by G. B. Shaw; Secker & Warburg Ltd. and Miss Sonia Brownell, *The Road to Wigan Pier* by George Orwell; S.C.M. Press Ltd., *Church, Community and State; a World Issue* by J. H. Oldham; S.P.C.K., *The Lambeth Conferences, 1867–1948.*

Thanks are also due to the Board for Social Responsibility of the Church Assembly for permission to quote from an article entitled 'Copec Then and Now, Part 2' by C. E. Raven which appeared in the January 1963 number of *Crucible*, and to the *Radio Times* Hulton Picture Library for permission to reproduce photographs.

INDEX

Reference may be either to the text or to the notes on the page concerned